WOMEN WRITE IRAN

Women Write Iran

. . . .

Nostalgia and Human Rights from the Diaspora

Nima Naghibi

University of Minnesota Press
Minneapolis
London

A portion of chapter 1 was published in an earlier form as "Diasporic Disclosures: Social Networking, Neda, and the 2009 Iranian Presidential Elections," *Biography* 34, no. 1 (Winter 2011): 56–69. A portion of chapter 5 was published in an earlier form as "Revolution, Trauma, and Nostalgia in Iranian Women's Autobiographies," *Radical History Review*, no. 105 (Fall 2009): 79–91.

Published by the University of Minnesota Press
111 Third Avenue South, Suite 290
Minneapolis, MN 55401-2520
http://www.upress.umn.edu

Library of Congress Cataloging-in-Publication Data
Naghibi, Nima.
Women write Iran : nostalgia and human rights from the diaspora / Nima Naghibi.
Includes bibliographical references and index.
ISBN 978-0-8166-8382-6 (hc) — ISBN 978-0-8166-8384-0 (pb)
1. American prose literature—Iranian American authors—History and criticism.
2. Iranian Americans—Biography—History and criticism. 3. Exiles' writings, Iranian—History and criticism. 4. Autobiography—Iranian American authors—History and criticism. 5. Autobiographical memory in literature. 6. Nostalgia in literature.
7. Human rights—Iran. I. Title.
PS647.I73N34 2016
818'.6030992870899155—dc23 2015019413

Printed in the United States of America on acid-free paper

21 20 19 18 17 16 10 9 8 7 6 5 4 3 2 1

For Andrew, Safianna, and Cyrus,
for enriching the narrative of my life

Contents

Righting the Past

WHAT IS AT STAKE IN THE WRITING OF A LIFE? In what ways can the *writing* of a life narrative *right* the wrongs of a traumatic past? Vital to the writing, reading, and circulation of life narratives that contain, at their core, traumatic memories and accounts of human rights violations is the recognizability of the subject as human, and the validation of her story as authentic. As scholars who work on trauma and human rights have observed, the role of a willing reader-spectator-witness is crucial to the process of narrating and working through traumatic memories.[1]

Drawing on Joseph Slaughter's work on human rights and narrative (1997), Kay Schaffer and Sidonie Smith (2004) observe that human rights organizations and tribunals rely on an "international commitment to narratibility" (3). Stories of abuses of human rights, of genocide, of torture are disclosed to human rights advocates through victim narratives and testimonies. Life narratives that recount experiences of trauma and acts of human atrocities demand a willing witness "to recognize the humanity of the teller and the justice of the claim; to take responsibility for that recognition; and to find means of redress" (Schaffer and Smith 2004, 3). Understanding the recent and continuing proliferation of life narratives from this perspective, then, requires us to take up our roles as responsible global and civic citizens and engage with others' narratives and their humanity with empathy and with a meaningful commitment to social justice.

Since the 1990s, there has been a surge in the popularity of the genre of life writing: more people are choosing to write memoirs and more publishers are willing to publish them in response to what appears to be an insatiable market demand.[2] In 2001, Leigh Gilmore observed that "suddenly, it would seem, memoir has become *the* genre in the skittish period around the turn of the millennium" (1). The popularity of memoirs has not abated since Gilmore's statement; indeed the number of memoirs continues to proliferate, crossing generic boundaries from print to visual mediums to online forums such as Facebook and YouTube (discussed in chapter 1), as well as to documentary film and auto/biographical comics (discussed in chapters 3 and 4, respectively).[3]

This book takes as its case study the popular trend among diasporic Iranian women to produce auto/biographical narratives—in the shape of published memoirs, documentary films, and online disclosures. Since the late 1990s, a growing number of Iranian women have been deploying a range of auto/biographical forms to narrate their personal experiences of life in postrevolutionary Iran and/or in the diaspora. In her now-canonical book in Iranian studies, *Veils and Words: The Emerging Voices of Iranian Women Writers* (1992), Farzaneh Milani argues that the genre of autobiography has been traditionally discouraged for Iranian women because it is seen as a form of metaphorical unveiling that challenges the notion of "sharm," a combination of shame and charm valued in the modest Iranian woman. However, something decidedly has changed since Milani made her remarks on the scarcity of women's autobiography;[4] in the first decade and a half of the twenty-first century, diasporic Iranians, many of them women, have written and published their life narratives. Living in the diaspora, then, appears to be the main condition for producing these narratives: both making it necessary to address the loss of home and providing the authors with a cultural environment more permissive of such self-revelation.

Additionally, most of these writers have chosen to write in English. In her memoir, *Journey from the Land of No: A Girlhood Caught in Revolutionary Iran,* Roya Hakakian (2004) explains why she feels compelled to write in her second language: "To write about Iran in Persian would be daunting. Instead of re-examining the memories, I feared that in Persian, I might begin to relive them. Persian could summon the teenager at sea. English sheltered the adult survivor, safely inside a lighthouse" (15). For those whose auto/biographies recount experiences of suffering, English offers emotional and temporal distance from the trauma to which they were exposed in the (Iranian) culture and the (Farsi) language with which they are most intimate.[5] One of the challenges of the testimonial process is that the act of testifying requires the sufferer to relive the traumatic experience a second time through narration. Recalling a traumatic episode in a language that is at an emotional remove from one's experience could ease some of the stress of the testifying process. For the generation that has come of age in the West, however, English might simply be the language in which they feel most at home. Regardless of their reasons for writing in English, many of these life narratives have met with significant interest and market success in North America. But their mass-market appeal has not translated into similar success within an Iranian context.[6] What, then, are the cultural conditions that have led to such a receptive popular market for diasporic Iranian memoirs in the West?[7]

The memoirs discussed in this book are all written in English and published in the diaspora; as such, they can be understood as part of a late twentieth-century phenomenon in North America and Western Europe that Gilmore (2001) has termed the "memoir boom" (2). Scholars such as Babak Elahi, Persis Karim, and Amy Motlagh, who (like me) straddle the disciplinary borders of English studies and Iranian studies, have enriched the study of these texts by looking at questions of belonging, displacement, and cultural translation. Karim has been instrumental in creating a space for scholarly discussion and debate about diasporic Iranian literary production; she has coedited two groundbreaking special issues of academic journals, one with Nasrin Rahimieh, titled "Writing Iranian Americans into the American Literature Canon," in *MELUS* (2008), and the other with Elahi, titled "Iranian Diaspora," in *Comparative Studies of South Asia, Africa and the Middle East* (2011).[8] Both issues have contributed significantly to this academic field and have enabled a growing body of scholarship on the Iranian diaspora.

Nevertheless, the majority of the scholarship on diasporic literatures, and particularly of memoirs, has been seen through an Iranian American lens, classifying these literatures as part of the development of ethnic American literature. While my colleagues offer compelling analyses, their arguments that these texts are part of a tradition of ethnic American writing does not take into account the popularity of this genre by diasporic Iranians writing in English in other countries, such as Canada, England, or Australia.[9] In their introduction to the special issue on "Iranian Diaspora," Elahi and Karim (2011) do recognize that, to date, scholarship on the Iranian diaspora has tended to focus on the United States, writing:

> Iranians can also be found in significant populations scattered throughout Canada, Europe, Asia, and Australia. These Iranian immigrants and their second-generation, and now third-generation, children and grandchildren reflect diverse experiences and cultural contexts depending on when they left Iran and how they have been greeted or represented in their host nations. (381)

Despite this recognition on their part, to date, most of the scholarly engagement with memoirs in particular has involved a claiming of this phenomenon as part of an American tradition of writing. For me, recognizing the widespread phenomenon of memoir writing by Iranian women (and increasingly Iranian men) globally, and not as part of "ethnic (American) literatures," requires that we understand these memoirs as part of a larger phenomenon: a diasporic Iranian "memoir boom."[10]

Not only are autobiographical narratives the genre du jour in contemporary Western societies, but they are also the genre of choice for diasporic Iranians, many of whom place the trauma of the 1979 revolution at the heart of their personal narratives. This seems a good time to point out the obvious: not all Iranians experienced the 1979 revolution as a trauma; indeed, some welcomed the revolution and the social and political changes ushered in through the establishment of an Islamic Republic. As mentioned in chapter 5, in some ways, women were the beneficiaries of the postrevolutionary period as the majority of university students are now female, and women hold many lucrative and professional posts in Iran as doctors, engineers, lawyers, and professors. Far from suggesting, however, that Iran is a nation committed to gender equality (it is important to point out, for instance, that a woman's legal status is considered half that of a man's, so in legal and official government terms, she is understood to be a second-class citizen), it bears repeating that for some women from the traditional and religious classes, the revolution made possible a university education and a professional mobility previously not available to them. The revolutionary trauma at the heart of the recent wave of diasporic memoirs discussed in this book, however, is experienced largely by a population who suffered painful losses as a result of the revolution: the loss of family and friends, the loss of economic and social status, and the loss of their home country. This is a population whose direct ties to Iran were disrupted after the 1979 revolution.

The authors discussed here, women whose lives were interrupted by the events of 1979, repeatedly return—in the telling of their stories—to the revolution as a defining moment in their lives. The majority of the life narratives discussed in this book (with the exception of those in chapters 2 and 3) are produced by a generation who were children at the time of the revolution, old enough to understand what was happening but too young to participate in the protests or to act as political agents. This is the generation *to whom the revolution happened* rather than the generation who brought about revolution.[11] For them, the revolution features as a central, life-changing event, and their narratives are often infused with nostalgic longing for lost opportunities. Theirs is a mourning for their imagined, future selves that can no longer come into view.

Tara Bahrampour and Gelareh Asayesh are at the forefront of what we can now call the diasporic Iranian women's memoir boom. Their memoirs, *To See and See Again: A Life in Iran and America* (Bahrampour 1999) and *Saffron Sky: A Life between Iran and America* (Asayesh 1999), chronicle the narrators' hyphenated lives as they move between America and Iran in the aftermath of the 1979 revolution. They are at once neither/nors who do not belong to any one particular place, and simultaneously cosmopolitan subjects who cross geographical, linguistic, and cultural borders with ease and can therefore comfortably position themselves anywhere in the world. The publication of *To See and See Again* and *Saffron Sky* acted as a catalyst for other diasporic Iranian women to produce their own life narratives—in the shape of literary and online texts, and documentary films.[12] A shared feature among these narratives is that they tend to represent the 1979 Iranian revolution as, very often, *the* key traumatic moment in the authors' personal histories.[13]

Initially, these memoirs faced a distinctly chilly reception from scholars who work on Iranian literature and culture.[14] Some have critiqued what they have identified as an imperialist agenda or complicity in these memoirs identifying what they believe are Orientalist representations of Iran and of Iranian women; others have gone further and traced connections between some memoirists and neoconservative institutions in the United States.[15] It is worth noting that much of the resistance to these memoirs comes from a historical suspicion of the genre of memoir itself. As Thomas Couser (2012) has observed: "Until quite recently, 'memoir' was minor and 'autobiography' major; 'memoir' subliterary and 'autobiography' literary; 'memoir' shallow and 'autobiography' deep; 'memoir' marginal and 'autobiography' canonical" (18). In part, the general prejudice against the genre of memoir compared to that of autobiography seems to emerge from the view that autobiography, with its long retrospective lens on a life (usually of a known personality—often male), connotes a thoughtfulness, an ability to observe and assess critically, that the memoir—with its focus on a shorter period of time, or on a single event in a person's life—does not. The memoir tends to be understood as more "emotional" and impressionistic, and therefore less reliable in its recording of events than an autobiography, which is seen as a more rational, balanced reflection on a person's life. The claim that the memoir is a limited and even compromised form of expression is one that some scholars have made in relation to its diasporic incarnations. Often seen as a stepping stone to full literary and cultural articulation, the memoir has been represented as an almost necessary evil until such time that Iranian writers come of age and (presumably) enter the adult world of literature.[16] This bias against the genre of memoir is transcultural; memoir has been historically viewed—and not just in discussions relating to diasporic Iranian memoirs—as the inferior and feminized relation to other literary forms, including autobiography.[17]

Diasporic Iranian memoirists have thus had to contend both with a suspicion of the genre in which they write and of their political motivations. While the anti-imperialist critique is certainly valid, there is more to be said about these memoirs, and about their popularity in the West, than that they are complicit with a neocolonial and imperial system of knowledge production about the East, and the lives of Eastern women in particular. This study suggests that understanding diasporic Iranian women's memoirs as part of a (predominantly North American) memoir boom opens up possibilities for reading these texts beyond their perceived political agendas; it also proposes that the diasporic Iranian women's memoir boom began in earnest with the publications of *To See and See Again* and *Saffron Sky* in 1999.

Edward Said (1975) has noted that beginnings are not arbitrary, and neither are they indisputable or absolute. Choosing where to locate the starting point of an argument is always somewhat arbitrary as all beginnings refer to something that has occurred prior; for Said (1975): "A beginning immediately establishes relationships with works already existing, relationships of either continuity or antagonism or some mixture of both" (3). Understanding 1999 as "the beginning" of the boom of diasporic Iranian women's memoir writing, then, situates this body of work in relation to, and indeed as part of, a cultural and literary phenomenon in North America (and to a lesser extent in Western Europe). But if, as some scholars have argued, the diasporic Iranian memoir boom should be understood to begin with the 2003 publication of Azar Nafisi's *Reading Lolita in Tehran,* then the appearance—and great success—of her memoir on the American literary stage only two years after 9/11 needs careful consideration.[18] Connecting the memoir boom with Nafisi's work politicizes, in very particular ways, the framework through which we come to read diasporic Iranian women's memoirs. Marking 2003 as the beginning of the diasporic memoir boom places the discussion about the proliferation of memoirs squarely within an imperialist context; it privileges the volatile post 9/11 political context that fueled an inflated U.S. rhetoric positioning Iran as part of an "axis of evil," encouraging readers to consider these memoirs as yet another manifestation of anti-Islamic sentiment. This study of diasporic Iranian women's memoirs (and not just Iranian American memoirs) offers an alternative framework from within which these narratives can be read: that of revolutionary trauma and nostalgic longing.

Following Said's observation that beginnings should remain cognizant of what has come before, it is important to recall that the late 1980s and the early 1990s saw the appearance of several memoirs by diasporic Iranian women, some of them ghostwritten, many of them by members of the former Iranian aristocracy.[19] Shusha Guppy's two compelling memoirs, for instance, *The Blindfold Horse: Memories of a Persian Childhood* (1988) and *A Girl in Paris* (1991), may be seen as legitimate forerunners to the diasporic Iranian memoir boom since like the more contemporary diasporic Iranian women's memoirs discussed here, her narratives posit a nostalgic view of her idyllic, Persian childhood and describe the loneliness of (in her case, self-imposed) exile in Paris. However, her memoirs are also notably different from the more contemporary manifestation of diasporic Iranian memoirs. In significant ways, Guppy's memoirs fit more comfortably alongside the works of a Western literary elite who penned their recollections of a distinctive (and often privileged) past; "Persia" does not even appear in the title of Guppy's second memoir, which focuses exclusively on her life in Paris. Guppy's memoir of her childhood records her personal memories of a Persia that was on the cusp of modernization; her memoir traces, through her family and personal experiences, the changes Iranian society underwent in the 1920s and 1930s as then-monarch Reza Pahlavi was attempting, through sheer force of will, to transform the country from a traditional society to a westernized, industrialized nation.

Her second book chronicles her adventures in Paris as a young student in the 1950s. This is an experience to which only a very small percentage of Iranians, particularly Iranian women, had access. Hers is a compelling text about the romance of being "ailleurs":

> Indeed as far back as I could remember I had dreamed of being *"ailleurs"*—elsewhere—and that for me meant Europe, and more

> precisely Paris. . . . It would take me half a lifetime to realize that *"ailleurs"* is unattainable, that it recedes as you approach it, and that whenever you think you have at least reached it, it has gone "elsewhere." (Guppy 1991, 6)

For Guppy, this romantic description of *ailleurs* captures a general feeling of malaise that is part of her artistic temperament. She weaves a compelling tale of self-exile, and while she indulges in nostalgia for home, she also revels in the stimulating creative and intellectual milieu of postwar Paris. As such, Guppy's Paris years evoke the writings of other celebrated exilic writers and artists in Paris such as Ernest Hemingway, Gertrude Stein, Pablo Picasso, and Samuel Beckett, among others. Indeed, Guppy moves in high-brow literary circles, frequenting the famous Café Flore in Saint-Germain-des-Prés, the celebrated haunt of intellectuals and writers such as Jean-Paul Sartre, Albert Camus, and many others. She meets and befriends the French poet Jacques Prévert, who was instrumental in the recording and release of her collection of Persian folk songs, *Persian Love Songs* (1993).[20] Thus, for Guppy, her period of "exile" was, in fact, for her, an exciting and privileged time of artistic growth and intellectual development. Ultimately, her privilege leads her to a life of self-imposed exile in London; however, her displacement is voluntary, and not related to the revolution that was yet to come.

Remarking on the fact that, years later, some of the Iranian students she had known in Paris found themselves back in France as a result of the 1979 revolution (an event Guppy [1991] does not even name except to refer to it somewhat cryptically as "a cataclysm not of their doing" [278]), she recognizes that her exilic state has little in common with theirs: "But they have a community, a sense of belonging, to which I can lay no claim—my exile had different roots" (278). Guppy, who was born into Iranian privilege and married into British aristocracy,[21] pursued the romance of self-exile as a way of escaping traditional Iranian expectations of gender roles and in order to pursue her artistic and musical talents. For Guppy (1991), the nostalgia she feels and writes about in her memoir is the vague nostalgia and dissatisfaction of a perpetually restless artistic temperament: "But now I know that the feeling of nostalgia that overwhelms me is not for anything, but is objectless and stems from the unassuageable longing for that original *'ailleurs,'* whose genesis far back beyond memory is the loss of paradise" (278). This, finally, is what marks a significant difference between

Guppy's memoirs and the memoirs that can be considered as part of the current diasporic Iranian memoir boom. Diasporic Iranian writers are in fact keenly aware of the object of their nostalgic longing: their homeland, Iran.

Contemporary diasporic Iranian memoirs are particularly interesting in their mediation of the diasporic experience through the authors' memories of prerevolutionary 1970s Iran, placing the concepts of memory and nostalgia, and questions of testimony and witness, at the heart of these narratives. Rather than being haunted by a desire for the ever-elusive "ailleurs," these authors pen nostalgic reflections of their past inflected with a keen longing for "home." For diasporic writers, it is *the return* that is the fantasy, *not* the departure; for them, there is little romance in being elsewhere.

In extreme cases, the pain of remembering eclipses narrative capability; the person who cannot narrate her own story, because she has yet to work through traumatic memories of revolution or of imprisonment and torture, can be understood with the aid of a term coined by Paul John Eakin (2008): the *de-storied individual.* For Eakin, the "de-storied individual" suffers from aphasia, a neurological disorder; this is a condition usually caused by a stroke that affects a person's memory and language centers in the brain, preventing her from piecing together a coherent narrative about her life. Not wanting to minimize the neurological dimension of aphasia, it seems to me that Iranians scarred by their experiences in revolutionary or postrevolutionary Iran, those who are unable to articulate and narrate their traumatic experiences in the form of a coherent narrative, can be usefully understood through the category of the "de-storied" individual. While some remain in an aphasic space, others work through their traumatic memories through the successful articulation of their life narratives. The process of healing involves moving the de-storied individual into a space of narrative possibility, a space where traumatic life narratives can be articulated and heard.

The need for a willing and empathic witness to render stories of pain and suffering meaningful and potentially productive has been noted by many scholars. According to Cathy Caruth (1995), the "history of a trauma, in its inherent belatedness, can only take place through the listening of another" (10). Gilmore's (2001) theory about the convergence of testimonial and confessional narratives also offers a crucial framework for an exploration of how narratives of trauma and narratives of self-representation dovetail in ways that enable a necessary witnessing to transpire (2–3); these narratives seek out a sympathetic audience affected by the stories they hear.

Essential to the therapeutic process of writing and testimony is the willingness of the spectator-reader-witness to recognize the humanity of another, and the legitimacy of their suffering. The life narratives discussed in this book all contain deeply affecting stories; feelings of nostalgia, empathy, guilt, and shame run through all the narratives discussed here. How do these affects circulate in these life narratives? How do they affect us as readers?

In my discussion of diasporic Iranian memoirs, I explore the political and social possibilities of affect, and use the terms *affect* and *emotion* interchangeably, although there is a significant body of theoretical work outlining and debating their differences: in brief, emotions are understood to be experienced socially, whereas affects are seen as abstract and physiological reactions. One of the foremost scholars of affect theory, Brian Massumi (1995), marks a clear difference between emotion and affect; for him, emotions are social expression of personal feelings whereas affect experienced as "intensities" are "embodied in purely autonomic reactions most directly manifested in the skin—at the surface of the body, at its interface with things" (85). Ann Cvetkovich (2012) distinguishes between affect and emotion similarly by observing: "[Affect] signals precognitive sensory experience and relations to surroundings, and [emotion] cultural constructs and conscious processes that emerge from them, such as anger, fear, or joy" (4). Ruth Leys (2009), however, critiques Massumi's model of affect as disconnecting the emotion from its object: the "antiintentionalist" or "nonintentionalist" understanding of affect perceives them to be "elicited or 'triggered' by what we call the object, but the object is nothing more than a stimulus or tripwire for an inbuilt behavioral-physiological response" (136). For Leys, viewing affect as a thoughtless physiological reaction makes mobilizing it toward politically relevant discourse and action a futile endeavor.

For me, the idea that emotion circulates provides a particularly useful lens through which to study diasporic Iranian memoirs and consider why some are more popular (or affecting) than others. While I am interested in how emotions circulate within and between texts, and how they are "transmitted" between the text and the reader-spectator-witness, these emotions, or affects, are not what Leys (2009) calls "objectless" (135).[22] Rather, my interest lies in the political potential of emotions in the context of testimonial writing. As Kay Schaffer and Sidonie Smith (2004) have observed: "Affective dimensions always attend the telling and reception of stories. Stories may generate strong sensations, feelings, and embodied responses for tellers and their audiences, at times of first and subsequent witnessing" (6). This study of diasporic Iranian life narratives considers how the circulation of emotions engages the reader-witness with the subject of the narrative. Allowing ourselves to be moved by the emotions in the text is critical to the process of recognizing the subject of the narrative as human, as someone with a story worth hearing. At their best, the circulation of affect in these texts inspires caring. This feeling of caring and empathic engagement allows the autobiographical subject of a life narrative to come into full view as recognizably human, as someone with a legitimate story to tell.

This monograph focuses on the contemporary compulsion among diasporic Iranian women in particular to produce testimonial and personal narratives in response to two historical moments in Iran: the 1979 revolution and the 2009 postpresidential election protests.[23] The 1979 revolution and the short-lived revival and brutal squelching of the revolutionary energies of 2009 have produced possibilities of articulation and self-expression for diasporic Iranian women in particular, and these forms of autobiographical expression have emerged in various print and digitized media. The life narratives discussed in this study constitute only a sampling of the testimonies of revolutionary trauma alluded to above; by no means does this study aspire to an exhaustive catalog, as the sheer volume of these texts precludes the possibility of offering a comprehensive analysis of disaporic Iranian life narratives.

Chapter 1, "Claiming Neda," examines how the widely circulated video footage of the death of Neda Agha-Soltan on the streets of Tehran in June 2009 triggered a profusion of life narratives by Iranians in the diaspora on social media platforms, particularly Facebook. The claiming of Neda as a symbol of freedom, and as a symbol of all Iranians (the common chant heard at public protests was "we are all Neda"), afforded diasporic Iranians the opportunity to share their personal stories of exile, of diasporic nostalgia, of personal and political trauma through the figure of Neda.

In death, Neda came to represent for diasporic Iranians "what could have been" (had the Green Movement succeeded in its goals).[24] Neda's death, then, registered for diasporic Iranians as the death of an imagined and presumably hopeful futurity. This chapter draws on Julie Rak's (2004) term *autobiographical discourse* as a particularly useful way of thinking through the autobiographical nature of online posts by diasporic Iranians. This material is of a decidedly autobiographical nature; the posts constitute snippets of lives that surface outside of a linear biographical narrative; they are pieces of life stories that surface in unconventional contexts. This chapter posits that the narratives of self-disclosures that erupted online in response to the events of June 2009 can usefully be viewed as part of the same proliferation of diasporic Iranian life narratives that began with the 1999 publication of *To See and See Again* and *Saffron Sky*.

Chapter 2, "Human Rights, Humanitarianism, and Empathic Witnessing: Prison Memoirs," explores the tension between the claim to truth and authorship and unclaimed trauma in these highly charged prison memoirs. The project of autobiography requires a commitment from the listener to bear witness to the traumatic event: "When this fails to occur, trauma can remain trapped as 'unclaimed experience' within the individual psyche and within the shared confines of the immediate community" (Whitlock 2007, 79). This chapter examines the tension between "marketable" narratives of trauma that secure a sympathetic listening audience and autobiographical accounts of those experiences that struggle, in a homeless and unclaimed state, in search of an audience. The memoirs discussed in this chapter include Marina Nemat's (2007) *Prisoner of Tehran: A Memoir,* Camelia Entekhabi-Fard's (2007) *Camelia, Save Yourself by Telling the Truth: A Memoir of Iran,* the collection *We Lived to Tell: Political Prison Memoirs of Iranian Women* (Agah, Mehr, and Parsi 2007), Zarah Ghahramani's (2008) *My Life as a Traitor,* and Shahla Talebi's (2011) *Ghosts of Revolution: Rekindled Memories of Imprisonment in Iran.* As mentioned above, these narratives are also part of a wave of testimonial literatures that foreground suffering, mobilizing what Gillian Whitlock (2007) calls a "rights discourse" that impels the reader to take up a compassionate stance (77). But what are the effects or the ramifications of compassion? How do we understand the eliciting of compassion in these testimonial narratives? This chapter explores the ways in which some of these narratives of prison trauma compel a politics of compassion, and so force an ethics of response in the reader. But it also considers why some contemporary diasporic Iranian prison narratives are more affecting, and more successful in their circulation as humanitarian narratives, than others.

Chapter 3, "Feeling Nostalgic, Feeling Guilty: Remembering Iran in Documentary Film," investigates the convergence of the genres of autobiography and documentary in contemporary documentary films. Here, the focus is on the social and political functions of nostalgia and memory in auto/biographical documentaries. Golkou Parhizgar's (2010) documentary *Round-Trip* chronicles her trip "home" to Iran from her disaporic home in

London. In Iran, she focuses her lens on the generation of young people born after the revolution, and through them, explores how feelings of loss and nostalgia are experienced both by diasporic subjects who pine to return "home" and for Iranians in Iran who feel like exilic subjects in their own country. Nahid Persson Sarvestani's (2008) *The Queen and I* also explores the politically and socially generative emotion of nostalgia. This film narrates the development of a rather unlikely friendship between Farah Diba, the former queen of Iran, and Sarvestani herself, a former member of a communist opposition group during the 1979 revolution. The work Sarvestani undertakes in this film, particularly the emotional experience of revisiting her revolutionary past in her conversations with the queen, inspire her next documentary, *My Stolen Revolution* (2013). Here, she confronts her overwhelming feelings of guilt regarding the death of her brother, Rostam, who was arrested and executed by the newly established Islamic Republic. Having encouraged him to join the communist group to which she belonged, she has carried the guilt of his execution with her since the revolution. This chapter then explores the predominant feelings these documentaries inspire: nostalgia (for another place and another time), and guilt and shame (for having left Iran, and in Sarvestani's case, for having managed to escape the country while her brother was arrested and eventually executed).

Chapter 4, "Repetitions of the Past: Marjane Satrapi and Intergenerational Memory," examines the work of the acclaimed graphic novelist Marjane Satrapi. Having attained international fame as a result of her first two auto/biographical works, *Persepolis I: The Story of a Childhood* (2003) and *Persepolis II: The Story of a Return* (2004), Satrapi extended her auto/biographical project with *Embroideries* (2005) and *Chicken with Plums* (2006). Borrowing Gilmore's notion of the "serial autobiographer," this chapter explores how Satrapi's various deployments of auto/biography interweave Satrapi's autobiographical avatar, Marji, into the narratives pertaining to family and nation.[25] Marji positions herself in her texts as witness to the intergenerational narratives of trauma and revolution, drawing on the empathic engagement of the reader-spectator.

Chapter 5, "Revolution, Nostalgia, and Memory in Diasporic Iranian Memoirs," discusses the prominent place of the 1979 revolution in these narratives, and argues that the experience of the revolution was both formative and destructive: formative because it occurred in their childhood or early adolescence, and destructive because it destroyed their known worlds. The first half of this chapter focuses on Gelareh Asayesh's (1999)

Saffron Sky, Tara Bahrampour's (1999) *To See and See Again,* Donia Bijan's (2011) *Maman's Homesick Pie: A Persian Heart in an American Kitchen,* Roya Hakakian's (2004) *Journey from the Land of No: A Girlhood Caught in Revolutionary Iran,* and Afschineh Latifi's (2005) *Even after All This Time: A Story of Love, Revolution, and Leaving Iran,* arguing that these texts all share a similar understanding of the revolution as causing a traumatic break in their lives. These narratives convey a nostalgia for an idealized time: prerevolutionary Iran, and an idealized period in the authors' lives: childhood. While Asayesh in particular, and Hakakian to a certain extent, dwell on feelings of loss in the diaspora, Bahrampour, Bijan, and Latifi appear more willing to embrace the diasporic space of the border.

The second half of this chapter examines Azadeh Moaveni's two memoirs: *Lipstick Jihad: A Memoir of Growing up Iranian in America and American in Iran* (2006) and *Honeymoon in Tehran: Two Years of Love and Danger in Iran* (2009). Both texts express a powerful nostalgia, albeit mediated through her parents' memories, for Iran. Born in California, Moaveni's longing for Iran is an inherited one, characterized by what Marianne Hirsch (2001) has called "postmemory," a term describing the intergenerational quality of memory, which lends itself productively to an analysis of how Moaveni's desire for a better time and a better place is (initially) mediated through her parents' memories of Iran. Her nostalgia, as powerful as it is, propels her "home" to Iran, where she constructs her own relationship with Iran and builds her own memories of the home that she, like her parents before her, is forced to leave behind.

This book builds on the important work Zohreh T. Sullivan (2001) began with *Exiled Memories: Stories of Iranian Diaspora.* Hers is a collection of transcribed interviews with diasporic Iranians who share with her their memories, many of them describing the trajectory that led them to their current lives in the United States. Sullivan (2001) observes that this collection of life stories "speaks to the reconstruction of memory and identity through diasporic narratives, to the conjuncture of the Americas and not to Iran itself" (xvii). *Exiled Memories* is one of the earliest efforts in diasporic Iranian studies to "link the palimpsest of autobiography and identity to that of diasporic history" (Sullivan 2001, 1). *Women Write Iran* attempts to extend the work Sullivan began in 2001 to understand how diasporic identities are formed in a space of exile and "forced deterritorialization" (Sullivan 2001, 1). Sullivan's contribution to an understanding of how life narrative, exilic identity, and traumatic memories shape diasporic identities precedes the diasporic Iranian memoir boom, yet offers some prescient insights into this recent phenomenon.

Anticipating the power that the recounting of life narratives holds for a diasporic Iranian population carrying the scars of revolutionary trauma, Sullivan (2001) writes: "What follows are the interrupted narratives of self, nation, and belonging, new stories that begin to be told in the new circumstance of exile, migration, or diaspora when we see people knitting the story of themselves with the story of the collective after it has been torn apart" (20). Sullivan recognizes the healing power of telling stories, and of reconstructing one's own identity through storytelling; if the experience of trauma is a dehumanizing process, then the act of recounting her memories is essential to the rehumanization of the subject. But equally important in this process is the role of the reader-witness, who must open herself up to being affected and moved by the stories that are told. *Exiled Memories* recognizes the therapeutic power of articulating life narratives, and offers the exilic writers in its pages a space in which their stories can be articulated, and so heard.

The goal of this book is to explore the phenomenon of diasporic Iranian women's life narratives in English in the late twentieth and early twenty-first centuries. I am suggesting that what ties these sometimes very disparate narratives together are the experience of the 1979 revolution as a traumatic event and the expression of a powerful nostalgia for an idealized past. The subtitle of this introductory chapter, "Righting the Past," invokes a double entendre that draws attention to the important work of *righting,* or of setting right, historical injustices through the act of *writing* life narratives. This book posits the importance of writing as an articulation of memory, and as an assertion of human rights; by drawing on the empathy of the reader-spectator-witness, life narratives offer the possibility of extending to the subjects a recognition of their humanity.

· CHAPTER 1 ·

Claiming Neda

Autobiography is not merely something we read in a book; rather, as a discourse of identity, delivered bit by bit in the stories we tell about ourselves day in and day out, autobiography structures our living.

—John Paul Eakin, *Living Autobiographically: How We Create Identity in Narrative*

THE QUESTION OF HOW A "HUMAN BEING BECOMES HUMAN" is one that preoccupies scholars who work on human rights narratives (Sliwinski 2011, 17).[1] This chapter considers that question by examining the overwhelming global responses to the death of Neda Agha-Soltan on the streets of Tehran in June 2009. The international response to the June protests in Iran and particularly to the death of Neda offers a glimpse at how social media—and Facebook in particular—played an instrumental role in constructing and circulating the story of Neda's life and diasporic Iranians who identified with her with such intensity. The sudden eruption and circulation of life narratives on Facebook was triggered through affective responses to the figure of Neda. The global digital network of life narratives was thus made possible by laying claim to the life of an individual whose story resonated effectively and affectively with large numbers of people across the world.

Global responses to the death of Neda took a variety of forms, including social media posts, Internet tributes, and public gatherings, and were expressed, for diasporic Iranians, through a shared autobiographical narrative containing, at its core, nostalgic claims to a past Iran and fragile hopes for an imagined futurity. But it was not just diasporic Iranians who were affected by the death of Neda. People with no personal connection to Iran felt themselves swept up by the diasporic community's claiming of her, and of their nostalgic memories of prerevolutionary Iran. The widespread, public circulation of Neda's death and the global reaction to it illustrate how "mass culture makes particular memories more widely available, so that people who have no 'natural' claim to them might nevertheless incorporate them into their own archive of experience" (Landsberg 2004, 8–9). This global sharing of life narratives was made possible through social media, particularly Facebook status updates and Tweets around the time of the 2009 protests, through which diasporic Iranians shared their affective responses to the political unrest in the country. They disclosed their feelings about the protests in Iran while drawing on the emotional support of a community of Facebook and Twitter users, Iranian or not, who found themselves affected by and identifying with the narratives that were emerging out of and in response to the protests.

The death of Neda was the crystallizing media event of the 2009 post-presidential election protests in Iran. As is now well documented, the protests—and their coverage—garnered breathless claims of a "Twitter revolution" from social media enthusiasts such as Andrew Sullivan and Clay Shirky. In *The Daily Dish* blog, Sullivan (2009a) enthused about the power of Twitter as a revolutionary tool for the Iranian opposition: "You cannot stop people any longer. You cannot control them any longer. They can bypass your established media; they can broadcast to one another; they can organize as never before." In an interview on the use of Twitter in Iran, Shirky exclaimed: "This is it. The big one. This is the first revolution that has been catapulted onto a global stage and transformed by social media" (Anderson 2009). Sullivan's and Shirky's hyperbolic views of the power of Twitter and new media to effect change—and even bring about revolution—were echoed in numerous online sources during and after the protests.[2]

Western news networks broadcast scenes from major cities in Iran where millions of Iranians, draped in green, demonstrated in a visible show of support for presidential candidate Mir-Hossein Moussavi, and a rejection of President Mahmoud Ahmadinejad. On June 12, within hours of the polls closing, Ahmadinejad was declared by Iranian state media to have won over 60 percent of the popular vote. Holding signs demanding, "Where is my vote?" Iranians took to the streets again, marching peacefully but claiming their right to a fair electoral process. The fact that some of these signs were in English might suggest to some that protestors were signaling supporters in the West. However, rather than interpreting this signaling as an encouragement to participate or intervene in an Iranian struggle, this gesture should be understood as a kind of global wave, an invitation to see Iran and its youth as other than that of the blinkered fundamentalist shouting, "Death to America." In other words, these English signs imply a conscious effort, on the part of demonstrators, to rewrite the narrative of Iran as a place of intolerance and xenophobia in the eyes of the West.

The Iranian government's response to these protests was, as is by now well known, swift and brutal. The peaceful demonstrations were crushed violently with beatings and mass arrests. The Western media were evicted from the country while the Western world remained transfixed by the footage of street demonstrations and the regime's merciless response, recorded on cell-phone cameras and posted online by Iranian activists. At the height of the Iranian protests, and at the height of the Western coverage of those protests, which dominated North American media from June 13 until the death of Michael Jackson on June 25, the mood online and in the media was exultant, rejoicing in the power of social media to facilitate global solidarity in a heretofore unprecedented way.[3] Social networking sites were thus central to publicizing and circulating, for a global audience, the political crisis that unfolded in Iran in 2009.

There was undoubtedly an electric charge to the circulation of news about the June protests, and this charge was conveyed largely at the level of affect. Major television news networks made repeated reference to the unmediated emotional content of the data coming out from mobile phones, YouTube uploads, and Tweets. Viewers were continuously cautioned to prepare themselves for the emotionally raw footage that they might find disturbing. On social networking sites such as Facebook, postings of events on the streets of Iran were carefully parsed, and hotly debated.

Online forums in which the political scene in Iran was discussed and debated thus generated powerful affective responses fostering a sense of global connection. The circulation of images and narratives about the June 2009 protests and their aftermath is an example of how affect gets transmitted, a process described by Teresa Brennan (2004) as a physiological phenomenon, referring to the general sense of being affected by the atmosphere, or by a particular mood in a room (1). Understanding the phenomenon of the global response to the Iran protests through the circulation of affect allows for a productive analysis of the emotional reach of the events of 2009. According to Brennan (2004), affect is transmitted in the following way: "The origin of transmitted affects is social in that these affects do not only arise within a particular person but also come from without. They come via an interaction with other people and an environment" (3). Affect theorists emphasize the *social* nature of affect; the transmission of affect illustrates how our moods, our bodies (since affective reactions occur at the level of physiology), respond to and are affected by others. In the case of the circulation of information about the Iranian protests, the general sentiment of excitement, of political possibility, and even of vicarious danger was transmitted to users of social media. In *The Times Online,* Sullivan (2009b) writes: "It was impossible not to *feel* connected to the people on the streets, especially the younger generation, with their blogs and tweets and Facebook messages—all instantly *familiar* to westerners in a way that would have been unthinkable a decade or so ago. . . . Reading personal messages from individuals on the ground prompts a whole other *sense* of involvement" (emphasis added). Shirky's reference to the relationship between emotion and speed bears some further consideration. Much of the celebratory language around social media has to do with its speed, its conflation of immediacy with intimacy, its ability to make us connect emotionally with one another through the reading of each other's personal narratives.

In a *New York Times* article on the function and uses of Twitter, or "microblogging," Clive Thompson (2008) describes how the online medium allows for the development of life narratives through the repetition of the seemingly mundane and trivial sharing of information:

> Each little update—each individual bit of social information—is insignificant on its own, even supremely mundane. But taken together, over time, the little snippets coalesce into a surprisingly sophisticated portrait of your friends' and family members' lives, like thousands of dots making a pointillist painting.

Scholars of life narrative have observed that the term *life narrative* is an open one that makes possible a range of auto/biographical expression. Marking a distinction between life writing and life narrative, Sidonie Smith and Julia Watson ([2001] 2010) write:

> We understand *life narrative* . . . as a general term for acts of self-presentation of all kinds and in diverse media that take the producer's life as their subject, whether written, performative, visual filmic, or digital. In other words, we employ the term *life writing* for written forms of the autobiographical, and *life narrative* to refer to autobiographical acts of any sort. (4)

Other critics, such as Thomas Couser (2012), have argued in favor of the term *life narrative,* which "comprehends all sorts of records of our lives. . . .

And it also comprehends modes of representation made possible by new technologies, like the Internet, which hosts YouTube, social media like Facebook, and the blog" (27).

Referring to the footage streaming out of Iran as a type of "extreme reality TV," the essayist and online activist Setareh Sabety (2010) calls attention to what is most alluring about modes of life narrative such as reality television: their promise to disclose and provide access to the "raw reality" of personal lives. These types of narratives can be understood as forms of what Julie Rak (2004) has called "autobiographical discourse," an expansive term that considers autobiographical expression in unconventional texts and locations (ix). The terms *life narrative* and *autobiographical discourse* then allow for particularly fruitful ways of thinking about the circulation of personal stories and observations online during the summer of 2009. Understanding autobiographical discourse and life narrative "as an integral part of a lifelong process of identity formation" allows for a consideration of a range of texts, including Facebook status updates and Tweets, as part of "the self-narration we practice every day" (Eakin 2008, 34).

In an edited collection about online auto/biographical narratives, Anna Poletti and Julie Rak (2014) observe: "Nowhere is the power and diversity of the autobiographical more visible than online, where it is the raison d'être for many of the activities and practices associated with Web 2.0" (3). Thus, scholars of auto/biographical studies have observed that social media encourages and makes possible articulations of life narrative in ways that differ significantly from how we understand the more conventional published autobiography. Facebook status updates, for example, disclose autobiographical information about the user through brief yet sometimes deeply personal statements. Arguing that the status update feature on Facebook "coax[es] life narratives" from its users, Aimée Morrison (2014) states: "There is no question—particularly since the introduction of the Timeline interface—that Facebook and its users are producing life narratives" (127). While status updates can be (but are not necessarily) brief, the decision of what to share with one's Facebook friends, and what to include as part of one's public profile, reveals biographical information about the user. Sometimes these disclosures appear inconsequential or even banal; sometimes they are deeply personal and emotional.

Alongside auto/biographical disclosures of the more mundane kind, social networking sites also provide a space for individual and emotional engagements with global injustices. This phenomenon of what Schaffer and Smith (2004) call "e-witnessing" requires us to distinguish this type of witnessing from a more "traditional" form of witnessing, one that takes place within a human rights framework and foregrounds "storytelling, empathy, response, action" (228). E-witnessing takes place within a "diffuse and decentralized" (228) network of information exchange: "Given that virtual audiences are themselves indefinable and fragmented, e-witnessing may or may not coalesce into a claim of collective identities or a sense of solidarity" (Schaffer and Smith 2004, 229). E-witnessing is a responsive mode in that it is emotional and reflexive, responding to the quick uploading and sharing of information that circulates online. The speed of the medium elicits and encourages powerful personal and emotional responses, compelling the social media user to bear witness to social and political wrongs.

"We Are All Neda"

Without a doubt, the most emotionally charged narrative to come out of Iran in June 2009 and into social media networks, and one that subsequently invited autobiographical responses, was that of the death of Neda Agha-Soltan. The story first made its way onto YouTube as a forty-second video clip that shows the twenty-six-year-old Neda collapsing to the ground after being shot by a sniper. The shooting took place at a demonstration the day after the religious leader Ayatollah Khamenei's ominous warning that should the protests continue, the demonstrators would suffer the consequences of their actions. The last moments of Neda's life were captured by a cell-phone video camera, and after the gruesome footage was posted on YouTube, it immediately became one of the site's most watched videos. *Time* magazine named Neda one of the heroes of 2009, declaring hers "the most widely witnessed death in human history" (Mahr 2009). Cable news stations played the footage of Neda's death on a loop accompanied by the caveat that what they were about to broadcast was extremely disturbing—even as they continued airing it. But the video clip—and the photograph of her bloodied face—circulated persistently on the Web.

Diasporic Iranian communities made prodigious use of social media, particularly Facebook, during the emotionally tumultuous period, much of it centering on Neda's death. For many diasporic Iranians, the compulsive posting and circulating of information on the political unrest in Iran reopened the wounds of exilic life and ignited powerful expressions of longing to be part of the movement on the streets of Iran. This public display of emotional intensities manifested itself through a certain authentication of "Iranianness" through autobiographical disclosures in their status updates and the comments they left on other people's posts.

Facebook status updates that shared news about the political situation in Iran were also part of the user's online profile through which they would post nostalgic remembrances of Iran by uploading old music videos and photographs of Westernized, urban Tehran scenes or family photographs from the 1970s, and through the sharing of personal memories. For Poletti and Rak (2014), the "constant directive to 'share' personal information on social media sites such as Facebook or Linked In is an example of a media affordance, which asks for users to create a specific type of identity, one that can be shared" (5). The performative dimension of social networking sites such as Facebook thus made possible a space in which a traceable Iranian "pastness" was both asserted and contested even as it was "shared." This claim to Iranian authenticity was further intensified by access to information: those who had the fastest access to information positioned themselves as more authentic native subjects, more closely affiliated with Iran, and so more deeply affected by the political events unfolding there.

Ulric Neisser's term *the extended self* offers an instructive way of thinking about how diasporic Iranians felt motivated to disclose their political and personal narratives online during the turbulent summer of 2009.[4] Paul John Eakin (2008) describes Neisser's term as "the self of memory and anticipation, the self existing outside the present moment," stating that it is "the primary subject of autobiographical discourse" (3). The death of Neda crystallized for diasporic Iranians their own intensely emotional reactions to the Islamic Republic, serving also as an affecting reminder of the trajectory of their own lives and the historical events that had led them to live in the diaspora. In a short commemorative piece on the anniversary of Neda's birthday, Hamid Yazdan Panah (2013) remarks: "Neda's story is symbolic of the story of so many Iranians, full of potential and on the cusp of greater things, but cut short by confrontation with power and repression." Through Neda's image, and what she represented—a young woman tragically killed as she demonstrated her dissatisfaction with the Islamic regime—diasporic Iranians were thrown into a crisis of identity. Relocated in various national locations in the West, they found themselves occupying an alternate, cyber universe where they felt profoundly affected by the protests in Iran. Following Eakin's (2008) claim that "autobiographical memory and autobiographical narrative are oriented to the future," diasporic Iranians seized upon the imagined possibilities of the "Green Wave" in a desire to reassert their connection to an Iranian past with an unspoken but excited projection toward the possibility of future return: the ultimate fantasy of the diasporic subject (155).

The diasporic claim to an authentic Iranian past and projected future culminated in laying claim to the image of the young and photogenic Neda. The mass circulation of the YouTube video of Neda's death, and the ensuing frenzy to identify and name her, illustrates Gillian Whitlock's (2007) claim that the drive to attach a "biography" and "celebrity status" to a face has to do with an "ethics of recognition that carries life narratives across cultures" (73).[5] The video of Neda's death elicited powerful emotional responses from diasporic Iranians and non-Iranian citizens in North America and Western Europe. The video, and the subsequent reproductions of her image on poster placards, in Facebook avatars, and on other online venues, transformed Neda's image into an icon of the "Green Movement."[6] Referring to what they call the "global career of Neda's image," Aleida Assmann and Corinna Assmann (2010) observe: "What had started as an *image of* ends up as an *image for*. Neda's conspicuous image today stands in for the many anonymous others who protested and suffered at the hands of the Iranian government" (235). Neda's image, then, recounts the story of postrevolutionary Iran as diasporic Iranians like to tell it: young, Westernized, and full of promise, Neda's desires for democracy and self-expression were ruthlessly crushed by an oppressive government. For many Iranians, this narrative resonates deeply with their own personal narratives and the larger narrative of the nation. The photograph of Neda's bloodied face turned toward the cell-phone camera that captured her last moments quickly became an iconic photo of the Green Movement and of its brutal suppression.

Like the iconic photo of Sharbat Gula, "the Afghan girl" on the cover of the June 1985 *National Geographic* issue, the image of a young and attractive Neda resonated and circulated through Western humanitarian rescue narratives. Writing about the global circulation of the photograph of Sharbat Gula, and its connections to life narrative, Whitlock (2007) states: "'The Afghan girl' story is contained within a framework of humanitarian concern, which organizes the commodification of subaltern lives as appropriate subjects for compassion" (71).[7] Like the gaze of the Afghan girl, the forty-second video clip of the death of Neda Agha-Soltan and her dying gaze into the lens of the camera "pierce[s] the skin" and "sears the heart" of witnesses:

> On these occasions, testimony can summon its witnesses to *feel* that their lives and privileges are enmeshed in others and that interdependencies and responsibilities follow from this. The picture of the Afghan girl is one such testimonial artifact, it "sears the heart" and remains memorable. (Whitlock 2007, 74)

Naming Neda one of the most memorable people of the year in 2009, *Time* magazine focused on the affective impact of her gaze: "For one gut-wrenching moment, as she lay dying from the bullet in her heart on that Tehran side street last June, Neda stared directly into the cell phone that was about to immortalize her. . . . Neda's dying gaze drew the eyes of the world. We neither look away nor forget" (Ghosh 2009).[8] Both Sharbat Gula and Neda hold the Western spectator with their gaze, and by doing so, compel the viewer to recognize their humanity. For Sharon Sliwinski, the spectator-witness plays a key role in recognizing the humanity of another; the spectator sees the other as human and *feels* the other's suffering. Thus the process of recognizing someone as human requires the affective engagement of the spectator who extends to another the recognition of a shared humanity. Some of the questions raised by scholars who work on human rights narratives include: What makes a person recognizably human? Whose suffering is witnessed (and therefore legitimated as suffering) while the suffering of others remains invisible? Such questions require the spectator-witness to take responsibility for her affective engagements and think about how and when she chooses to bear witness to another's trauma, another's narrative of pain. Such questions are pertinent to understanding the global reaction to the death of Neda.

Immediately after the video of Neda's death went viral, social media was abuzz with emotional responses to the protests in Iran. Diasporic Iranians were laying claim to Neda, whose story was being framed as that of a young, Westernized woman who longed for freedoms that were taken for granted in the West. Describing her own emotional reaction upon receiving the YouTube video of Neda's death through her Twitter account, Sabety (2010) focuses on Neda's "Westernized appearance":

> Her blue jeans and Adidas-style striped red and white sneakers also signify the type of woman Neda was. . . . Her thin figure, perfectly plucked eyebrows, and signature Iranian nose job also suggests the kind of woman she was: one of the thousands of

> young, beautiful women who try to look as Western as possible despite or in outright defiance of the imposed hejab and thirty years of Islamist indoctrination. (123)

Thus for diasporic Iranians and non-Iranians in the West, the emphasis on Neda's Westernized looks and fashion choices rendered her recognizable and appealing as an icon of freedom and democracy: "Both in words and images the notion of 'Western lifestyle,' as invoked graphically by the detail of Neda's black cloak falling open to 'reveal Western jeans and sneakers,' is symptomatically part of a neo-liberal concatenation of 'freedom' with 'democracy,' and of 'democracy' with 'capitalism'" (Tulloch and Blood 2012, 4). There were many spectator-witnesses to Neda's death—and her life—as represented by the photographs that later emerged on the Web. Those photographs showed a vibrant and smiling Neda without the state-enforced *hijab,* or veil. These images helped secure her place as a fully recognizable human subject because of her familiarity; she could have been *any* young woman living in the West. The story of (an unveiled) Neda, then, was claimed as a *universal* story.

Figure 1. The second photograph of Neda Agha-Soltan that circulated widely on social media. This photogenic image of an unveiled and Westernized Neda *became the rallying cry for diasporic Iranians in the West to claim that "we are all Neda." Photograph by Associated Press.*

Very quickly, Neda's image was transformed into a universal pop icon for democracy and freedom. At rallies around the world protesting the post-election crackdown on Iranian civilians, Iranians in the diaspora chanted, "We are all Neda," thus transforming the narrative of Neda's death into a shared autobiographical narrative about the sufferings—and desires—of all Iranians, in Iran and in the diaspora. This claiming of Neda manifested itself visually in numerous ways; for instance, a popular Facebook avatar in June 2009 was of Neda's bloodied face set against a green background—in a collapsing of Neda's image with that of the Green Movement and with the identity of the Facebook user. Many diasporic Iranians added Neda as their middle name on their Facebook profiles, sandwiching her identity into their own. Numerous websites surfaced, dedicated to a memorializing of Neda, where people posted comments and mourned her death. A short YouTube video, "I am Neda," deeply affecting in its use of melancholic music, features young people holding up signs demanding "democracy," "freedom," "respect," and declaring, finally, "I am Neda." The video concludes with these words: "Neda was the face of the faceless, We are the voice of the voiceless." This video, much like other such videos, websites, and images devoted to Neda's memory, ends up flattening her into a surface that can be applied equally over its diasporic and Western audiences, as well as over the protestors on the streets of Iran, thus transforming Neda's life—and death—into a narrative about the (diasporic) self.

Seizing on the moment, diasporic Iranians claimed the Green Movement and the image of Neda as if to declare to the West, "This is who we are. We are people who understand and value democracy. We are not crazy fundamentalists pounding our fists in the air. The story of Neda is *our* story." In a dramatic visual statement, Reza Deghati, a Paris-based Iranian artist and National Geographic photographer, devoted his studio, his staff, and hours of his time to the creation of hundreds of "Neda Masks" for "Neda Mask action day" in front of the Eiffel Tower in Paris on July 25, 2009. This project was part of his larger goal of staging similar visual protests in front of major international landmarks. Neda's image—as unveiled, as modern—thus became a vehicle through which diasporic Iranians countered dominant Western narratives about Iran and Iranians. Assmann and Assmann (2010) have also observed that "the dispersion of Neda's images was not random . . . but steered by a political frame of attention. Its driving force were exiled Iranians and other citizens who sympathized with the Iranian protestors and organized demonstrations in which they declared their solidarity" (227–28). Thus diasporic Iranians claimed Neda's narrative as one that echoes their own personal trajectory, and that told the tragic narrative of the Iranian nation: a Westernized country that fell into the clutches of Islamic fundamentalists. This is a narrative that also appeals to a liberal Western consciousness and goes some way to explaining how deeply Neda's story affected so many people.

The bronze sculptures of Neda by the American artist Paula Slater is another telling example of how Iranians in the diaspora directed the narrative about Iran and Iranian women through the careful management of Neda's image. Moved by the story of Neda's death, Slater created a bronze sculpture based on one of the first available photographs of her wearing the mandatory hijab.[9] Calling it the "Angel of Iran," Slater dedicated it to the Iranian people and presented it to the diasporic Iranian community in San Francisco. The community expressed their appreciation for her work, but requested that she make another sculpture—this time of an unveiled Neda. Slater did so, naming it "Angel of Freedom." Thus Neda's image (without the state-imposed hijab) has been claimed by diasporic Iranian subjects

Figure 2. This bronze sculpture of Neda Agha-Soltan, titled "Angel of Iran," was based on the first photograph of her wearing the state-sanctioned hijab. Photograph by Paula B. Slater. www.PaulaSlater.com

as how they see themselves and how they want to be seen by the West. Her unveiled image also served as a reminder of *how things once were.* It is perhaps not too far-fetched to propose that the diasporic Iranian community—and indeed the Western world—really claimed Neda with such intensity after seeing the famous unveiled photograph of her, along with others of her on vacation in Turkey with her boyfriend. Before that, when the graphic and violent video of her death was broadcast, people reacted in horror and with compassion toward the sight of a young woman mercilessly gunned down in the street. But the universal claiming of her as a symbol (and a martyr) for a "Free Iran," and the universalized identification with her, only became possible after she became recognizable as someone like "us." It was only through this moment of recognition that the claim "I am Neda" could be taken up by all.

Indeed, everything that was known about Neda, such as her desire to travel, her love of music and dance, and her boyfriend, was conveyed through a Western framework. Soon after her death, the photo of Neda's bloodied face crossed the threshold into pop art by adopting the similar style and

Figure 3. This bronze sculpture of Neda, titled "Angel of Freedom," was based on the photograph of the unveiled Neda (see Figure 1). Sculptor Paula Slater made this sculpture in response to requests from the diasporic Iranian community. Photograph by Paula B. Slater. www.PaulaSlater.com

colors of Shepard Fairey's famous "Obama Hope" poster. The aesthetic similarities to the hope poster are richly evocative: during the 2008 presidential campaign, Obama represented a rejuvenated and renewed hope for a U.S. democracy that had been seriously undermined during the presidency of George W. Bush. Fairey's poster of Obama highlighted the campaign slogan of hope, underlining the promise of future change in the American political and social landscape. In similar fashion, Neda's image was taken up as a symbol of hope, despite—or indeed because of—her tragic death, and for a change in political leadership in Iran.

The Fairey poster itself carries echoes of Andy Warhol, one of the pioneers of U.S. pop art who both celebrated and ironized capitalism and art as mass production. Warhol's work carries within it an awareness and critique of consumer culture in capitalist societies: he recognized both the power of an iconic image and its capacity to be forgotten and discarded upon quick consumption. Thus, using Neda's photograph within the Warhol style gestures (perhaps unintentionally) to the mass consumption of her image by millions of people, the majority of whom would go on to forget about her within the year. But the use of an aesthetic style that also contains a celebration of capitalism and democratic ideals, and one that is so strongly associated with American popular culture, also works to affirm Neda's rightful place within the democratic West.

The narrativization of Neda through Western frameworks such as American-style democracy and mass consumer culture is particularly evident in the HBO documentary film *For Neda,* which takes a clear political stance very much in line with hawkish U.S. policies; the documentary's political leanings are immediately evident through its choice of Shohreh Aghdashloo as narrator. Aghdashloo, a popular Iranian actor living in Los Angeles since the Iranian revolution, and a one-time darling of the Iranian diaspora, has fallen out of favor with some Iranians of late because of her recent decisions to accept acting roles that perpetuate negative stereotypes of Iranians and Middle Easterners more generally.[10] The documentary has a star-studded lineup of interviewees, including the controversial literary scholar Azar Nafisi and the former CNN broadcaster Rudi Bakhtiar (now Director of Communications for the International Campaign for Human Rights in Iran), both of whom focus on the oppressiveness of women's hijab, an issue that was never raised—at least not explicitly—by Iranian protestors. The focus on the oppressiveness of the veil in this documentary illustrates how the internal political issues of June 2009 became distorted in the diaspora. While it may be true that Neda resented having to wear the hijab, as her mother indeed states, the documentary does not make clear that the principal reason she and millions of other Iranians turned out to protest in the streets was their anger at what they understood to be the fraudulent results of the Iranian presidential elections, not the issue of mandatory hijab.

Worth noting here is the fact that a documentary that has Neda's life story as its main focus invites autobiographical recollections from its interviewees such as Bakhtiar, who shares her own memories of growing up under the Islamic regime and chafing beneath the imposed hijab. The documentary features accounts about women's oppression in Iran by such personalities as the best-selling memoirist Nafisi, a highly divisive figure in the Iranian diaspora.[11] The tragedy of Neda's narrative consequently became a vehicle through which diasporic Iranians in particular began sharing their own life narratives not just through social media but also in documentary film, as well as through more conventional ways such as the autobiographical memoir (discussed later in this chapter). Saeed Kamali Dehghan, the investigative journalist who risked his life to go to Iran and secretly interview Neda's family for the documentary, has published at least two autobiographical articles about his personal experiences in the making of the film. In one piece, he writes of his intense fear while in Iran during the clandestine filming of the documentary, and of his terror at the Tehran airport as he waited to board his (delayed) airplane, convinced that his interview tapes would be discovered, and that he would be arrested by Iranian authorities (Dehghan 2010). In the space of a fairly brief article—the focus of which is at least ostensibly his pivotal role in the documentary about the life of Neda—Kamali Dehghan also manages to recount his own memories about growing up in Iran. In a moment of disclosure, he reveals that unbeknownst to his family, he is gay, and that had he remained in Iran, he and his partner would have been at risk of execution. This example demonstrates once again how Neda serves as a catalyst for narrative revelations by others. It also illustrates the force of the desire to bear witness to Neda's life and death; the inclination to narrate her story was so powerful that people like Kamali Dehghan were willing to risk their own lives in order to narrate hers.

The story of Neda's life and death has thus resonated in powerful ways around the globe, eliciting and encouraging disclosure of intense personal narratives. Perhaps the most theatrical of these was conveyed at a press conference the day after she died. Iran's exiled Crown Prince Reza Pahlavi, claiming Neda as his very own, reached into his breast pocket and pulled out photographs of his wife, his three daughters, and Neda, declaring: "'I have added her [Neda] to the list of my daughters. She is now forever in my pocket'" (AFP 2009). By configuring himself as Neda's father—she who had now become the daughter of Iran—he very astutely positions himself as the father of the nation, in a not-too-subtle attempt to rearticulate his claim to the throne, which would have been his had it not been for the 1979 revolution. Pahlavi's claiming of Neda, who had come to embody the struggle for Iranian democracy, can be read as a rather cynical—and unfortunate—political strategy on his part, particularly in light of the fact that his father, the deposed monarch, Mohamad Reza Pahlavi, was himself no fan of democracy. Pahlavi attempts to intersect his life narrative with that of Neda's by including her in his family, and thus write himself back into the unfolding history of Iran.

At a speech at the National Press Club in Washington on June 22, Pahlavi restated his commitment to the establishment of Iranian democracy and his horror at the abuse of human rights in postrevolutionary Iran. In a *Washington Post* article about the speech, Dana Milbank (2009) quotes Pahlavi:

> "No one—no one—will benefit from closing his or her eyes to knives and cables cutting into faces and mouths, of our young and old," he said, and then, choking up, he took a sip of water. "Or from bullets piercing our beloved Neda," he went on, before a sob escaped his mouth at the mention of the girl shot in the protests. . . . Finally, gripping the lectern determinedly, he vowed that "a movement was born" that "will not rest until it achieves unfettered democracy and human rights in Iran."

In the summer of 2009, there were numerous peaceful demonstrations in support of Iranian protestors by Iranians in the diaspora; these gatherings served an important function as they signaled to demonstrators inside Iran that the world was behind them, and that they had international support. For diasporic Iranians, they also served to counter the feeling of exilic disconnect, forging a connection (real or imagined) with Iranian protestors. At one such gathering in Washington, D.C., several days after Neda's death, Yasmine Pahlavi, the wife of the former crown prince, and two of their daughters, Noor and Iman, joined a group of diasporic Iranians, chanting slogans in Farsi, such as "Neda jan, Neda Jan, we heard your voice" and "Don't be afraid. We are all together" ("khanvadeh shahzadeh" 2009). These chants, uttered by diasporic Iranians across the Western world, were attempts at bridging the diasporic narrative with a national one. A feature of the diasporic Iranian experience is the discomfiting feeling of guilt for having left their homeland in the first place; during the protests, many diasporic Iranians shared their feelings of longing and guilt for not being there, for not being able to be part of the protests and to be "on the ground" in Iran. These chants were thus a form of bringing diasporic Iranians closer to Iranians "at home" ("khanvadeh shahzadeh" 2009).

Another one of the chants at the Washington, D.C., gathering, "Ma Bache Ha Ye Kourosheem" (We are all the children of Kouros/Cyrus the Great), carries within it echoes of another time in history: the spectacularly lavish 1971 celebration of 2,500 years of Persian civilization at the ruins of Persepolis, the former seat of the Persian Empire, an event that has been roundly criticized in both popular and academic circles.[12] As part of the same celebrations at the tomb of Cyrus the Great in Pasargad, the shah famously assured Cyrus that he "'could repose in peace for we are awake'" (A. Milani 2011, 338). His self-aggrandizing gesture has been subject to much ridicule as the claiming of Cyrus alongside the claiming of Neda at a demonstration featuring the Pahlavi family in Washington, D.C., brings to mind another less-than-glorious moment in Iranian history. Thus the protest chants in the diaspora carried with them the force of nostalgia. While Iranians in Iran were expressing their hopes for the future, the chants of Iranians in the diaspora bore the weighty memoires of their past connection to Iran, and in this case, of a romanticized, ancestral past celebrating the glories of the Persian Empire. Alongside this chant conjuring a bygone political era, the YouTube video also shows Yasmine Pahlavi chanting, "Yes we can," evoking a more contemporary political context, and an obvious reference to Obama and his signature 2008 presidential campaign slogan.

These gestures to American (or American-style) democracy through affiliation with Obama exemplify Wendy Hesford's (2011) point regarding "the human rights spectacle" (7). There are a number of ways to interpret the claiming of Neda's image as an icon of freedom and democracy by the Pahlavi family as well as by other Iranians in the diaspora. On the one hand, this claiming can be understood as "appropriations of human suffering in activist, cultural, and legal contexts, as well as Western democratic nations' use of images to deflect attention from their own human rights violations by turning other nations into spectacles of violence" (Hesford 2011, 7). Certainly, focusing on the image of Neda as the victim of the human rights abuses of the Islamic Republic obscures not only the human rights record of the United States but also the documented human rights abuses under the Pahlavi regime in prerevolutionary Iran. At the same time, though, Neda's death has served as a productive catalyst for the expression of life narratives by diasporic Iranians deeply affected by the spectacle of her tragic death. While Neda became a vehicle through which diasporic Iranians shared their own memories and stories of Iran, non-Iranians around the globe were equally affected by her death through what Alison Landsberg (2004) has called "prosthetic memory." This type of nonessentialist memory, which is not anchored by a specific geography or particular cultural identity, is unique to the era of global capitalism and mass culture and encourages "a sense of collective social responsibility" (Landsberg 2004, 152). This overwhelming feeling of collective empathy and feeling of social responsibility is what made the global reactions to Neda's death so remarkable. The story of her life and her death recorded on a cell-phone video camera was transformed into such a forceful narrative that many people who previously had no connection to Iran felt themselves moved by her story and by the story of political turmoil in Iran. Neda's narrative managed to inspire a global affect; her tragic story inspired, even if only for a brief moment, a powerful sense of global and collective citizenship.

The outpouring of personal narratives in reaction to Neda's death demonstrates that in certain instances, and "despite our differences in location and history . . . it is possible to appeal to a 'we,' for all of us have some notion of what it is to have lost somebody. Loss has made a tenuous 'we' of us all" (Butler 2004, 20). Understanding public mourning through a collective "we" as proposed by Judith Butler, through prosthetic memory as proposed by Landsberg, or as an act of citizenship, following Robert Hariman and John Louis Lucaites, enables our comprehension of the global outpouring of emotion and the sharing and circulation of life narratives. The video of Neda's death has inspired numerous songs by both professional and amateur musicians. Popular artists such as Madonna and groups such as U2 dedicated concerts to the Green Movement, and to Neda as the martyr of that movement. Many artists and musicians—both Iranian and non-Iranian—dedicated their works, and their concerts, to Neda. Bri Hermanson, an American illustrator, uploaded a portrait of Neda on her blog on June 26, 2009, writing: "Her story has struck a chord with me in many different ways, especially since we were born in the same year, and I felt strongly compelled to make a portrait of her" (Hermanson 2009).[13]

One approach to understanding the universal claiming of Neda, and the ways in which the narrative of her life and death became a vehicle through which diasporic Iranians and non-Iranians disclosed stories of their own lives, is by drawing on Hariman and Lucaites's (2007) observations on mourning: "While seemingly mourning our own loss, we actually are affirming the deeply social nature of our being in the world . . . by grieving for a stranger cut down in public, the mourner affirms an elemental sense of civic friendship" (159–60). Thus, if something positive can be said to have emerged from those dark days in Iranian history, it was the strong sense that, if only for a brief period, there was a powerful and shared global feeling, a universal sense of the importance of *caring* for others. The global reaction to the video of Neda's death thus demonstrates how acts of public mourning can reveal the ways in which our lives are both constituted—and undone—by others (Butler 2004, 23).

Much has been made of Neda's final gaze into the cell-phone camera recording her death and of the fact that she died with her eyes open; the images that have been reproduced of her death show her with her head turned toward the camera, with blood on her face and her eyes fixed on the lens of the camera. Faced with her dying gaze, the viewer as witness is challenged to take a stand, and is thus denied the comfort and privilege of neutrality. In their analysis of the iconic photograph of the 1970 Kent State shootings, Hariman and Lucaites (2007) propose that "the photo reconstitutes citizenship as an emotional act" (144). Hariman and Lucaites (2007) describe the act of viewing, of observing the iconic photograph that marks a traumatic national moment as an example of what they call civic solidarity or civic friendship through the affective bonds of citizenship: "Citizenship is transferable from one body to the other, not by legal entitlement or any contractual relationship, but through acts of empathy, affectional identification, and emotional expression on behalf of the other" (145). The viewing and circulating of Neda's iconic photograph thus inspired a powerful feeling of global citizenship and empathy for all Iranians who were protesting on the streets. Through the global witnessing of Neda's death, the "spectator-witness" felt moved to recognize the humanity of Iranians. This feeling of empathy was conveyed and sustained through the proliferation and circulation of personal narratives by diasporic Iranians (and non-Iranians) online.

Social media, and Facebook in particular, was the principal arena in which diasporic Iranian life narratives, in response to the circulation of Neda's tragic story, flourished. Through the posting and reposting of reflections on the street protests, and specifically of Neda's death, diasporic Iranians shared fragmented recollections of a past life in an attempt to reconnect with the larger Iranian national narrative from which they had felt disconnected. But Neda's life narrative also inspired the publication of the more "conventional," published memoir. Arash Hejazi, the doctor-publisher who featured prominently in the video of Neda's death as he tried to save her life, and who was repaid for his efforts with a life in exile, published his own memoir, *The Gaze of the Gazelle: The Story of a Generation* (Hejazi 2011). Written about the events of Neda's death—and of his involvement in the last few seconds of her life—Hejazi's (2011) memoir is dedicated to Neda, to his friend, Emad, who filmed and uploaded the video of Neda's death, and to "the hundreds of other innocents slain, detained or tortured during the post-election protests, most of whom belonged to a generation that was not even born when its destiny was sealed during the Islamic Revolution of Iran in 1979" (v).

Hejazi (2011) begins his memoir by demonstrating how the end of Neda's life has shaped the rest of his own:

> I have already shown and told your story to the world, Neda; millions of people know how you were murdered, just because you wanted to have a voice. You are the martyr. People are chanting your name all over the world like a mantra, crystallizing the accumulated hopes and dreams of the Iranian nation. . . . I have lost everything because I told your story; my career, my country, my family, my security. (xvi)

Defining himself and the trajectory of his life with that of Neda's, Hejazi (2011) declares: "I saw her gaze before she passed, the gaze of the gazelle that has been running from the hunter for many hours and now lies on the ground, exhausted and with an arrow deep in her side" (xiv). By claiming responsibility for globalizing her story and her name, Hejazi (2011) also claims ownership of her story, stressing: "I was there when she died. I tried to save her but failed. It was a friend who captured the tragedy on his camera-phone; it was I who sent it out anonymously" (xiv).

Hejazi's memoir thus begins with Neda. Now so much a part of her story, he maintains that his witnessing of Neda's death, and his commitment to recounting the narrative of her life (and death), resulted, for him, in emotional trauma. Telling her tragic story has cost him the ability to live in Iran, thus drastically altering the trajectory of his own life. In order to heal the traumatic break that the circulation of her narrative effected in his life, he decides to write and share memories of his past life. Bookending his memoir with references to the need to write to restore himself emotionally, a process Suzette Henke (2000) calls "scriptotherapy," Hejazi (2011) declares: "I cannot be healed: not until I tell my own story, the story of a generation that was there to see everything, bear everything and lose everything," and ends his memoir expressing the hope that "this is the story that may help me heal" (xvi, 362). The impulse to write or to tell stories as a form of healing is a theme that runs throughout this study of diasporic Iranian life narratives; the authors discussed here narrate their lives as a way of coming to terms with their traumatic experiences.

Hejazi's memoir of the Neda event begins with an account of another moment of rupture in Iranian history. He explains one moment of national crisis—the 2009 postpresidential elections—through the narration of another, earlier period of national upheaval: the 1979 revolution. Hejazi (2011) positions himself as a member of the Burnt Generation, the generation between the ages of

> seven and 15 at the time of the Islamic Revolution. We were the generation that witnessed the murder of its uncles during the Revolution and the execution and imprisonment of its parents afterwards. . . . We were the true witnesses of our nation. . . . We survived to bear witness to what we had endured for the next generation: Neda's generation. (xvii)

Claiming that he does not believe in the idea of destiny, he goes on to contradict himself, suggesting that witnessing the death of Neda was indeed his destiny (Hejazi 2011, xvii). Hejazi's memoir is in fact a somewhat confusing read in part because it is so intensely emotional, suggesting that perhaps his role in the Neda narrative is too recent, and that the trauma of his experiences are too fresh, preventing him from writing a clearly articulated narrative.[14]

Every aspect of Hejazi's memoir is (understandably) deeply bound up with Neda's story. Even the foreword, written by the Brazilian writer Paulo Coelho, begins by claiming a deeper, more intimate connection to Neda. Referring to the viral video of her death, he states: "For me, however, it was more personal. There was a young man in the video trying to save Neda. He was my friend, Arash" (Hejazi 2011, ix). Coelho proceeds to recount the development of his friendship with Hejazi, and of his own personal experiences of Iran. In many ways, then, the narrative of Neda's life and death has inspired the expression of other narratives, other life stories. Neda's tragic story has thus served as a catalyst for the expression and articulation of other life narratives, from the staccato forms of self-disclosure posted to social media, to the longer, meditative memoir form. Either way, the outpouring of personal narratives, memories, and self-disclosures localizes Neda's story at the center from which other narratives reverberate in wider, concentric circles.

Claiming the "Wrong" Neda: Whose Life Narrative?

The global desire to claim Neda and her life story resulted in near-catastrophic consequences for another Neda, the "wrong" Neda. As discussed above, during the intensely emotional aftermath of Neda's death, many felt a powerful impulse to capture, claim, identify with, and circulate her image. During that period, however, a photograph of another woman with a similar name, Neda Soltani, began circulating through social media networking sites, producing unforeseen and tragic complications of a different kind. The image was picked up by CNN and other major news networks, erroneously identifying this photograph of another (very much alive) Neda as the famous video's innocent victim. The young woman, Neda Soltani, sent out desperate pleas to news media and social media, asking people to remove her picture from their blogs, websites, and videos, but her photo continued to circulate—in fact, many used Soltani's photograph as their Facebook avatars in a collapsing of Neda's identity with their own, and while eventually the mistake was corrected in most instances, Soltani's photo remains—at the time of this writing—online in some places as the face of resistance and of the Green Movement. Fearful for her life, Soltani—the "other" Neda—was, like Hejazi, eventually forced to flee the country, seeking asylum in Germany.

In 2011, Soltani, a former professor of English literature at Azad University in Tehran, published her own memoir, *My Stolen Face,* describing the nightmarish scenario that resulted in her eventual exile from Iran. In their desperate search to locate the identity of the young woman who was shot and killed on the street, to tie the film clip to a "real" life narrative—diasporic

Iranians and Western media began circulating Soltani's Facebook profile picture, a photograph of her wearing a flower-patterned headscarf, as the photograph of the murdered Neda. This incident offers a fascinating glimpse into the role of Facebook in the construction—and destruction—of life narratives. According to her memoir, and the various media interviews she has given since living in exile, Soltani first realized that something was amiss when she checked her Facebook account on the evening of Neda's death and noticed that she had—suddenly and inexplicably—received hundreds of "friend" requests from people around the world. She realized that people had mistaken her name, Neda Soltani, for that of Neda Agha-Soltan, so she accepted their requests and explained the mistake. But by then mainstream news channels were circulating her Facebook profile picture around the world. When she realized, to her horror, that the photograph she had uploaded as part of her Facebook profile was being identified as that of the murdered Neda, Soltani removed the photograph from her Facebook account and tried to contact the Western media to sort out the confusion. She was soon to discover that, despite her requests, the media would do nothing to correct the mistake: "I thought about all those journalists, news people, reporters, TV people. They did not care what would happen to me. Whatever awaited me in the end, they would just say I was another victim of the brutal Islamic regime and create a sentimental story out of it'" (Soltani 2011).

What happened, in fact, was a denial of her life by various sources: the Western media and diasporic Iranian activists who used her photo (and initially her name) in their zeal to identify Neda Agha-Soltan and to bring to "life" the girl who died on video were determined to claim her as an icon of democracy and freedom in Iran. "When I saw people all over the world demonstrating with my photo, putting up shrines, lighting candles—it was just like sitting there and watching my own funeral. Of course I knew that it could have been me—I could well have suffered the fate of that poor, innocent woman" (Soltani 2012). A question worth asking here—and one that Soltani also raises in her memoir—is why so many people were sending friend requests to someone whom they presumed was dead. Bizarrely, the Facebook page assumed to be that of the deceased Neda Agha-Soltan had come to stand in for her life. By becoming "friends" with Neda in an alternate, cyber reality, and thus incorporating her online narrative into their individual Facebook profiles, Facebook users in the West could claim a piece of Neda's life. The Iranian government quickly saw, in this debacle, a window of opportunity through which to control the damage that the killing of Neda had wrought on the country's international image and reputation. In other words, they saw an opportunity to rewrite the narrative of the 2009 events. The Ministry of Information began harassing Neda Soltani to recount her story and in so doing, to deny an identity and story that were focusing the world's attention: the death of Neda Agha-Soltan. Because she proved unwilling to cooperate with the state by repudiating the narrative of Neda's life and death, government officials began threatening to charge Soltani with endangering national security. Soltani soon realized that her life was in danger and that her only option was to flee the country, which she did with the help of friends who arranged passage and bribed an airport official.

After several unsuccessful attempts at disentangling her life narrative from that of the other Neda, Soltani (2011) decided that she would begin giving media interviews to explain the mistake:

> With each interview that I gave, the complication that I feared the most reoccurred: hate mail. People, especially my own fellow countrymen and fellow countrywomen, accused me of being a puppet of the Islamic Republic who wanted to distort Neda's image. Others said I was an opportunist charlatan, who was taking advantage of Neda's death to seek asylum in Germany. Still others claimed that they had never seen my photo before. 'What kind of animal is this slut to take advantage of the cruel death of a young woman?!' Several people even took it further by calling my lawyer, and others involved in the publication of articles relating my story, threating to file a lawsuit against me for fabricating a story meant to distort the face of their heroine.

Worth noting here is how the story of Neda Agha-Soltan's life was claimed and circulated in such uncritical and destructive ways by all parties: diasporic Iranians and others in the West as well as the Islamic Republic. Claimed as a martyr for freedom by supporters of the Green Movement in the West, she was also claimed by the Iranian state, which was only too aware of the revolutionary potential of martyrdom in an Iranian cultural context. Initially the Iranian government made significant efforts to contain Neda's image as martyr, and then quickly realizing that this was impossible, they tried to redirect her image in the service of the state. Recognizing the politically explosive possibilities of Neda-as-martyr, the Islamic Republic initially demanded that the Agha-Soltan family remove the black banners signaling mourning from outside their home. The government also prohibited the family from holding a public funeral for their daughter, fearing that a large crowd gathered at her gravesite might trigger more antigovernment protests. Later, the Martyr Foundation of the Islamic Republic approached Neda's family, offering her official martyrdom status, rendering the family eligible for a regular pension and other benefits. The family rejected the offer, not wanting the state to claim her as their own martyr.[15]

At stake in the contest between the so-called Green Movement and its Western supporters, on the one hand, and the Islamic Republic, on the other, to claim Neda as their own martyr is a commitment to two particular and differing visions of the political future of Iran. Butler's (2004) work on the framing of subjects as recognizably human is particularly important for thinking through the implications of these competing claims to Neda as hero-martyr, requiring us to consider "the question of the representability of life itself: what allows a life to become visible in its precariousness and its need for shelter, and what is it that keeps us from seeing or understanding certain lives in this way?" (51). It is thus important to think about the structures of recognition that enable such a profound and intense global engagement with the spectacle of Neda's death. The claiming of (one) Neda's life at the expense of another's requires sober reflection on the ways in which we come to place value on a life. In their zeal to claim a martyr for the antigovernment cause, some diasporic Iranians were willing to destroy and deny the existence of another life—that of Neda Soltani. At the same time, Iranian government officials exerted their efforts in claiming and managing her story in order to deny the death (and life) of Neda Agha-Soltan, whose narrative threatened the self-representation of the Islamic Republic as a government "for the people."

The widespread circulation of Neda's image and of the tragic final moments of her life through social media and mainstream media enabled the articulation of a host of other life narratives: diasporic Iranian, and non-Iranian, through expressions of affinity with what Neda had come to symbolize—an icon for Western-style democracy and freedom. Butler's (2004) remarks on the social function of the obituary as "the means by which a life becomes, or fails to become, a publicly grievable life, an icon for national self-recognition, the means by which a life becomes noteworthy" (34) offer insights into the Neda phenomenon. Neda's life was indeed deemed "note-worthy," as attested by the numerous obituaries that her death inspired. But the question regarding how certain lives—and narratives—become more visible than others remains to be explored. The widespread circulation of Neda's story occurred at the expense of another Neda—whose life was appropriated, misrepresented, and then denied. The trajectory of Neda Soltani's life was interrupted and radically altered as she was forced to start a new life in exile.

But Neda Soltani was not the only one whose life was denied or obscured in the shadow of the globalization of Neda's narrative. In fact, through the publication of *My Stolen Face* and her various media interviews, Soltani has succeeded in writing a "counterstory" to Neda's tragic life (Eakin 2008, 12). The act of writing about our lives affirms both the content of our stories—and us—as the principal actors of our stories (Eakin 2008, 5). In writing our life narrative, writes Eakin (2008), "we establish ourselves as persons: I am someone, someone who has lived a valuable life, a value affirmed precisely by any life story's implicit claim that it is worth telling and hearing" (5). If the act of writing establishes us as persons and affirms our lives, then what of the life narratives that never rise to the surface, those that remain submerged beneath the stories that have been successfully articulated and widely circulated? What of those whose voices are silenced, whose lives are so brutalized that they are unable to find a space through which to come into sight?[16]

Rewriting a Life: The Story of Taraneh

In mid-July 2009, a devastating story began circulating online about a young woman, Taraneh Mousavi, who, according to some reports, was arrested during the time of the postelection protests, although whether or not she was participating in the protests remains unclear. She was reportedly held in detention for several days without permission to contact her parents until they eventually received an anonymous telephone call informing them that she had been admitted to the hospital "following an unfortunate 'accident' in which her womb and anus had been damaged" ("Was Taraneh Raped" 2009). Her parents reportedly never managed to see her: by the time they arrived at the hospital, she had been taken away, although the hospital staff confirmed that a woman with her description had been admitted there. A few days later, Mousavi's burnt corpse was found near Karaj, west of Tehran.

Mousavi's story was publicized on several blogs, and was corroborated by the reformist candidate Mehdi Karroubi, but the Iranian government launched a counteroffensive in the media denying the story and indeed her very existence. Official Iranian reports claimed that this story was false and based entirely on unsubstantiated rumors. Iranian state television aired a report on the Taraneh Mousavi case, referring to the various websites that had made reference to her story, and declared that the entire story had been exposed as baseless rumors and lies ("IRIB Television" 2009). The television station featured an interview with two women whom they identified as Taraneh Mousavi's mother and sister, and claimed that Mousavi herself was living in Vancouver, Canada. This is a disturbing report not least because the interview clearly looks staged, and the women interviewed appear awkward and tense. The interviewer, whose voice we hear but whom we cannot see, sounds friendly—albeit patronizing—and he manages the interview in such a way as to convey the utter absurdity that such a person could ever have existed, let alone that such a tragedy could have befallen her.

The women's and interviewer's (affected) chuckling at the apparent preposterousness of the suggestion that a young woman could be so brutalized by a benevolent government is truly chilling. At the request of the interviewer, the women place a telephone call to a Taraneh Mousavi in Vancouver (presumably the sister and daughter of the two women being interviewed). She picks up the phone, asking if everything is alright, to which her sister responds with "Yes—everything is fine. It's just that your photograph has been on various sites—and they are claiming you have been burnt." At this point, she and the (off-camera) interviewer giggle. The phone line goes dead. The interview ends with the "mother" calling on the government to help find the people who have been spreading such lies so that similar stories do not circulate in this way again.

The unconfirmed and uncorroborated story of Taraneh Mousavi is an unsettling and distressing one. Although the story did gain some traction online, her image is clearly not as recognizable as that of Neda's, nor is her story as well known. Unlike Neda, Taraneh did not die in front of a camera, and so the events of her life and death could be buried—even negated. It is worth remembering, however, that the Islamic Republic also went to great lengths initially to deny Neda's death, maintaining first that Neda faked her death and was actually killed by the doctor, Arash Hejazi, and another man who were only pretending to help her; the state then declared she was in fact still alive by coercing Neda Soltani to claim Neda's identity. Neither one of these attempts to rewrite Neda's story was successful. The Iranian government's attempts to erase and rewrite the narrative of Neda's death only serve to expose the horrifying story of the murder of Taraneh Mousavi. The Islamic Republic has demonstrated its investment in rewriting the life narratives of its victims as a way of controlling the official narrative of the state, but what their efforts demonstrate is that every story that is peeled away reveals another even more condemnatory account about the tactics of the regime.

The official government attempts to deny the Taraneh Mousavi story, complete with the coerced television interview in which her life—indeed her very existence—is denied, is a signature strategy of the Islamic Republic.[17] There are many other stories of Iranian youth tortured and killed in the aftermath of the postelection protests in 2009. Some of these, as in the case of Sohrab Arabi, a young man who was arrested during one of the protests and later murdered while in state custody, are names that circulated online to some degree, but many more of them remain anonymous. This raises the question, then, of whose stories matter. Whose lives get eulogized? At what price do life narratives circulate? Social media plays an increasingly important role in the circulation of such narratives. Fragmentary and incomplete as these narratives may be, their circulation reveals the heightened stakes of life narrative when they can be so easily narratized outside of an individual's control (as in the case of Neda Soltani or Taraneh Mousavi), and mobilized for any number of purposes, both noble and less noble.

This chapter began with Sharon Sliwinski's (2011) question of how a human being becomes recognized as human, and draws on the works of Butler (2004) and Hariman and Lucaites (2007) as it claims that recognizing another as human constitutes an act of global citizenship and civic responsibility. But the process of recognizing another's humanity occurs both through the telling and the *hearing* of life narratives. The question of which stories are told, thus eliciting the necessary claim on the spectator-witness to recognize another's humanity, is the focus of the next chapter.

· CHAPTER 2 ·

Human Rights, Humanitarianism, and Empathic Witnessing

Prison Memoirs

The human capacity to injure other people has always been much greater than its ability to imagine other people. Or perhaps we should say, the human capacity to injure other people is very great precisely because our capacity to imagine other people is very small.

—Elaine Scarry, "The Difficulty of Imagining Other People"

ELAINE SCARRY'S POWERFUL ESSAY on the limits of human empathy and the seemingly limitless capacity for human cruelty provides a useful starting point to this chapter, as it gestures to some of the questions with which this book, and this chapter in particular, is concerned: How is suffering expressed in narrative? And what do narratives of suffering do? How can we, as privileged readers, bear witness to the traumatic experiences endured by political prisoners in a meaningful way, in a way that goes beyond merely expressing sympathy in the face of another's suffering? How can we, as readers located in the West, read and engage with narratives of violence, torture, imprisonment, and suffering, particularly when these narratives depict experiences in cultural and national locations with which the West has a compromised—and often vexed—relationship?

Beginning with Marina Nemat's (2007) *Prisoner of Tehran,* 2007 saw the proliferation of diasporic Iranian women's prison narratives written in English. Other prison narratives published that year include Camelia Entekhabi-Fard's (2007) *Camelia, Save Yourself by Telling the Truth* and the collection *We Lived to Tell: Political Prison Memoirs of Iranian Women* (Agah, Mehr, and Parsi 2007). These were followed by Zarah Ghahramani's (2008) *My Life as a Traitor,* Haleh Esfandiari's (2009) *My Prison, My Home: One Woman's Story of Captivity in Iran,* Roxana Saberi's (2010) *Between Two Worlds: My Life and Captivity in Iran,* and Shahla Talebi's (2011) *Ghosts of*

Revolution: Rekindled Memories of Imprisonment in Iran.[1] These prison narratives are part of a wave of testimonial literatures that foreground suffering, drawing on a relatively recent (since the late eighteenth century) genre of the humanitarian narrative.[2]

The prison memoir, as humanitarian narrative, requires us to consider the pressures of ethical response placed on readers of autobiographical accounts of imprisonment, torture, and human suffering. While human rights and humanitarian acts "share many attributes and emerged from the same intellectual origins in liberal political philosophy of the eighteenth century," the relationship between the two is somewhat ambiguous, even fraught (Wilson and Brown 2009, 4–5). As Richard Ashby Wilson and Richard D. Brown (2009) have claimed, "The historical divergence between 'humanitarianism,' the wish to promote human welfare, and human rights is critical. . . . The humanitarian seeks to assist fellow human beings and to alleviate suffering, and does not necessarily act to defend violated rights" (11). This chapter, then, explores the problems of narratizing trauma, a central concern in trauma studies being the "problem of witness testimony, and of memory" (Hodgkin and Radstone 2006, 99) and the tensions between the affective impact of humanitarian narratives and the human rights imperative.

The emotive power of humanitarian narratives generates ethical and moral responses to the suffering body. However, as Sophia A. McClennen and Joseph R. Slaughter (2009) have argued, we live in an era in which the language of human rights is everywhere—and thus nowhere—since it has become a tool wielded by both the left and the right to serve their own political agendas.[3] Bearing in mind the constant threat of the possible co-optation of human rights discourses, cultural critics should engage with the question of humanitarianism and of human rights while remaining vigilant against "the possibility of further emptying out the power and language of human rights in the process of making them commonplace" (McClennen and Slaughter 2009, 5).[4]

In his work on the similarities between the humanitarian narrative and the bildungsroman, Slaughter has argued that the humanitarian narrative reasserts the modern individual (with rights, and with a voice) and explores what happens to this modern subject when faced with a denial of these rights. According to Wilson and Brown (2009),

> The narrative form not only prompts emotional engagement, sympathy, and guilt; it can also promote a remarkable variety of

> types of action. In particular . . . individual victims' narratives seem to be a necessary component in the mobilization of empathy, and in the formation of global political constituencies to end the suffering of others. (20)

Responding with empathy (which recognizes difference—unlike sympathy, which assumes sameness) to stories of pain and trauma allows us to begin the process of reading our privilege and others' suffering by attending to an understanding of compassion as an emotion that impels action, and by redirecting the expression of compassion to one of internal redress: to a claim on the privileged witness to "became an ameliorative actor" in the face of suffering (Berlant 2004, 1).[5] Thus, the politics of compassion in these prison narratives disallow a neutral stance. In Sara Ahmed's (2004) words, "emotions are relational"; they engender feeling in the reader that can be a socially and politically transformative response to another's traumatic experience (8). This more hopeful view of an empathic engagement with—through the witnessing of—others' suffering is challenged by Thomas Laqueur's (2009) claim that "the very term 'humanitarianism' has long been suspect precisely because sentiments for humanity generally did not translate easily into care for humanity at hand. . . . It is, and was, far easier to be moved than to be moved to action, far easier to see clearly at a distance than nearby" (33). Kay Schaffer and Sidonie Smith (2004) claim that the circulation of stories of suffering that take place in distant lands can humanize otherwise vilified cultures and peoples, but at the same time, "empathetic identification became a means to the reader's own self-affirmation as an empowered agent, here an agent of social change and humanitarian betterment" (12). Elspeth Probyn (2005) has argued that

> through the media's representation of different forms of suffering, privileged citizens get a glimpse of pain and thereby gain a certain sense of empathy, without, of course, having to endure the conditions that produce pain. This constitutes a climate of second-hand, or vicarious, feeling. . . . It seems that a little bit of pain can make you feel better about yourself. (7)

With these caveats in mind regarding the potential pitfalls of expressions of humanitarianism, of feeling moved without being "moved to action," and of the simultaneous dangers of expressions of sympathy that serve to reconsolidate the self as a feeling and humane subject, this chapter explores the relatively recent proliferation of diasporic Iranian women's prison memoirs written in English and considers the context of their reception in the West (Laqueur 2009, 33). Some of the questions explored in this chapter include a consideration of why some narratives become more popular or more palatable or more affecting than others. For example, how can we make sense of the far-reaching sympathetic responses elicited by some well-known prison narratives—for example, Marina Nemat's (2007) *Prisoner of Tehran*? How can we understand the expression of compassion in relation to Nemat's text against a marked lack of affective response to those unrepresentable subjects of trauma whose narrative reach does not extend as far, whose sufferings do not register as deeply upon readers in the West? Schaffer and Smith (2004) claim that some "empathetic identification . . . recuperates stories of radical differences into their more familiar frameworks of meaning. Such acts of consumption of other peoples' lives enable them to dispel the fear of otherness by containing it" (12). Some narratives of trauma are thus more easily recuperable and more relatable than others. Some narratives of suffering invite humanitarian expressions of sympathy while others do not.

In thinking about the emotional impact of these prison memoirs, we might consider not just the story of suffering told but also how experiences of suffering are narrativized. What kinds of cultural and literary codes do these memoirs draw upon? Part of the answer lies in the generic conventions upon which these narratives draw. In *Boom! Manufacturing Memoir for the Popular Market,* Julie Rak (2013) argues for a return to genre in helping us understand the seemingly insatiable public thirst for memoirs in North America, stating: "Genre is a powerful organizing set of principles, preconceptions, and practices that without calling attention to itself, drives much of the way memoir is produced, consumed, and received" (18). Rak (2013) proposes a compelling theory for the generic appeal of the memoir, arguing that what makes a genre both recognizable and pleasurable is the promise of repetition—but with a difference:

> If we think of genre as the non-identical repetition of familiar elements, it is possible to understand why, unlike literature with its features of uniqueness, generic writing is popular with many people. If literature generally works on the principle of difference—a great work of literature must be different from others or the

> works of an author are similar, but are different in kind and quality from what other authors write—then generic writing works because the recognition of repetition is pleasurable. (29)

The proliferation of humanitarian narratives through the genre of the prison memoir has been critical in engendering Western sympathy for the suffering Iranian subject, particularly at this historical juncture when the Iranian state remains deeply unpopular in the West. Thus, the humanizing of subjects living under a widely vilified state relies on rendering the unfamiliar familiar. At times that process is enabled—and at times hindered—through the deployment of recognizable narrative codes, tropes, and genres: for example, those of the captivity narrative or the romance novel.

The captivity narrative can be traced back to an early modern Western literary tradition that reflects Western anxieties about colonial exploration and exploitation. North America is where the captivity genre originated and flourished, capitalizing on white settlers' fear of "Indians" and the physical threat they presumably posed to the vulnerable American or British female body.[6] This popular genre with roots in seventeenth-century New World "contact narratives" experienced a resurgence in popularity with Betty Mahmoody's (1987) *Not without My Daughter,* as both Farzaneh Milani and Gillian Whitlock have observed.[7] According to Whitlock (2007),

> It is Mahmoody's story of her incarceration in Iran after the revolution that revitalized the captivity narrative in contemporary harem literature (and, incidentally, the legend of the innocent American confronted by fanatics). . . . This fear of captivity is the dark side of harem literature: here is the horror of the white Christian woman incarcerated and subjected to the veil against her will. (103)

In *Words Not Swords,* Milani (2011) also refers to the echoes of the genre of the captivity narrative in some recent memoirs about Iran. Milani takes especial care, however, to make a distinction between the hostage narrative and the prison narrative.[8] Indeed, there are important differences between the two genres, but it would not be too far-fetched to suggest, as I do, that the appeal of prison memoirs such as Nemat's, for instance, has to do precisely with the fact that her narrative straddles the border between the two genres. In other words, because Nemat's memoir affects at once the posture of a prison narrative while working within the generic conventions of the less taxing (in terms of readerly experience) captivity narrative, it has succeeded in drawing upon a broad audience.

Thus, the popularity of prison memoirs such as Nemat's (2007) *Prisoner of Tehran*, Ghahramani's (2008) *My Life as a Traitor*, and, to a lesser extent, Entekhabi-Fard's (2007) *Camelia, Save Yourself by Telling the Truth* can be in part attributed to the fact that they fulfill (North American) readers' expectations of what constitutes a female captivity narrative. In the tradition of the captivity genre, their stories are both racialized and eroticized.[9] The truth of these authors' accounts of their brutalizing experiences in prison is decidedly *not* the issue here; rather, Rak's (2013) claim about the recognizable, familiar, and pleasurable elements of genre provides a useful approach to considering the far-reaching humanitarian responses elicited by these memoirs. According to Wilson and Brown (2009), "Because a commitment to humanitarianism can frequently be fulfilled and rewarded more promptly in the here and now than can a commitment to human rights, humanitarianism more reliably delivers emotional rewards" (11–12). Thus, the recognizable genre of the captivity narrative plays on affective, humanitarian responses to a familiar threat: the vulnerability of young women in the face of powerful, dominating men—often in a racialized context. This humanitarian response can be articulated in isolated terms, directed toward a suffering individual, without taking into account the larger political and social forces that have led to unjust conditions. In other words, the humanitarian response demands less from us: we express feelings of sorrow or pity regarding an isolated case without turning a self-reflexive, critical eye toward the larger social and political system, which creates inequalities and hierarchies, a system in which we may be ourselves complicit.

Working within the generic tradition of colonial stories of captivity, Nemat's *Prisoner of Tehran* sets up a dichotomy between Nemat's own more civilized Christianity and the barbaric (in this case, Muslim) worldview of her captors. Thus, the fictional tropes of the captivity narrative (which has Christian inflections) are familiar to a Western readership and risk confirming, rather than contesting, generalized images of a threatening Iran. In her memoir, Nemat details the conditions of her arrest and imprisonment at age sixteen in Iran's notorious Evin Prison. Nemat is tortured and sentenced to death, but she is dramatically rescued moments before her execution by her interrogator, who forces her to marry him. It is a sensational story in which her interrogator/husband is soon murdered by his own colleagues in Evin, but thanks to the help of her in-laws, Nemat is released, and eventually escapes to Canada, settling and raising a family in Aurora, Ontario.

In *Prisoner of Tehran,* Nemat repeatedly reminds us of her Christian faith. Of her first interrogation in prison by her future husband, Ali, she writes: "Maybe I was the only Christian he had ever seen in Evin. He probably had expected me to be like most Muslim girls from traditional families—quiet, shy, and submissive—but I didn't have any of these qualities" (Nemat 2007, 13). In a discussion with her captor/husband, Ali, Nemat asks him why the other interrogator dislikes her so much: "He explained that Hamehd and many others like him didn't care for those who are different and have different ways. I sighed. I didn't understand this strange Islamic society" (166). This representation of Hamehd "and others like him," presumably other Islamic fundamentalists, feeds into a civilizational discourse at the heart of captivity narratives. This civilizational discourse that fixes the representation of Muslim societies as always out of time or as somehow deficient in relation to Western societies is articulated through feelings of humanitarianism and expressions of compassion.

In *My Life as a Traitor,* Ghahramani, arrested at age twenty and held in Evin Prison for participating in student protests, foregrounds her mother's Zoroastrian faith, invoking a romanticized image of ancient Persia and the Zoroastrian values of peace and kindness:

> As a child, I felt utterly at home in the Zoroastrian community. I loved the costumes (really, versions of ancient Persian national dress: billowing silks of many colors, scarves, dainty slippers) and the celebrations of seasons. The temperament of the men, women, and children I met at celebrations added to the attraction. There was nothing hard-line about them, nothing dogmatic. (Ghahramani 2008, 20)

Despite her avowed preference for Zoroastrianism, she nevertheless expresses a respect for the "true" values of Islam as practiced by her father (Ghahramani 2008, 18–20). Camelia Entekhabi-Fard, a journalist with the now-defunct daily newspaper *Zan,* has a Muslim background but takes pains early in the book to situate herself within a secular, Westernized, and pro-Pahlavi family:

> At home in our house, we had neither listened to the personal communiqués from Ayatollah Khomeini who was arriving from Paris, nor did we join the throngs of revolutionaries burning tires in the streets. When revolutionaries tossed their manifestos into our courtyard at night, my father would throw them back out onto the street. We didn't want to know where they planned to gather, and we weren't interested in the mullahs or that surly old man with the crooked black eyebrows either. (Entekhabi-Fard 2007, 13)

Thus, Nemat, Ghahramani, and Entekhabi-Fard take pains to signal to readers that they are writing about Iran from minority positions; they foreground their minority religious status (in the case of Nemat and Ghahramani) and their secular Westernized identity (as in the case of Entekhabi-Fard and Ghahramani). All three emphasize their Persianness as opposed to a Muslimness mistrusted in the West, positioning themselves as "other" enough to represent their subject authoritatively and familiar enough not to alienate their Western audiences.[10] The tension between a familiar "sameness" and a more ominous "difference" is essential to generating the anxiety on which the captivity narrative operates.

Nemat's, Ghahramani's, and Entekhabi-Fard's narratives are also highly eroticized following the tropic conventions of both the captivity genre and the Harlequin/desert romance, which hinge on the anxieties that emerge in response to the sexual threat posed by the figure of "swarthy" men. In *Prisoner of Tehran,* Nemat evokes her fragility throughout; just before her interrogators lash her feet, one of them declares: "'Ali, look; she has such small wrists! They'll slide out of the cuffs,' said Hamehd. He forced both my wrists into one cuff and dragged me to the bed" (Nemat 2007, 17). The crucial scene in which her execution is stayed is reminiscent of a Harlequin or desert romance (a genre that often draws on the racialized captivity narrative) in which the ingenue is abducted by a threatening, often dangerous, man consumed with sexual desire and against whom she is powerless:

> His eyes focused on mine, Ali walked toward me. I wanted to run. . . . Ali untied me from the pole. I collapsed. He caught me, lifted me, and walked toward the car. I could feel his heart beat against my body. I uselessly tried to struggle out of his arms. . . . Ali dropped me in the front passenger seat of his car and slammed the door. I tried to open it, but it wouldn't open. (Nemat 2007, 40)

Here, Nemat's heightened awareness of his beating heart against her body, and her struggle, despite her physical frailty, against his overpowering masculine strength sexualizes the dynamic between them, drawing on what Tania Modleski (1982) has identified as the formulaic plot of Harlequin romances. In her description of the Harlequin formula, Modleski (1982) refers to a 1976 Harlequin text, *Goblin Court:*

> Knowing the hero will eventually imply or state that he has loved the heroine from the beginning, the reader can attribute the hero's expressions of hostility and derision to his inability to admit, perhaps even to himself, how much the sight of the woman "sprawled at the side of the road looking like a collapsed puppet" inflames his passion and rouses his admiration. Male brutality comes to be seen as a manifestation not of contempt, but of love. (40–41)

The reference to the woman as a collapsed puppet arousing the man's passions is strikingly similar to Nemat's description of herself collapsing into Ali's arms after he unties her from the pole. At the risk of trivializing the undoubtedly harrowing prison experiences of Nemat, Entekhabi-Fard, and Ghahramani, it is difficult to overlook the Harlequin romance tradition upon which they appear to be drawing in their personal narratives.

In *Camelia,* Entekhabi-Fard, like Nemat, focuses on her physical attractiveness. She even cites her distinctive looks as one of the major sources of conflict with her teachers at school. Both Nemat and Entekhabi-Fard emphasize their feminine delicacy in a way that renders them appealing and that invokes the narrative conventions of romance and captivity narratives. Entekhabi-Fard (2007) writes of her female guard's jealousy of her appearance and even of her undergarments: "She was fascinated with my yellow ruffled Victoria's Secret underwear that I had bought in New York. And when my mother sent me underwear from home, she sent fine lingerie, and it became another source of jealousy for little Leila" (44).

The theme of feminine good looks as jarringly out of place in prison also surfaces in Ghahramani's *My Life as a Traitor.* After an interrogation session in which she is beaten and suffers a cut to her face, Ghahramani (2008) writes of her fear:

> I will not be given any medical treatment, the wound will suppurate, I will become deformed and ugly, I will no longer be a pretty

> Persian girl, people will pity me, boys will avoid me, I will never marry. How powerful my vanity is! My world is toppling into ruins around me, and the only thing I can think of is my pretty face! (91)

Ghahramani is understandably terrified by the violence to which she has been subjected, and by the overall atmosphere of arbitrary rule in Evin, but this sense of terror is further magnified as she emphasizes her delicate, feminine features, invoking the literary trope of female fragility in the face of powerful and arbitrary masculine force common to the captivity and romance genre.

All three texts work within a framework of sexualized power relations between the male captor and the female captive, but Entekhabi-Fard (2007) underscores her agency as a female subject by claiming her freedom through her self-professed "seduction" of her interrogator:

> We had never seen each other, as I always faced the wall in the interrogation room. I used my voice and my hands to draw him in—my voice soft and contrite as I confessed, and my hands dancing like swans. I could sense him changing slowly. I knew he couldn't wait for the moment he could turn me toward him, when we would face each other. (45)

Other Harlequin elements of this narrative are evident in passages like the following: "Love, like a wisp of fresh air from paradise, had been blown deep into the heart of this hardened man. I knew, even when he punched me, that he felt he was touching a delicate flower. His mood swings were harsh because this love confused him" (Entekhabi-Fard 2007, 219). Entekhabi-Fard's representation of her interrogator as possessing a rough, hardened exterior that will eventually soften in the face of his unexpected love for the bewitching ingenue is, as Modleski (1982) has argued, a defining feature of romance novels, from Samuel Richardson's *Pamela* and Charlotte Brontë's *Jane Eyre* to twentieth-century Harlequin novels:

> The heroine is confused by the hero's behavior since, though he is obviously interested in her, he is mocking, cynical, contemptuous, often hostile, and even somewhat brutal. By the end, however, all misunderstandings are cleared away, and the hero reveals his love for the heroine, who reciprocates. (36)

This is certainly the case in Nemat and Entekhabi-Fard's texts: both manage to transform a prisoner-interrogator relationship into a romantic one.

The figure of the brutish lover won over by a diminutive, meek young woman, conventional in popular romance, is thus a feature shared in both *Camelia* and *Prisoner of Tehran,* although Entekhabi-Fard presents herself in a more active role as her interrogator's seducer, while Nemat remains an unwilling and passive victim. Nevertheless, the familiarity of this romance/captivity narrative in *Prisoner of Tehran* is what may account for its wide appeal, and the generally sympathetic response from a Western readership (indeed, Nemat has become a minor celebrity in Canada), as well as its angry denunciation by some former Iranian political prisoners, many of whom now live in Canada or Europe.

The very basis of the story, which has elicited humanitarian responses from Western readers, has been angrily rejected by leftist Iranians living in the diaspora. The heated reactions to Nemat's book were documented on Shahrzad Mojab's University of Toronto website, Memories, Memoirs and the Arts: Women Political Prisoners of Iran. (This website was updated and relaunched in the spring of 2014 with a new title, Political Prisoners: The Art of Resistance in the Middle East.) In its earlier incarnation, the website included a letter by former political prisoners addressed to Mojab in her capacity as (then) director of the Women and Gender Studies Institute at the University of Toronto, dated July 22, 2007:

> Based on what each one of us experienced and witnessed in our long imprisonment terms in the Islamic Republic's prisons, we strongly believe and can prove that *Prisoner of Tehran,* by Marina Nemat, is a fabrication. Not only does it distort the depiction of real events, it is, in fact a work of fiction and imagination. . . . The book serves to contaminate and discredit the image of former political prisoners, their struggles, and their resistance in prison. Above that, this book is a blatant insult to the people of Iran, and to the thousands who were executed in the Islamic Republic's prisons. (Mojab n.d.)

These former political prisoners also wrote to Penguin Canada in protest, stressing the difference between fact and fiction, truth and falsehood: "If Ms. Nemat had presented this book as a novel or story, it would be another matter. But time and time again in public interviews, she has insisted that the book is documentary and factual."

These letters, and other statements in response to Nemat's book, underscore the importance of "autobiography as a form of witnessing which 'matters to others'" (L. Anderson 2001, 126). What Suzette Henke (2000) has termed "scriptotherapy" (writing as a form of therapy) can only be successful if there is an audience willing to bear witness to the articulated trauma (xii); without this form of public witnessing, trauma becomes pathology. The mere act of writing is not in and of itself therapeutic; the testimonial relies upon an exchange between the speaker and the listener, the traumatized and the witness. If this relationship does not occur, trauma remains trapped in what Caruth (1996) has called an "unclaimed experience." Underlying the protests of former Iranian political prisoners is this very frustration—and anxiety—that their testimonials do not have the reach of Nemat's Penguin publisher, leaving their trauma unclaimed and unheard.

The anger generated regarding the "truth" of Nemat's narrative is a criticism often launched against the writers of memoirs. But as Thomas Couser and other critics of memoirs and life narrative have emphasized, the term *memoir* "derives from the French word for memory. . . . Calling a narrative about yourself a memoir usually signals that it is based primarily on memory, a notoriously unreliable and highly selective faculty" (Couser 2012, 19). Bearing in mind the origins of the term, locating the truth and accuracy of a particular memoir is less my concern here than an exploration of the narrative conventions employed in such accounts, the kinds of feelings these stories generate in readers, and in turn what kinds of actions such feelings might inspire.

Despite pointing out the recognizable fictional tropes within which Nemat's, Entekhabi-Fard's, and Ghahramani's texts operate, my intention is not to dismiss their accounts of torture, imprisonment, and suffering. Rather, following Rak (2013), I explore how certain life stories are told through the mobilization of recognizable generic conventions and the (social) effects of these texts' public circulation. What engages my interest here is a reflection on the emotional impact of certain humanitarian narratives and a consideration of why some narratives of suffering appear more persuasive and more affecting than others. Why do some narratives invite humanitarian responses and not others? *Prisoner of Tehran, Camelia,* and *My Life as a Traitor* all have circulated quite widely in the West, and a quick Google search reveals "book club" questions prepared by their publishers in order to encourage discussion in informal reading groups, suggesting, then, that these books are widely read or at least that they are understood as appealing to a large audience.[11] *Prisoner of Tehran,* however, has achieved an astonishing level of fame—at least in Canada, where the book was a contender for the annual "Canada Reads" competition sponsored by the Canadian Broadcasting Corporation.[12]

Another feature common to all three books, and to the captivity genre, is an individualist narrative of personal freedom and escape. Schaffer and Smith (2004) claim:

> The "triumph" of global capitalism and the dominance of the West, particularly in the United States, have meant that the culture of the individual, with the belief in the individual's uniqueness and unique story, and in individual rights, has gained an international currency as it has been exported to ever expanding areas of the globe. (11)

Indeed, *Camelia, My Life as a Traitor,* and *Prisoner of Tehran* all invoke a celebratory model of individualism, and all three texts work within a framework of sexualized power relations between the (male) captor and the (female) captive as discussed above. Nemat's memoir concludes on a note of individualist, middle-class triumphalism in quiet, suburban Aurora; Ghahramani's narrative ends with her escape to Australia, with the assistance of the journalist Robert Hillman and his wife, who encourage and facilitate her departure from Iran and her immigration to Australia; Entekhabi-Fard flies to New York City after she persuades her captor/lover that she will work as a spy for the Iranian government, but once there, she refuses to return to Iran.

Entekhabi-Fard's self-representation as an agential subject, at once a triumphant individual fighting against an oppressive state and an unapologetic female temptress, forms the core of her memoir and is further reflected in the ambiguity of the title of her text. At a glance, the somewhat awkward title, *Camelia, Save Yourself by Telling the Truth,* can be taken as a reference to the act of bearing witness to injustice, or a call for courageous truth-telling in the face of oppressive power. Midway through her memoir, however, Entekhabi-Fard (2007) reveals that the imperative to truth-telling appears on the forms on which prisoners are forced to confess and to repent their sins: "I began the 'homework' my interrogator had given me—several sheets of paper marked 'Ministry of Intelligence, Interrogation Form.' An expression in Arabic was printed in bold black ink at the top of each page.... Below the Arabic, the Persian translation read, 'Nejat-e shoma dar rastgui ast'" ("Your deliverance comes through truth-telling," or in Entekhabi-Fard's own translation, "save yourself by telling the truth") (101). What is intriguing here is how slippery categories of truth-telling become: what one claims to be testimony and witnessing becomes collaboration with the system in another instance. Embedded in this statement of truth-telling and saving the self is the imperative to deliver a "truthful" narrative that implicates friends and family. Entekhabi-Fard (2007) writes frankly of her collaboration: "Then I confessed to him, I told him about everything.... I felt like a nun, I felt that I *needed* this confession" (44). It is not insignificant that Entekhabi-Fard here compares herself to a nun, drawing on a religious and Catholic model of penance and confession, a moral and spiritual cleansing ritual that would be familiar to a Western readership, albeit a specific one. In light of Entekhabi-Fard's professed seduction of her interrogator, the reference to a model of Catholic confession and absolution cannot be accidental.

The ominous-sounding counsel on the confession forms, however, if heeded, transforms the subject from a valiant prisoner of conscience into a much-derided confessant/*tavvab,* a despised and feared figure of "the repentant prisoner" unique to the prisons of the Islamic Republic of Iran. According to Ervand Abrahamian (1999), the Islamic Republic created and fostered the category of the *tavvab* or repenter as an insidious method of internal control:

> Prisoners were closely watched by repenters ever eager to win privileges and their freedom. Not surprisingly, prisoners detested these *kapos* and *antenss* (antennas) on the lookout for incriminating information.... The wardens set up a Repenters' Society, a newspaper called *Payam-e Tawabin* (Repenters' Message), and special wards named Bandeh Jehad (Crusaders' Wards). They offered them incentives—more generous rations, lighter sentences, even amnesty, and access to the prison workshops, where women could earn pocket money as garment workers and men could earn pocket money as metal workers. They also encouraged women repenters to marry eligible guards. This fueled the rumor—mostly unfounded—that they condoned sex between guards and prisoners. (168)[13]

In her introduction to the collection of stories *We Lived to Tell,* Mojab (2007) describes the category of *tavvab* as follows:

> The state enforces religious morality through the creation of informants. The *tavvab* is a prisoner who is being forced to denounce her politics and be somebody other than herself: an interrogator, a pious woman, a believer, a spy; a *tavvab* is the ears and eyes of her captors, an executor of rules within the cell, an arbitrator among inmates and prison guards. . . . To show her religious devotion, she shoots the last shot of executions; she accompanies guards on the streets to identify activists and bring them into captivity. (10)

Although the religion to which the *tavvab* pledges allegiance is Islam, the *tavvab* in prison and the Christian subject in the Catholic Church's confessional box both confess and repent their sins, whether sexual or political in nature, and their confessions ultimately work to buttress existing systems and relations of power. Describing her own transformation into a confessant/*tavvab,* Entekhabi-Fard (2007) writes:

> I didn't want to become a spy, to criticize and investigate my colleagues. My stomach turned at the thought, yet I agreed to everything. I had entered into an agreement not to be "me." I melted at the sound of my interrogator's voice. I let him mold me into a new person, the person he wished me to be: a soldier waiting on the orders of her commander. (77)

There are, of course, important differences between the confessional in a Catholic church and the dehumanizing process of repentance specific to the prisons of the Islamic Republic, a process that creates a new category of being—the *tavvab*/repenter—that results in the imprisonment and murder of others. What is notable, here, is that Entekhabi-Fard is keen to draw a comparison between her confession and the confession of a nun, appealing in that moment to the sympathy of a Western audience for whom the idea of confessing one's sins resonates quite differently than for an Iranian readership familiar with the *tavvab* phenomenon and for whom "confession" may signal the betrayal of one's friends and fellow inmates. Further, the image of a nun conjures a sanitized and desexualized image, an image at a significant remove from Entekhabi-Fard's (2007) admission:

> I'd hear him coming down the hall for me, and I couldn't wait—I would imagine he wasn't coming to torture me but to love me. I needed this peace of mind to keep from going crazy and to store up energy to stay strong. How could I force him to love me, too? He thought of me as *mofsed,* deserving execution. I couldn't change him and I couldn't change the world. But I'd fallen in love, and I felt it, real love. I couldn't control my heart's beating when I heard him approaching. (45)

Scarry (1985) has claimed that the untranslatable nature of pain, as in instances of torture, accounts for the disdain most people express toward political prisoners who confess under duress of physical torture.[14] In his study of prisons and torture in modern Iran, however, Abrahamian (1999) takes a different view from Scarry. Describing the development of the category of the *tavvab,* or recanter, Abrahamian (1999) traces the perceptible shift in public attitudes toward recanters, noting that in light of information regarding the brutal conditions of torture in (postrevolutionary Iranian) prisons, there is greater public sympathy toward them:

> This rising awareness about torture led many to be more understanding of recanters—even to empathize with them. This again contrasted sharply with the past. Traditionally, the term *e'terafat* (confession, recantation) had connoted betrayal and defection. By the late 1980s, it could mean no more than a measured response to unbearable pain. Similarly, the term *towab* (repenter) originally had the associations of active collaboration. But by the late 1980s, it could mean no more than passive and limited submission. The prisoners themselves sharply differentiated between "tactical" and genuine "repentances," between halfhearted and full-hearted recantations, between harmless and deadly confessions, and between those "broken" into passive submission and those induced into active collaboration. (224)

Herein, according to Abrahamian, lies the main difference between "recanters": while most people have now come to understand the televised confession as evidence of the brutality to which the prisoner is subjected, there is a perceived difference between the strategic (and reluctant) recanter and the recanter as active collaborator, one who is so broken by conditions in prison that she is willing to spy on her cellmates, often former colleagues and friends.

Writing about the popularity and the marketing of life narratives, Schaffer and Smith (2004) observe that "publishing houses . . . convert stories of suffering and survival into commodified experiences for general audiences with diverse desires, and also for an increasing number of niche audiences interested in particular kinds of suffering" (11). Thus the confessing subject/*tavvab* upholds the status quo in the first instance of confession, in prison, and later in the second instance in books whose target market is a North American or European audience. In both cases, the confessant's narrative acts as the truth that the audience in question (the interrogator/captor in prison, or the reader in the West) wants to hear. Former Iranian political prisoners now in the diaspora have expressed their anger at Nemat's representations of conditions at Evin and have questioned the veracity of her narrative. Indeed, three things appear to be at stake here: the truth of her narrative, the truth of her suffering, and a contestation of her claim to compassion. All three prison narratives discussed above compel a humanitarian response from the reader as witness; these narratives engender some kind of feeling in the reader that can be a socially and politically transformative response to another's traumatic experience. However, while this engendered compassion or "'sociality' of emotion" may have transformative political or personal potential for the Western and Iranian reader of the prison memoir, we need also to bear in mind Ahmed's (2004) caution that

> the charitable discourses of compassion more broadly show us that stories of pain involve complex relations of power. . . . The over-representation of the pain of others is significant in that it fixes the other as the one who "has" pain, and who can overcome that pain only when the Western subject feels moved enough to give. (22)

Similarly, Lauren Berlant (2004) has argued that "compassion is a term denoting privilege: the sufferer is *over there*" (4). The gap that opens up between the object of compassion and the compassionate subject is where expressions of humanitarianism are articulated, underscoring how feelings of compassion and humanitarianism are inextricably bound up with complex relations of power.

The prison memoirs of Entekhabi-Fard, Ghahramani, and Nemat illustrate the crossing vectors of compassion and humanitarianism. The foregrounding of Nemat's Christian identity in particular is an important element of her marketing success. Nemat repeatedly reminds us of her Christian faith, of the fact that on the night of her arrest she took her rosary beads with her to Evin, and that she was forced to convert to Islam while there. In the media literature on Nemat's book, there are frequent comparisons to Zahra Kazemi, the Iranian Canadian photojournalist who was brutally raped and murdered in Evin. Nemat (2007) herself mentions Kazemi in a postscript to her book, and claims to give her and other political prisoners voice through the writing of her memoir:

> If the world had paid attention earlier, if the world had cared, Zahra would not have died; many innocent lives would have been saved. But the world remained silent, partly because witnesses like me had been afraid to speak up. But enough was enough. I was not going to let fear hold me captive any longer. . . . I had a story to tell. Zahra had given Iran's political prisoners a name and a face; now it was my turn to give them words. (276)

This statement, noble as it sounds, is misleading: the Kazemi case actually received significant international attention, and resulted in very tense relations between Ottawa and Tehran. In response to Iranian intransigence over the Canadian government's request to have her body repatriated to Canada, Ottawa recalled its ambassador from Tehran. While it is true that this heated exchange between the two governments took place after her death, Nemat's claim—"if the world had cared," Kazemi would still be alive today—sounds rather disingenuous.

By claiming the position of one who speaks the truth at her own risk, Nemat authenticates her narrative through association with Kazemi, whose violent death in Evin has come to symbolize the brutality of the Islamic regime. Nemat's invocation of Kazemi thus validates the truth of her own experiences, thereby establishing her as worthy of her readers' compassion. Her second memoir, *After Tehran: A Life Reclaimed,* is about the writing of her first book, the emotional turmoil she endured as a result of its publication, and the backlash she experienced in the Iranian community. Here, she constructs herself as a victim once again—not only of the memories of prison haunting her but also of the unfavorable reaction to her prison memoir by her family and Iranian audiences alike. This follow-up memoir is dedicated to Neda, the young woman who was shot and killed on the streets of Tehran in the summer of 2009 and became the iconic face of the Green Movement.[15]

The object of compassion has to be at least somewhat familiar, or recognizable, to the compassionate subject, marking a critical difference between feelings of compassion and pity. Using the work of Hannah Arendt, Elizabeth Spelman (1997) describes compassion as a sharing in the suffering of another; pity, on the other hand, allows us to feel the suffering of the other in such a way that "reflects and announces the distance" between the sufferer and the witness to suffering (67). Marjorie Garber (2004) makes a further distinction between compassion and sympathy, arguing that while compassion points to hierarchies and unequal structures of power, "*sympathy* remain[s] historically a condition of equality or affinity" (23). By focusing on their positions as minorities within Iran, and through a constant negotiation of this dialectic of familiarity and otherness, writers such as Nemat, Ghahramani, and Entekhabi-Fard attempt to navigate the precarious terrain of their readers' feelings of compassion, sympathy, and pity. For example, these narratives have solicited the compassion and benevolence of the Western subject through a reconsolidation of Iran as a place of intolerance and suffering Iranians as objects of pity.

In an article titled "Looking for Peace, Not Pity" in the *Sydney Morning Herald,* Robert Hillman (2007), coauthor of Ghahramani's prison memoir, describes the development of what appears to be a perturbing degree of interest in Ghahramani and a compulsive drive to protect her. While working as a journalist in Tehran, Hillman and his wife befriend Ghahramani and her family and friends. In the article, he describes himself watching her and thinking about her with an intensity that borders on the disquieting. Hillman repeatedly urges Ghahramani to come to Australia, a plea with which she eventually complies. In the article, he rationalizes his absorption in her life as somehow connected to his anxiety over Australian immigration policies and the inhospitable climate for Muslim immigrants in that country. However, Hillman (2007) chooses, rather disturbingly, to disclose a somewhat unhealthy preoccupation with her appearance:

> My concern for Zarah extended to her wardrobe. I was most relaxed when her choice of clothes matched that of every other casually dressed young woman on the streets of Melbourne:

> low-cut jeans, broad belt, simple top. Then, perversely, I began to worry that she looked too much like every other young woman. When we went to meet publishers to discuss a book we'd written together, I almost suggested that she wear a head scarf with her jeans. (4)

As he recognizes his growing preoccupation with her appearance and with her life in Australia, he simultaneously disavows his fixation by emphasizing his concern for her well-being in the context of Australian nationalist discourses on Muslim immigrants specifically and multiculturalism more generally. Hillman (2007) concludes on a self-reflexive note: "At least let them [Muslim immigrants] be free of the pity of people like me" (5). In this moment of self-awareness, Hillman recognizes the way his liberal politics—through expressions of compassion and humanitarian concern for the immigrant other—re-cements hierarchies of Western liberal democracies and Islamic fundamentalist states.[16] Further, the mobilization of compassion and pity participates in an unequal economy: the liberal democratic subject extends compassion, or worse, pity, to the object suffering at the hands of "anti-liberal" or "totalitarian" oppression *in exchange* for the spectacle and consumption of the abject suffering body.

Ghahramani is a particularly desirable object of compassion as she is young and photogenic. The shaving of her head becomes, for her, an act that constitutes the pinnacle of her degradation while in Evin:

> My head feels—wrong. Not on the inside, on the outside. I want my hair back. Nothing that has happened to me in prison has distressed me like the shearing of my head. And I know it is shallow, I know it is all to do with vanity. But, I was pretty once. I liked being pretty. So, what is this? A character-building opportunity? A chance to accept how superficial being pretty is? I don't want the opportunity! I want to be a pretty Persian girl dutifully attending to her studies and having nothing to do with politics. Nothing. (Ghahramani 2008, 72–73)

As mentioned above, Entekhabi-Fard, Nemat, and Ghahramani emphasize their good looks in their respective narratives. This singling out of themselves as physically attractive is coupled with repeated references to Entekhabi-Fard's Westernized secular family, Ghahramani's Zoroastrian roots, and Nemat's Christian faith. This is an effective rhetorical strategy aimed at making themselves both physically and ideologically appealing to readers located in the West.

Nemat as a Christian, Ghahramani as a secular Persian/Zoroastrian, and Entekahbi-Fard as secular and Westernized are seen as tolerant (or tolerated/tolerable) subjects who "fit" in the West by virtue of their minority status in Iran and because of their recognizable and familiar subjectivities for the Western reader. Their stories of imprisonment and struggle for freedom inspire the compassion of like-minded liberal subjects. But these testimonial narratives of suffering and pain, which impel us to bear witness and to feel the suffering of those represented in these texts, and also presumably the suffering of those who cannot represent themselves (Kazemi would be one such example), remind us that "claims of shared human suffering can do as much to reinforce claims of superiority and inferiority as they can to undermine them" (Spelman 1997, 9). How, then, do we engage with testimonial literatures, with stories of suffering, without reproducing inequities between compassionate readers and differently constituted subjects of suffering? The proliferation in testimonial narratives, in narratives of trauma and pain, force us into a crisis of witnessing. How can we make sense of the far-reaching compassionate responses elicited by testimonials such as Nemat's *Prisoner of Tehran* and, to a lesser extent, Entekhabi-Fard's *Camelia* or Ghahramani's *My Life as a Traitor*? How can we understand this articulation of compassion against the marked lack of affective response to those unrepresentable subjects of trauma whose narratives do not travel as far, whose sufferings cannot circulate as effectively, and thus do not inspire feelings of humanitarianism, let alone a sustained engagement with and commitment to human rights?

The collection *We Lived to Tell: Political Prison Memoirs of Iranian Women* (Agah, Mehr, and Parsi, 2007) is an example of a prison narrative that has not circulated as widely as those discussed so far. In light of the fact that this collection was published in the same year as Nemat's and Entekhabi-Fard's prison memoirs, and one year before Ghahramani's, the question of the difference in their reception requires some attention. *We Lived to Tell* is a collection of three separate stories by three women political prisoners. These narratives offer unrelenting accounts of the psychological and physical torture to which the authors and their cellmates were subjected during their time in Evin. Certainly none of these stories can be said to fit the genres of the captivity narrative or the Harlequin romance. These are stark descriptions that recount the suffering of mothers as they bear responsibility for their children living the first years of their lives behind prison bars, and then endure the pain of separation as they send their children out of prison, to be raised by family members while they themselves languish in prison, paying the price for their political convictions. The stories relate an atmosphere of terror where women prisoners feel total powerlessness in the face of the arbitrary exercise of authority and the menacing presence of *tavvabs*/repenters in their cell blocks. But these stories are also meant to work as inspirational descriptions of lasting bonds between women and the gratifying humanity that can sometimes be found in the most inhumane conditions.

The stories told here, however, do not work within the same familiar and recognizable storytelling conventions as do the prison memoirs discussed above. There is, for example, very little—if any—character development; the social and familial context of the narrators is barely mentioned, offering little sense of the history of the protagonists in these stories, or of what led them to their political activism. There is not much information about the narrators, leaving us with little sense of the characters, their families, and their personalities outside of the context of their political convictions. These narratives do not work within the genre of the bildungsroman with a suffering-redemption arc of personal growth. This absence of conventional narrative plot goes some way to explaining why this collection was not picked up by larger publishers such as Penguin or Farrar, Straus and Giroux (as in the case of Nemat's and Ghahramani's memoirs). These are narratives that work primarily as bleak testimonials, foregrounding experiential authority and ardent political convictions over and above narration.

In *We Lived to Tell,* the reader is faced with accounts of suffering, relentless in their descriptions of terror and abuse, and, as a result, extremely demanding in their affective claim upon the reader as witness. The collection's more limited circulation and its lesser emotional impact on readers in the West (as compared to Nemat's memoir, for instance) can be explained through what Whitlock (2007) describes as the "withdrawal of empathy" in the face of testimonials that demand witnessing but fail to register the necessary response in the reader (80). Whitlock (2007) considers the fact that "compassion fatigue . . . from affective overload in the mass media" might partly account for an audience's unwillingness to be compassionate witnesses to trauma (80). However, as she points out, affective overload is only a partial answer to narratives that fail to elicit a compassionate response.

We Lived to Tell tests the limits of human empathy, illustrating Scarry's (1996) contention that

> the way we act toward "Others" is shaped by the way we imagine them. Both philosophic and literary descriptions of such imagining show the difficulty of picturing other persons in their full weight and solidity. This is true even when the person is a friend or acquaintance; the problem is further magnified when the person is a stranger or "foreigner." (98)

The unembellished prose, the absence of character development, the dearth of information about the characters outside of their political activism, and the narrative's refusal to work within recognizable generic forms are contributing factors to the text's relative public invisibility.

In large part because the stories do not draw on narrative conventions (of plot or character development), and because the prose is unpolished and at times uneven, *We Lived to Tell* has not succeeded in inspiring large numbers to act as, in Ann Cubilié's (2005) words, "witnesses to the witnesses."[17] In order to inspire people to move to the assistance of others, there has to be a familiarity (of genre, of character), an element of recognition for the reader. Unfortunately, *We Lived to Tell* has not inspired a humanitarian response similar to that evoked by Nemat's or Ghahramani's memoirs. The starkness of the stories in this collection, and their disclosure of the bare facts of prison life, make a basic and uncompromising appeal to human rights, demanding more of the reader than simply "feeling moved." But in the absence of narrative conventions, the collection's too aggressive claim on the reader for an affective response remains unheeded.

Shahla Talebi's *Ghosts of Revolution* (2011) is a prison memoir that operates in a different register than any of the ones previously discussed. Unlike the prison memoirs considered above, Talebi offers a historical contextualization of Iranian society and politics that does not lend itself to hastily drawn conclusions about the country as a unilaterally brutal place. Rather than working within the limits of the genres of the captivity narrative or the romance novel, *Ghosts of Revolution*—and indeed, *We Lived to Tell*—can be described in terms of what John Beverley (2004) calls the "testimonio," which translates as "testimony," the act of bearing witness to injustice (32): "*Testimonio* represents an affirmation of the individual subject, even of individual growth and transformation, but *in connection with a group or class situation marked by marginalization, oppression, and struggle*" (41). The authors' recounting of their political activism under the Islamic Republic (and under the shah) is fueled by a class consciousness and a commitment to political change, thus marking their narratives as more obviously *testimonio* than Nemat's, Ghahramani's, or Entekhabi-Fard's prison memoirs.

However, unlike the authors of *We Lived to Tell,* Talebi writes in graceful prose, intertwining her memories of suffering and torture in prison with those of her fellow inmates and of their collective efforts to keep their selves intact under the dehumanizing effects of torture. Talebi's memoir, an emotionally challenging read, is a story of defiance against oppression and binding love between those who have suffered the unimaginable torments of political prisons. This is a powerful text that bears witness to the traumatic effects of torture and imprisonment in pre- and postrevolutionary Iran and the horror of the mass executions of 1988 during which thousands of political prisoners—including her own husband—were summarily killed and thrown into unmarked graves.[18] Now a faculty member in the Department of Religious Studies at Arizona State University, Talebi engages with questions of torture and suffering through a deeply personal and complex theoretical lens.

Building on Scarry's (1985) claim that "physical pain . . . is language-destroying" (19), Slaughter (2007) argues that "as a human rights violation, torture is paradigmatic in its implementation as a tool to destroy a speaking subject. Human rights violations target the voice, and therefore, the voice should be the focus of international human rights instruments" (2). The proliferation of diasporic Iranian women's prison narratives in recent years, however, contests Scarry's and Slaughter's claims about the destruction of the voice of the tortured subject. In response to theories of trauma as inarticulable and unrepresentable, Wendy S. Hesford (2011) poses a salient question: "Given the translation of pain and suffering into the language of agency and witnessing in human rights discourse, we might ask why we should hold on to the notion of its inexpressiblity" (55). Indeed, Talebi's narrative works, in deliberate and thoughtful ways, as a challenge to Scarry's formulation of torture as language-destroying; her memoir is a poignant and deeply affecting testimonial to both the cruelties and the generosities of human relationships.

In response to the attempted destruction of her voice, Talebi offers a moving account of her experience in prison and as a victim of torture. Describing her reaction to the fate of some of her former cellmates, who, shortly after their release, succumbed to the traumatic memories of torture and imprisonment by committing suicide or succumbing to madness, Talebi (2011) writes:

> I realized that I was not writing, or dreaming about my experience, or more accurately, did not know what I was dreaming about; nor was I aware if I was even dreaming at all. It was a state of despair, a space of silence and lost voice. I was no longer even singing to myself as I used to. Horrified by this realization, I reluctantly began to write, and my writings were saturated with the ghosts of the dead and the spirits of the mad. . . . It became apparent to me that I could not tell my story unless it incorporated all these other voices and worlds, as giving voice to anyone else would inevitably involve my own story. (52–53)

Putting pen to paper, she expresses her voice and shares her memories alongside descriptions of her friends and cellmates, articulating a vision of humanity that conceives of human relationships as interdependent, stressing her belief that the well-being of oneself is necessarily dependent upon the well-being of others. Unfortunately, this is also a model that does not have the cultural valence of narratives of triumphant individualism, such as, for example, the genre of the bildungsroman.

Every chapter in *Ghosts of Revolution* incorporates stories of other people whose lives became inextricably intertwined with Talebi's own in prison, and whose sufferings impress themselves upon her memory. With sensitivity and empathy, Talebi traces and narrates the trajectory of each individual's life. In extreme cases, as in the irrevocably damaged young Roya, who has removed herself cognitively and emotionally from her immediate surroundings, Talebi and her fellow prisoners hypothesize about her life before prison. Speculating about her middle-class background, Talebi fleshes out Roya's pre-prison life, thus offering her, in the fullness of generosity, and even without her awareness, memories of happiness, love, and security, a time before prison and before torture. Throughout her memoir, Talebi offers moving descriptions of her inmates, even humanizing a particularly despised recanter/*tavvab,* Fozi, by contextualizing her story through a sympathetic framework that challenges Scarry's (1996) claim with which this chapter began: "Our capacity to imagine other people is very small" (103). Talebi intertwines these descriptions of others' lives with memories of her own past, of her family, and of her husband, who was executed in 1988.

In *Ghosts of Revolution,* Talebi puts forward a vision of the individual as always already contingent on another. Conjuring Scarry's perception of torture as the total destruction of the boundaries of the liberal individual subject, Talebi (2011) draws attention to the fact that human lives are always relational:

> Free agency is an illusive modern liberal concept, true. But rethinking it in a context of the other and within a collective notion of human existence concerned with an ethics of living responsibly and responsively in relation to others is the ideal that, no matter how utopian it may be, is worth pursuing. (214)

In a moving illustration of how the dissolution of the boundaries of the individual under torture can challenge the modern construction of the self-contained individual, Talebi relates the story of Soudi and Behrouz, who were subjected to torture in the same chamber. As related by Soudi, even in the extremities of pain, Behrouz was full of love and empathy for her suffering, and gave her the tools with which to survive—even as he knew his own death under torture was inevitable: "But what was certain was the fact that for Soudi, Behrouz's resistance had generated a sense of hope and showed her a power beyond the destruction of torture that not only allowed her to survive the torture but taught her the art of living and dying. Refusing to bargain with his dignity and humanity, he confronted the system of individualization according to which all a person cares about is his own pain and happiness. Behrouz's attitude indicated how his ethics of care for the self was linked to his care for others" (Talebi 2011, 94). This collective sensibility offers redemptive possibility; yet, being at odds with the triumphant individualism favored in the genre, it does not have the means to reach wider audiences.

Thus, Talebi's memoir as humanitarian narrative in the form of *testimonio* makes claims on the reader to respond to narratives of suffering in ethically and politically responsible ways, but it also places stress on the modern conception of the individual as self-contained and autonomous. As Talebi relates her visceral account of pain and torture, she writes also of resilience and of the possibility of retaining one's humanity, one's ability to feel empathy even in the most brutal of conditions. As she recounts her experiences and those of others, however, Talebi (2011) is sensitive to the challenges of the genre in which she is writing, emphasizing the unreliability of the faculty of memory:

> It is impossible to provide an intact image of what happened in prison. Nobody is able to do that. I am talking about it, as others have, so I do not forget and yet to free myself from its haunting, imprisoning power. But in order not to forget, I must see it as outside of me, in narrating it, in remembering it as something that occurred in the past. The task is complicated. What I remember is my memory; it could never be an utter narration of what happened in the past, but rather what I remember and experience today as my feelings and memories of then. Yet it is the life that my mind and body remember and of which herein I write. (49)

Relying on memory to access a "pure" and authentic account of the past is, obviously, both chimerical and impossible. Talebi is sensitive to the multiplicity of ways in which she can narrate her story of imprisonment—depending on how she remembers events at any given time. Recognizing the centrality of memory in autobiographical writings underscores the importance of allowing ourselves to be "touched by the past," as Roger Simon (2005) describes it. For Simon (2005), to be touched by the past is not simply to feel empathy or pain in the face of another's traumatic recall:

> At stake in the touch of the past is the welcome given to the memories of others as a teaching—not simply in the didactic sense of imparting new information—but more fundamentally as that which brings me more than I can contain. To be brought more than one can contain is not a condition in which one becomes a symptom of a history one cannot possess, but rather a condition of possibility for true learning—one which bears the risk of being dispossessed of one's certainties. (10)

Ghosts of Revolution stands apart from the memoirs discussed above: this is not a sensationalist story in the style of the captivity narrative, nor is it a stark description of events in the style of a political manifesto (as is unfortunately the case with *We Lived to Tell*). Rather, Talebi's memoir is about the resilience of ordinary people in dehumanizing and degrading conditions. It is also, uncomfortably, the story of the evils committed by ordinary people in ordinary circumstances, such as her recounting of her memories of the torture and suffering inflicted on the village dog by a group of boys when she was a child, or of the pleasure with which her teachers inflicted corporal punishment on nonconformist students. Talebi interweaves her memories of the torture to which she and others were subjected in prison with her childhood memories of the physical and emotional suffering inflicted by other children on their peers.

A particularly disturbing episode for her family involved a group of young men who tormented and terrorized her good-natured but slow-witted cousin, Yousuf, by tossing him into a fast-moving river, in the full knowledge that he did not know how to swim:

> Gulping the water, frozen and paralyzed, he stared at death spreading over him. His last look at the world he knew till then was at the devilish expressions in his friends' eyes and their grinning faces enjoying themselves at his expense. This time of eternity for Yousuf was also the moment of exceeding pleasure for his coworkers—an instant during which Yousuf crossed the line to the world of the absolute other. (Talebi 2011, 164)

Drawing comparisons between this instance of group violence and the mass prison killings in 1988, Talebi (2011) writes:

> The way that everyone seems to have played a part in drawing Yousuf to his final destination reminds me of the massacre of political prisoners in the summer of 1988. The prison officials pursued a policy of having everyone's hands in the system covered with prisoners' blood. . . . It was to keep everyone silent about the massacre, for if they spoke, the secret of their own role in the crime would be revealed. (166)

Talebi's memoir thus extends a significant challenge to readers; it requires us to self-reflect in ways that can be deeply uncomfortable, asking us to imagine not only others' suffering when they are at a safe remove but also to reflect on the disturbing affinities between the cruelties to which human beings subject each other in their quotidian lives with the torture and betrayal of friends and cellmates in a heightened, harrowing context such as in prison. Talebi's memoir, then, compels us to contemplate and acknowledge, in profoundly unsettling ways, the limits of our own humanity.

Contrary to Scarry's statement regarding the impossibility of imagining and feeling empathy for others, and despite his own reservations about feeling moved without "feeling moved to action," Laqueur (2009) also recognizes that "narratives of suffering generate fellow feelings that are—and historically were—crucial to the origins and continuing success of an ever widening struggle for human rights" (31). Thinking about memoir as a genre that generates feelings of empathy for the suffering of another, and as a mode of expression that humanizes an other, affords us an understanding of the prison memoir both as a *testimonio* that bears witness against injustice and as a humanitarian narrative that demands that we rethink our conceptions of ourselves as self-contained individuals. Keeping in mind the limitations of the humanitarian impulse with which this chapter began, an absolute rejection of humanitarianism would be not only a tragic error but also a posture struck out of the myopia of total privilege. For those who have suffered the tragic misfortune of seeing inside the walls of prison, but who, thanks to a global campaign clamoring for their release, were able to escape relatively unscathed, humanitarian action literally saved their lives.[19] Talebi's prison memoir as humanitarian narrative thus places stress on our ability to feel empathy and challenges us to articulate an uncompromising commitment not only to the language but also to the implementation of an ideal of human rights that is all encompassing and uncompromising in its vision and its aims.

· CHAPTER 3 ·

Feeling Nostalgic, Feeling Guilty

Remembering Iran in Documentary Film

Nostalgia is about the relationship between individual biography and the biography of groups or nations, between personal and collective memory, individual home and collective homeland.

—Svetlana Boym, "Off-Modern Homecoming in Art and Theory"

While the first two chapters of this book concern themselves with the responsibilities of diasporic Iranian and Western witnesses to auto/biographical accounts of suffering and human rights abuses in Iran, the first half of this chapter takes a more meditative approach to the place of nostalgia in diasporic Iranian life narratives as represented in documentary films. Focusing on three auto/biographical documentaries made by diasporic Iranian women from two different generations, this chapter explores the overlapping of nostalgic feelings with private (familial) memories and public (official) narratives of the past. As discussed earlier in this book, life narratives, and specifically those by diasporic Iranians, have generated a significant amount of interest in academic and popular contexts in recent years. Most—if not all—of these life narratives, despite their diversity in style and content, tend to negotiate a common element: the Iranian revolution experienced as an emotional wound or trauma.

Understanding the revolution as a traumatic event accounts for its belated articulation into narrative, one of the defining features of trauma being its unassimilable nature (Caruth 1996, 4). Considering the revolution as traumatic betrays one's social and political class, however, since it assumes a certain suffering—political, economic, and social—as a result of the revolution.[1] Obviously, not all Iranians may have experienced the revolution as traumatic, but it would not be far-fetched to propose that the majority of Iranians currently in the diaspora—and irrespective of their social and political backgrounds—are now *here* because they can no longer be *there.* Thus, what they share is an experience of revolution as rupture, as traumatic break, interrupting the anticipated trajectory of their lives. Cathy Caruth's (1995) definition of trauma as the belated return of the repressed is one way of accounting for the outpouring of Iranian women's life narratives that invoke the seismic changes wrought by the revolution—some thirty-plus years after the event.[2] At the heart of diasporic Iranian autobiographical expressions that portray the revolution as both an individual and a collective trauma lies a nostalgic impulse to reclaim a lost (prerevolutionary) nation or home, and alongside a sense of home, a claim to a projected and imagined lost identity.

Nostalgia has tended historically to be regarded in negative terms: initially viewed as a curable medical disease, it was later considered to be a form of psychological trauma.[3] Once it was no longer diagnosed as a medical—and therefore treatable—ailment, nostalgia was recast, in cultural and literary contexts, as an emotional wound. These negative connotations have contributed to a view of nostalgia as implying movement backward, but as Svetlana Boym (2001) has argued, nostalgia is as much about projecting a future past as it is about claiming an irretrievable past. In other words, nostalgic remembrances of prerevolutionary Iran do not simply amount to mourning a "lost" Iran or a past life, they are also an expression of mourning *for one's future self that might have been.* In the nostalgic desire to reclaim an irretrievable place (Iran) and irretrievable time (pre-1979) lies an articulated grief for a future that *could have been.* At the level of the individual nostalgic, the desire for another place and another time involves a mourning for that (imagined) future self—who the diasporic subject imagines herself to have become had the traumatic event (in this case, the revolution) not taken place.

Golkou Parhizgar's (2010) *Round-Trip* and Nahid Persson Sarvestani's (2008) *The Queen and I* are autobiographical documentaries that explore the filmmakers' personal trajectories from Iran to the United Kingdom and Sweden (respectively). In his landmark essay, James Clifford (1994) has described the diasporic search for one's roots as a process of traveling along paths both emotional and physical (304). In *Round-Trip,* Parhizgar, born in the early 1980s at the peak of political turbulence and systematic terror in the early postrevolutionary years, traces the complex and circuitous path of her life from Tehran to London and (temporarily) back to Tehran again. As she traces the routes she has taken in search of her personal, familial, and cultural roots, she is careful to retain politics in the background. But as for most diasporics, politics is never very far removed from her personal story. Parhizgar's autobiographical documentary begins with an out-of-focus shot, an extreme close-up of an open music box with a Disney princess figurine twirling in time to the tinny music. The camera zooms out slightly to depict Parhizgar's eye reflected in the toy-size mirror. Gradually, the scene comes into focus and the viewer is drawn into the narrative unfolding through Parhizgar's eye, the autobiographical "I" of her story. For Leah Anderst (2013), the autobiographical "I," or what she has termed the "viewing I," "is a figure that highlights the autobiographical filmmaker as a self-aware practitioner who represents not only her story but also her thinking about that story, her filmmaking practices, and her role as arranger of the materials of her story" (214–15). The viewing "I" draws attention to the constructedness of the autobiographical narrative by recognizing the centrality of the autobiographer's role in piecing together different moments in her life to create what appears to be a seamless and linear story (223).

This chapter examines how life narratives are assembled and narrated in documentary film and how the visual medium of documentary lends itself to the role of witnessing in human rights documentaries. Although the films discussed here cannot be neatly categorized as human rights documentaries, all three films touch on the question of human rights and social justice. In particular, Sarvestani's *My Stolen Revolution* brings to the fore questions of witness and suffering in its depiction of the lives of former political prisoners.

In *Round-Trip,* Parhizgar begins her auto/biographical documentary by moving back into her childhood past from the present moment of filming by including photographs of herself as a child and of her parents; the movie also begins and ends with a close-up of one of her treasured childhood possessions: a music box. The movie thus begins with a self-conscious attempt at chronological order: over the tinkling sounds of the music box, Parhizgar's voice-over informs the viewer: "Some people are born a girl, some a boy. Some are born in the East, some in the West. Some people are born in a home. Some in a hospital. I was born at Evin political prison in Tehran in 1983." This startling revelation interrupts the fairy-tale fantasy invoked by the twirling Disney princess figurine, whose image is abruptly cut and replaced by a childhood photograph of Parhizgar wearing the required *maqn'aeh,* a form of compulsory *hijab,* or head covering, for all schoolchildren in postrevolutionary Iran. The image of the Disney princess conjures not only a particular Western fairy-tale tradition but also the global commodification of femininity marketed and distributed by the Disney corporation.

The sudden shift in focus from the image of the dancing Disney princess to the childhood photograph of the filmmaker in a *maqn'aeh* gestures to the radical rupture in the historical and political trajectory of Iran. The Iranian government, which in the 1960s and 1970s implemented nationwide policies to Westernize the nation and to encourage Western investment in the country, suddenly found itself facing a popular resistance movement that rejected all things Western.

The radical shift in the political atmosphere in late 1970s Iran is reflected in the documentary with the abrupt visual shift from the dancing Disney princess to the sober black-and-white photograph of Parhizgar wearing the state-ordained *maqn'aeh.* This photograph is followed with footage from the massive street protests during the 1979 revolution as Parhizgar narrates: "Like millions of other Iranians, my parents were involved in the revolution and were arrested for their political beliefs. They were imprisoned for three years. I left the prison to live with my paternal grandparents, Mamani and Babai, when I was six months old." After this remarkable beginning, the film makes an abrupt shift to the present time of the film: "Tehran 2009." Parhizgar continues: "After eleven years of living in England, at the age of twenty-six, I returned to Iran with a one-year round-trip ticket."

The documentary's out-of-focus image in the opening shot—the extreme close-up of the music box and the reflection of Parhizgar's eye in its mirror—gradually sharpens, centering on the eye/I, or "the viewing I," of the autobiographical narrator (Anderst 2013). This sharpening of focus reminds the viewer that this is Parhizgar's personal story, one that will be shaped, directed, and narrated by her. Notwithstanding the accepted notion in autobiographical criticism that the process of remembering and reconstructing a narrative of the past is both imperfect and selective, some of the omissions in Parhizgar's narrative are puzzling. For example, Parhizgar mentions the location and date of her birth—Evin Prison, 1983—only to gloss over this disquieting revelation. Parhizgar's parents were imprisoned in Evin during a terrifying period in the history of this notorious prison; the 1980s were a dark and fearful time in Iran, culminating with clandestine mass executions of leftist prisoners in 1988.[4] Astonishingly, Parhizgar does not mention this episode of terror in Iranian history when she discloses the fact of her parents' imprisonment—and of her birth—in Evin during this very same period. Although she states that her parents' political activism lands them in jail, she does not elaborate on the nature of their political activism or the details of their imprisonment and eventual release. Their subsequent divorce upon leaving prison also only garners a brief mention. Intertwined with a fraught history and politics, Parhizgar's personal story thus begs further elaboration. Hers is a somewhat reluctant autobiography, certainly a hesitant one, extending some information while withholding more. Although the selective remembering of one's past is part of the autobiographical process—requiring readers, and viewers, to remain attuned to "the role of remembering, and conscious forgetting, in the act of making meaning out of the past and present"—Parhizgar's fleeting and evasive mention of her birth in Evin during that terrifying period in Iranian history is quite extraordinary (Smith and Watson [2001] 2010, 30).[5]

It is worth remembering, however, that the reluctance for full self-disclosure is a distinctive feature of the diasporic Iranian condition: autobiographical statements by Iranians in the diaspora are often tempered with caution, as this is a population keenly attuned to the risks of revealing too much, particularly with respect to their political leanings. Always apprehensive about the possibility of encountering government informers, diasporic Iranians are acutely aware that venturing into controversial political terrain risks thwarting the diasporic fantasy of return to the "home" country. As a diasporic subject with the ability to move freely across borders, Parhizgar takes especial care not to jeopardize her mobility, her ability to travel unhindered between Tehran and London. This desire for continued access to Iran accounts for her relative reticence to share her views on Iranian politics as she focuses her lens instead on the personal and emotional effects of displacement. Nevertheless, the film brushes against the subject of internal Iranian politics as it emphasizes a feeling of optimism and upcoming change shared by Iranian youth. Parhizgar herself makes reference to a desire to be part of this (unspecified) change. In view of the fact that the documentary was filmed in the months before the controversial presidential election results of June 2009, this reference to "change" is not insignificant.[6] But, as with her reticence about her parents' and her own early childhood experiences in Evin, Parhizgar is reluctant to elaborate any further upon the changes to which she somewhat cryptically alludes and of which she desires to be a part. Her reluctance to disclose too much information can be further understood in the context of the volatile and terrorizing political atmosphere in Iran, particularly in the violent aftermath of the 2009 protests.

Rather than focusing on the politically charged idea of future change, the film dwells on the less fraught and risky emotion of nostalgia. *Round-Trip,* for the most part, dwells in a type of nostalgia that Boym (2001) identifies as modern, one that she defines as "a mourning for the impossibility of mythical return, for the loss of an enchanted world with clear borders and values; it could be a secular expression of a spiritual longing, nostalgia for an absolute, a home that is both physical and spiritual, the edenic unity of time and space before entry into history" (8). Parhizgar's auto/biographical documentary thus offers a meditation on the subject of nostalgia and on the concept of home: as a young child, Parhizgar chooses to leave Iran, where she was living with her grandmother, in order to join her mother, who had made a new home for herself in London. Later, as an adult, Parhizgar returns to Iran and explores the possibility of moving back to live in her homeland. Her documentary investigates feelings of displacement while recognizing, at the same time, that the experience of being "out of place" is not necessarily the exclusive circumstance of the diasporic subject; the emotionally disruptive experience of being out of place at home is a condition shared by disenfranchised peoples anywhere. This film focuses on feelings of alienation and unbelonging as the lot of the diasporic subject as well as of the modern Iranian subject currently living in postrevolutionary Iran.

Through interviews with friends and family, Parhizgar affords the viewer a glimpse into the bizarre, disjointed life of young people in Iran for whom the concept of home has become alien since the country in which they reside and to which they have emotional attachments is also the place that actively oppresses them, that curtails their freedoms and their movements. While "home" has become an alien place, the prospect of leaving, for many, is either an economic or political impossibility or an option they are not yet emotionally prepared to consider. Parhizgar interviews Iranians of her generation in an effort to locate her own internal compass and to fix her personal understanding of "home," but the more people to whom she speaks the more she uncovers a general, shared malaise, a heightened sense of displacement particularly among Iranian youth: "It's becoming clear to me that I'm not the only one struggling with matters of identity. Somehow young people here also feel like strangers in their own country."

These interviews disclose to the viewer the frustrations of and disenchantment with life under the Islamic Republic experienced by Iranian youth, and an abstract longing for the (imagined) past of their parents' generation; indeed, the documentaries discussed in this chapter all use the interview form through which to explore the filmmakers'—and their subjects'—nostalgic relationship to Iran. Given that all three films focus on the genre of the interview through which to recount auto/biographical narratives, Bill Nichols's claim about the hierarchical nature of the interview is an important one to recall here; interviews, for Nichols (1991), are part of what he calls "discourses of sobriety" that are "sobering because they regard their relation to the real as direct, immediate, transparent. Through them, power exerts itself. . . . They are the vehicles of domination and conscience, power and knowledge, desire and will" (4). Given that individual, personal narratives in these auto/biographical documentaries are disclosed through the structure of the interview, a healthy suspicion of the interview's claim to a direct representation of reality informs my analysis.

The strength of *Round-Trip* is in its engagement with nostalgia. The film focuses on a nostalgic longing for an irretrievable past and an imagined, hoped-for future, thereby challenging the notion that the return to a physical place, in this case, Iran, will function as a soothing balm applied to the feelings of pain and loss that are part of nostalgic longing. Through her documentary, Parhizgar offers a nuanced and complex understanding of nostalgia—as an emotion borne not only out of the fruits of exile but also one that can be keenly felt while still "at home." Boym's (2001) attention to the temporal aspect of nostalgia is key here: nostalgia is generated not just by a feeling of loss in relation to a former physical home but also by a mourning for another *time,* another period in history, that once held the promise of future possibilities.

The nostalgia in which the postrevolutionary generation of young people in Iran indulge, however, is a form of what Arjun Appadurai (1996) has called "armchair nostalgia, nostalgia without lived experience or collective historical memory" (78). While postrevolutionary generations do not have the same "lived experience" of prerevolutionary Iran as do their parents, some draw on the collective memory of the previous generation, and thus indulge in a nostalgic yearning for a historical time they did not experience except as mediated through their parents' memories.[7] So, the postrevolutionary generation's yearning for a better time, for a time other than the one in which they are currently living, is infused with their parents' nostalgic longings for their own youth during the Pahlavi period. Iranians born after 1979 appear at once *less* marked by the revolution that left its irrevocable scar on their parents' lives and *more* deeply scarred by its aftershocks, responsible as the revolution was (and continues to be) for the radical schism between public and private spheres in contemporary Iran. Thus the nostalgia of young Iranians is for a time when the separation between the public and the private was not so severely marked.

Parhizgar interviews various acquaintances, including her half sisters, her cousins, and her friends, most of whom express a desire to leave Iran but who, attuned to the emotional consequences of living in the diaspora, have yet to take the steps required to do so. The documentary also includes interviews with friends who comment on the mass exodus of young people from Iran to North America or Europe, young people who can no longer tolerate the extent to which the morality police infringe on Iranian society. One of Parhizgar's artist friends, Naghmeh, left Iran with her family at age sixteen, settling in Canada, but returned to Iran nine years later. While the desire to return "home" brought her back to Iran, Naghmeh admits that the very concept of home has become a fraught one for her:

> I don't think I will stay here. My ideal would be to know that I could always go and come back. But right now I can't say where I belong. I don't feel that I belong 100 percent to one place. I feel that people like us don't have roots in one special place or maybe we have roots in many places. This has made us feel homeless no matter where we are. But we can also adapt ourselves more easily to wherever we are. It has its good and bad aspects.

The concept of feeling out of place while at home, or of feeling homeless in one's native homeland, evokes James Clifford's (1994) claim about the complex routes one pursues in search of one's familial, national, or cultural roots. The homeless at home feel deracinated but are unable to reroute for reasons political, economic, or personal. *Round-Trip,* by its very title, suggests a circularity and an indulgence in the fantasy of return. In this case, the return is double: the round-trip ticket, purchased in London, also alludes to Parhizgar's return to her diasporic home in the UK. But the documentary also chronicles her return to Iran, the country of her birth and the one she left at age thirteen. According to Clifford (1994), the ability to reroute and cross borders is a feature of modern diasporic identities:

> Dispersed peoples, once separated from homelands by vast oceans and political barriers, increasingly find themselves in border relations with the old country thanks to a to-and-fro made possible by modern technologies of transport, communication, and labor

> migration. Airplanes, telephones, tape cassettes, camcorders, and mobile job markets reduce distances and facilitate two-way traffic, legal and illegal, between the world's places. (304)

Indeed, in *Round-Trip*—the subject and focus of the documentary being reroutings—traveling away from and back to Iran contends with questions of cultural and national identities and affiliations both at "home" and in the diaspora.

Driven by a powerful nostalgia for her childhood and a keen desire to reconnect with her old homeland, Parhizgar returns to Iran and attempts to document and reconstruct a narrative of her childhood while imagining the ways in which her future trajectory would have been different had she remained in Iran. Parhizgar, however, is in the privileged position of seeking her roots through a range of possible *routes* pursued by the diasporic subject, bringing to mind Marianne Hirsch and Nancy K. Miller's (2011) perceptive claim that "*rites* of return always invoke the question of *rights*" (7). The powerful driving impulse in narratives of nostalgia is the desire to return, and both *Round-Trip* and Nahid Persson Sarvestani's *The Queen and I* are propelled by this powerful longing. But while for Parhizgar, return "home" remains a possibility, Sarvestani's documentary foregrounds the pain of the political exile for whom the route home remains obstructed. For Sarvestani, a former communist activist, as for the former empress of Iran, Farah Diba, there is no right of return. Sarvestani's auto/biographical documentary film *The Queen and I* follows the development of an unlikely friendship between a former empress and a former communist involved in the 1979 overthrow of the Iranian monarchy who find themselves in the same painful predicament of living in the diaspora.

Both *Round-Trip* and *The Queen and I* begin with allusions to fairy tales: while the camera in *Round-Trip* zooms in on the Disney princess figurine in the music box, the opening scene of *The Queen and I* begins with the coronation ceremony of Mohammad Reza Shah Pahlavi and the queen, upon whom he bestowed the title of "Shahbanou," which translates as both "empress" and (literally) "wife of the shah." The documentary begins with footage from the coronation day, showing the shah and the jewel-bedecked Farah emerging from a Cinderella-like royal carriage. Sarvestani (2008) narrates:

> When I was growing up in Iran, we had a king and a queen. My first memory of the shah and Empress Farah is watching their coronation ceremony on television. At the time, my family was

> struggling to make ends meet. My father was gravely ill and my mother had to weave carpet [*sic*] fifteen hours a day to feed a family of ten. I could not believe that such a fantastic fairy tale could actually take place in reality. I became captivated by the queen, who lived an unreachable life of legend. But as I grew older, my childhood fascination was overshadowed by tales of torture and oppression under the shah's regime.

The scene then cuts to a photograph of Sarvestani as a young woman, followed by newspaper clippings and Amnesty International reports about acts of torture committed by the shah's secret police, then to scenes of revolution and chaos in the streets of Iran; she states: "I joined the revolution that forced the shah and the queen into exile" (Sarvestani 2008).

A dramatization of Sarvestani's altercation with Iranian airport officials during her trip home after the release of one of her films comes after the coronation scene in her documentary. The revolutionary guards interrogate her about her film and her political affiliations, accusing her alternately—and rather bewilderingly—of being both a communist and a monarchist. The airport confrontation led to months of house arrest for Sarvestani before she was finally released and allowed to return to her home in Sweden on condition that she stop making films about Iran.[8] Sarvestani signs her consent, but upon her return to Sweden she begins to wonder, in a voice-over commentary, about the Islamic Republic's condemnation of her as a "shah lover"; this reproach inspires her to seek out Farah, whom she describes as her "former enemy." Sarvestani's filmmaking style in both *The Queen and I* and *My Stolen Revolution* includes reenactment scenes (as described above) that, as Nichols (1991) has observed, "run some risk of credibility in reenacting an event: the special indexical bond between image and historical referent is ruptured. In a reenactment, the bond is still between the image and something that occurred in front of the camera but what occurred occurred *for* the camera" (21). Sarvestani's penchant for dramatizations of events thus works against the truth claims she puts forward through the documentary genre no matter how "factual" the events she depicts.

Both *Round-Trip* and *The Queen and I* begin with allusions to fairy tales, and both documentaries disrupt their fairy-tale beginnings with photographs of the filmmakers' childhood or youth followed by accounts of imprisonment (in the case of Parhizgar's parents), of imprisonment and execution (in the case of Sarvestani's brother), and of house arrest (in the case of Sarvestani herself). Thus both films deliberately construct a past Iran as a fairy-tale narrative and then disrupt that narrative through descriptions of violence, torture, and imprisonment. *The Queen and I* begins by presenting Sarvestani and Farah as polar opposites; indeed, at the start of the documentary, they appear almost as caricatures of the political and social positions with which each identifies. Sarvestani arrives for her first meeting with Farah with what appears to be an affected, even confrontational, casual attire and demeanor. Farah, on the other hand, is shown in the film's early scenes, walking the streets of Paris like a regal ghost, always perfectly made-up and coiffed, in the event that one of her former subjects should run into her and recognize her. At first glance, then, the film looks as if it might be setting up Farah as an easy target for Sarvestani's (and the viewer's) ridicule. Indeed, initially, that may well have been Sarvestani's intent, but before long, Sarvestani herself concedes, "this film has a mind of its own." Thus if the documentary begins by following one route—the easy one of condemning the former queen and the Pahlavi regime for the past and present political state of Iran—it quickly reroutes, exploring the more complex emotional, psychological, and physical paths along which these two very different women travel as they arrive at a place of mutual understanding, respect, and even friendship.

The scenes in the documentary featuring Sarvestani on her own, away from Farah, show her berating herself for not confronting the queen more directly and questioning the ruinous political decisions made by the shah in the past. On the one hand, Sarvestani feels that as a former communist she should be holding Farah accountable for the injustices committed by the Pahlavi regime. But on the other hand, she reluctantly admits that when in Farah's presence, she is charmed by her, and even begins to feel affection for her. Farah, on her part, vacillates between her suspicions of Sarvestani's motives and a sense of growing affinity between them. The surprising friendship that develops between them demonstrates the affective force of nostalgia, underscoring its productive possibilities. Through their shared, intense longing to return "home," and despite the undercurrents of this longing, each holding the other somehow accountable for their current rootlessness, Farah and Sarvestani *feel* their way toward a politically and socially transformative moment when a former revolutionary and a former empress can become friends.

The Queen and I, then, is notable in its exploration of the political and social effectiveness of nostalgia. This documentary offers an example of how nostalgia, as affect, gets "transmitted" between Sarvestani and Farah, raising the question of how shared feelings of nostalgia for an imagined and an elusive Iran enable the friendship between a former communist activist and a former queen.[9] Further, it raises the question of how and in what ways this documentary allows for the socially transformative possibilities of affects such as nostalgia and empathy. Among the autobiographical narratives by diasporic Iranians since the 1979 revolution, *The Queen and I* takes a somewhat unique position on nostalgia. Although the film dwells on "algia"—a sense of loss—it simultaneously highlights the generative possibilities of both nostalgia and memory by interweaving Sarvestani's autobiographical self-disclosures with her biographical portrait of Farah.

Sarvestani's and Farah's autobiographical stories overlap as they share the grief of losing a beloved family member in an untimely way, and Sarvestani draws attention to this overlapping of narratives in a voice-over: "For thirty years, I've lived with the guilt of feeling responsible for [my brother's] death. I've kept looking for diversions to avoid thinking about the past. Maybe it's the same with Farah. We both live with the pain of losing a loved one." Sarvestani is haunted by the traumatic memory of the execution of her younger brother, Rostam, whom she encouraged to join a communist opposition group during the revolutionary period. Rostam was arrested and eventually executed by the newly established Islamic Republic. Thus, the film, as indeed Sarvestani's life, resonates with her unresolved feelings of guilt about involving her brother in a political cause that ultimately cost him his life.[10]

Sarvestani's confessional moment is followed by Farah's reflections on the traumatic impact of the revolution on the lives of her children, particularly on her daughter Leila, who died of a drug overdose in 2001 amid speculations of suicide. Standing at Leila's gravesite in Paris's Passy Cemetery in the tony sixteenth arrondissement, each lost in her own thoughts, Farah says: "We lose our youth like this and see what kind of people live on. The outcome of the 'glorious' revolution. Both for you and for us. And for so many people in our country. What can one say?" This moment of intense, mutual pain experienced through the telling of stories and the sharing of memories about their lost home and about the heartrending loss of a beloved daughter and brother illustrates the productiveness of nostalgia. Two women whose social class and political affiliations are completely at odds forge a strong emotional connection through their shared nostalgia for another place and another time. At one point, Sarvestani remarks: "Today is the twenty-ninth anniversary of the revolution. How ironic that we are in the same room together: the queen and someone who fought to remove her from her power." While the film certainly gestures to the irony of this peculiar circumstance, it also demonstrates the possibilities wrought from revolution: that two women who occupied radically opposing social and political positions before and during the Iranian revolution can come together as friends through the sharing of their grief and their nostalgic recollections of a better time, or at least of a time that held promises of a more hopeful future.

While for Farah, the prerevolutionary period was a fairy tale in which she starred as the empress, Sarvestani's experience of that period was less fantasy than harsh reality and deprivation. Her family lived in extreme poverty, so the Pahlavi period is not one she recalls with fondness; as a child, she was acutely aware of the extreme disparities of economic and social class and felt deeply the injustice of her family's situation. Rather, for Sarvestani, it was the revolutionary period itself that held out the promise of change and betterment; it was that heady period of promise and excitement for a more equitable and just future for which she feels nostalgic, a promise that ultimately turned out to be tragically false.

Thus the theme of revolution, which as Boym (2001) has observed reflects two meanings—revolution as cyclical and repetitive, and revolution as radical break—is a key element in *The Queen and I.* This documentary is partly a revisiting of Sarvestani's activist youth as well as an attempt on her part to return to that moment in history and ask questions of the symbolic representative of the regime that she sought to topple. Thus, "revolution" in this context is cyclical—a return and a revisiting of Sarvestani's past through memory. But the film also invokes the idea of revolution as a radical break both at the national and the familial level. The two women hail from distinctly different worlds—socially, culturally, and economically—and Sarvestani makes this poignantly clear as she shows the moments in which their memories bring the two women together at the same time that their shared experiences reveal their radical differences. For example, in a Parisian art gallery owned by an Iranian artist, Farah comments on how much she loves the smell of paint; Sarvestani reminds her that she has also said that she loves the smell of gasoline. Farah laughs and affirms this is so because the smell of gasoline reminds her of home. But the home evoked by the gasoline smell for Farah is one of wealth, privilege, and power, thus for her, gasoline reminds her of the heyday of Iranian oil production and of her husband's, the shah's, seemingly unassailable power in the early 1970s.

Sarvestani approaches this question of class privilege with delicacy by musing:

> The smell of gasoline reminds me of my country too: the night we were going to be smuggled across the Persian Gulf to Dubai after months of being fugitives. On the boat, we were told to keep quiet under a heavy blanket. My one-year-old daughter was sick and coughing from breathing the smell of gasoline. I had to cover her mouth all night to stop her from making a noise.

In this instance, the smell of gasoline invokes feelings of terror and fear, feelings that emerge out of political, social, and economic vulnerability, of the dangers of illegal border crossing and of the insecurity that comes with not having money or power or connections.

Another moment in the film when Sarvestani's and Farah's narratives intersect and then diverge dramatically is during the story of their respective departures from their homeland. Farah recounts her family's flight from revolutionary Iran and the terror the family experienced—compounded by a sense of being adrift, rootless, and unwelcome as they were shuttled from country to country, not feeling safe or welcome anywhere. The traumatic narrative of the Pahlavi family's departure from Iran elicits Sarvestani's sympathy, triggering her own memories:

> Farah's exile story reminds me of the feeling of rejection and despair I experienced in the two years we lived in Dubai illegally. As soon as we got off the boat, we got arrested and jailed with all the other illegals. Once the authorities heard that if they send me back to Iran, I could face the same fate as my brother, they gave me permission to stay for two extra weeks on the condition that I would then leave the country. That was the beginning of two agonizing years living in hiding. Finally, we were able to leave for Sweden with fake passports.

Thus even the similarities in their stories of flight reveal the differences in the two women's social, political, and economic status.

Although the Pahlavis' departure from Iran was painful and difficult, and finding a safe place to land proved to be a challenge, the family obviously had both economic and social capital. After being shuttled from one country to another, the royal family received a warm welcome in Egypt by President Sadat, who offered them their own palace in which to live. Sarvestani's experience, on the other hand, was one shared by millions of refugees around the world: she had no money, no legal papers or status, and lived in perpetual fear of being discovered and sent back to Iran, where she would face certain execution.

However, despite these very real differences in status between the two women, the emotions that bind their auto/biographical narratives involve shared feelings of guilt and responsibility for the deaths of their loved ones and an intense longing to return home. The tragedy of the death of Leila Pahlavi, Farah's daughter, and the execution of Rostam, Sarvestani's brother, emerge as scars of revolutionary trauma impressed upon the minds of Sarvestani and Farah. The feeling of empathy generated by their shared grief and guilt at Leila's gravesite is further heightened for a contemporary viewing audience attuned to the fact that ten years after Leila's death, and only a few years after the filming of *The Queen and I,* Farah's younger son, Ali Reza, would commit suicide. The temporal gap between the filming and release of this documentary, and the privileged knowledge that emerges out of the historical present from where a contemporary audience views the film, heightens the sense of nostalgia and empathy generated by the documentary.

The overwhelming sense of loss Sarvestani and Farah feel as a result of the deaths of their loved ones also manifests into a longing for a lost homeland. United in their inability to return home, the documentary is informed by a profound longing for and nostalgic remembrance of an Iran that once held the promise of a hopeful and inspiring future. In an early scene in the film, Farah comes home to her Paris apartment to find a bag of black soil and a potted plant waiting for her. She turns to Sarvestani with an expression of joy mingled with pain: "One of my friends went to Iran and brought me this plant. From Iran." As she runs her fingers through the earth, she exclaims: "Oh! Black soil. I wonder where she got it from. Possibly from Niavaran Palace. It's wonderful. Now that I can't go back to Iran, at least I can feel its soil." This scene captures the power of the nostalgic feelings that, at times, appear to overwhelm both Sarvestani and Farah. The desire to feel the earth of the native country is a common feeling expressed in exilic communities. The sheer physicality of this scene, Farah's palpable nostalgia as she grabs a fistful of Iranian soil and lets it run through her fingers, Sarvestani's own nostalgic feelings as she observes the sample of

Iranian earth in Farah's hands, and the powerful nostalgic sentiment encouraged in the exilic viewer further demonstrate Sara Ahmed's (2004) claim that "emotions circulate between bodies" (4). The sample of Iranian earth that Sarvestani watches pass through Farah's fingers both fuels the nostalgia and becomes the object of nostalgia, as it stands in for the symbolic loss of home. Through the recounting of their memories, Sarvestani's and Farah's distinct autobiographical experiences intersect and find common ground in their shared nostalgia for Iran, revealing how nostalgia, in this instance, generates feelings of empathy and camaraderie through its expression.

While neither Sarvestani nor Farah have the privilege of the right of return to Iran, they both have the opportunity and the means to travel other routes, moving across the globe in a nostalgic pursuit of a reconstructed fantasy of an Iranian past. So, while they might not have the right to return to Iran, they do have the right—indeed the privilege—of mobility. Sarvestani's film follows Farah as she travels across the globe from her well-appointed Paris home: to Cairo, where a loyal group of exilic Iranians make an annual pilgrimage on the anniversary of the shah's death to pay their respects at the tomb of the deposed shah; and to events in Washington, D.C., where well-heeled Iranian exiles encircle the Shahbanou to dust off and relive their memories of the past at a charity function for the Foundation for the Children of Iran, founded by Yasmine Pahlavi, Farah Diba's daughter-in-law.

Viewing nostalgia exclusively as an overindulgence in and romanticization of a prerevolutionary past risks dismissing nostalgic remembrances of Iran as merely a luxury in which the diasporic or exilic subject indulges. But this film demonstrates that the transmission of nostalgia can work in socially and politically generative ways as it moves the viewer out of the realm of indulgent nostalgic memory and into a more productive space of empathy. Sarvestani ends the documentary with these words:

> When I started this film, I was intrigued by a woman whose life couldn't have been more different than mine. In the end, Farah is no longer the fairy-tale queen of my childhood fantasy, nor the mysterious antagonist of my revolutionary past. We have become two unlikely friends who share a profound longing for the Iran we both love, and dream the same dream to touch its soil again.

These words are delivered through voice-over commentary as the camera focuses its lens on an improbable pair, the former empress and a former communist revolutionary, sitting companionably beneath a tree. Both Sarvestani and Farah express a desire to reclaim a future past of Iran, a future that they had once imagined for themselves but that now exists only through nostalgic reimaginings. The film also plays on the tension between what Boym (2001) calls "restorative nostalgia" and "reflective nostalgia" (41). Restorative nostalgia, which stresses "*nostos*—return home," has a conservative strain as it seeks to restore an old system, whereas reflective nostalgia indulges in narratives of loss (Boym 2001, xiii). Reflective nostalgia, in Boym's (2001) words, "thrives in *algia,* the longing itself, and delays the homecoming—wistfully, ironically, desperately" (xviii). *The Queen and I* portrays "restorative nostalgia" as pitiable, and even ridiculous, mostly embodied by Farah's monarchist entourage in Paris, Cairo, and D.C., who are portrayed as unsympathetic figures, both sycophantic and preposterous, trotting out tired conspiracy theories about British and American orchestrations of the revolution that overthrew the shah. While Sarvestani depicts the monarchists as outlandish and ludicrous figures, she successfully rehumanizes a (for some) vilified Farah through their shared nostalgic articulations of an imagined and elusive Iran.

This documentary thus demonstrates the productive possibilities of nostalgic narratives as it shows how such narratives can work through the traumas of the past with an eye to future transformational possibilities. *The Queen and I* underscores how and when remembering moves beyond mere personal indulgence into a productive space where individual and collective agency through empathy is made possible. This documentary begins with Sarvestani identifying Farah as "her former enemy," but as it draws to a close, Farah tells Sarvestani: "I think we have reached a point where we need to place our efforts into a better future for Iran. After thirty years, we should, myself included, leave the past behind." The film thus encourages reflection on how nostalgic memories can transform the act of turning back to the past into opportunities for moving forward. The folding over of past memories into the present impels us to remember, but simply to remember is not enough: we need to transform the process of remembrance into a collective desire to reflect and reevaluate where we once were and where we are now.

Thus the repetition of nostalgic autobiographical narratives about Iran should not be understood as an exclusively individual or personal working through of trauma. The process of remembrance and the claim to memory demands that we confront our past, but it also forces us into a confrontation with our historical present, making us think of our place within a collectivity. The repeated incursion of the past, of a public and historical memory, into our present impels us to think in transformative ways about our place in the world, enabling us to transform our nostalgic memories from a place of solipsistic indulgence in broken narratives to a site of generative and collective future possibility.

While *The Queen and I* focuses its lens on the generation directly involved with and responsible for bringing about revolution, *Round-Trip* concerns itself with the generation that has come of age thirty years after the revolution and does not perceive it as the life-changing event that does the generation before them. The nostalgia in which the younger generation indulges is not necessarily nostalgia for a prerevolutionary era; rather, theirs is a meditative nostalgia that dwells on the *algia* of feeling and on the sadness of eluded opportunities. But in the interviews that Parhizgar conducts with Iranian youth in the film, there is a palpable excitement in their anticipation of the future. Many of the young people radiate a sense of optimism in the months leading up to the presidential elections in June 2009, permitting themselves to imagine that some kind of change was at hand; they allowed themselves the luxury of imagining alternative possibilities and future selves. The gap between the historical present in which we view *Round-Trip* and the past time of the actual filming of the documentary heightens the feeling of pathos that the film inspires. The optimism of the younger generation and the reality of the brutal crackdown after the 2009 elections—on which many were pinning their hopes—is heartrending.

The tragic similarities between 1979 and 2009 are made even more explicit in Sarvestani's (2013) most recent auto/biographical documentary, *My Stolen Revolution*. The connections she makes between these two historical periods draw attention once again to the cyclical nature of revolution; activists in 1979 believed that the revolution they were bringing about would initiate a significant change from the shah's oppressive regime. Instead, the familiar cycle of oppression, imprisonment, and torture was repeated with the notable difference that state terror and brutality were heightened after 1979. Protestors in June 2009 imagined their actions would initiate political and social change, only to find themselves undergoing the same experience of mass arrests and torture as the generation before them.[11]

In addition to the recurring themes of oppression and revolution, and nostalgia for a lost or imagined idea of an Iran that *could have been*, *My Stolen Revolution* extends the powerful emotions of guilt and grief that run throughout *The Queen and I.* The premise of *My Stolen Revolution* is Sarvestani's coming to terms with the guilt she has carried for over thirty years regarding the execution of her brother and the imprisonment of her friends in the notorious Evin Prison. The documentary follows Sarvestani as she seeks out her old friends and acquaintances, members of the political opposition to which she belonged during the revolution. Very quickly she discovers that most of her friends and fellow activists were executed in the 1980s, but she does manage to locate a handful of friends who survived prison, and who eventually escaped to countries in Scandinavia, Europe, and North America.

While the first half of this chapter offers an analysis of the social and political potential of nostalgic feelings in *Round-Trip* and *The Queen and I,* this second half, with a focus on *My Stolen Revolution,* considers the transformational possibilities of nostalgia through a consideration of human cruelty and empathy, of guilt and shame, of forgiveness and self-forgiveness. The documentary begins with a brief historical overview of the replacement of one oppressive system of government under the shah with an even more tyrannical regime under the Islamic Republic. Beginning with news footage from the 1979 revolution and ending with images of the brutal crackdown on activists on the streets of Tehran in the summer of 2009, the film, dedicated to former and current Iranian political prisoners, bears witness to the cruelties and injustices of Iranian governments—past and present. It also serves as an homage to those who fought for freedom during those critical historical moments and who paid the ultimate price with their lives. This documentary takes, as its starting point, Sarvestani's engulfing feelings of guilt and responsibility regarding the death of her younger brother, Rostam. The documentary includes footage of the June 2009 protests, including the much-viewed clip of Neda Agha-Soltan's death recorded on a cell-phone camera. Over the video footage of Neda's death, Sarvestani's voice-over informs the viewer: "For thirty years I've tried to keep those memories of Iran at arm's length. Yet events taking place in Iran today reawaken my memories." Thus, Sarvestani's decision to remember and revisit her past, and thus narrate the events of her life that have led her to where she is now, is propelled by her emotional reaction to the protests and the mass arrests in the summer of 2009. As discussed in chapter 1, many diasporic Iranians felt compelled to share their life narratives in response to the June 2009 protests and their aftermath. In particular, the death of Neda served as an emotional trigger for many people; Sarvestani's decision to include the famous footage of her death in *My Stolen Revolution* is further substantiation of how the story of Neda inspired the articulation of so many life narratives by Iranians in the diaspora.[12]

Drawing connections between the 2009 and the 1979 protests, Sarvestani recalls her activist youth. By the age of seventeen, she had become politically active with a left-wing organization, and recruited her younger brother, Rostam, to join their group. Rostam was eventually arrested by the newly established Islamic Republic, and was executed six months later. Throughout the film, Sarvestani returns to an overwhelming sense of culpability for his death; the revolutionary guards, she is convinced, were looking for her when they raided their house, as she was the older and more politically active sibling, but when they found Rostam at home, they arrested him in her stead. Ravaged by years of guilt, Sarvestani embarks upon a search for her former friends with whom she worked in the communist resistance movement in order to uncover information about Rostam's imprisonment and execution and to confront her feelings of tremendous responsibility for his death. She also bears the guilt of having fled the country while her fellow activists were arrested and tortured in prison. She begins her search by writing down the names of all her friends on a piece of paper and quickly comes to the shocking realization that out of the long list of names in front of her only a very few have survived prison. She succeeds, however, in finding her old mentor, Shahin, a former communist leader, and recalls: "I looked up to her. It was she who opened my eyes to injustices. Her word was law." Like Sarvestani, Shahin managed to flee Iran. She settled eventually in San Francisco, where Sarvestani arrives, with her daughter, for their emotional reunion.

The women greet each other tearfully, reminiscing about the last time they saw each other: Sarvestani's (now adult) daughter was a year old and they were in a military training camp. Their reunion thus begins with fond memories about their shared activist past, but the camera soon draws attention to incongruous images: Shahin, an ex-communist leader, now lives in a well-appointed home with a glimmering swimming pool in her backyard. The next jarring image is of Shahin, a formerly staunch atheist, performing her morning prayers. Behind her, Sarvestani leans against the wall, her face wearing an expression of shock and disgust at this unfathomable change in her former communist leader: "I'm deeply shocked to see my role model, my atheist role model, in a veil, praying to a fictitious god. I'm furious. For Rostam's sake. For my own. Is this the result of our struggle?"

Later, Sarvestani presses Shahin for an explanation, and Shahin struggles to justify how she manages to reconcile her former atheist beliefs with her current turn to religion. As she labors through an awkward defense in the face of a visibly angered Sarvestani, Shahin describes her devastating sense of culpability for involving so many young people—including and especially her own younger brothers—in a movement that ultimately cost them their lives. The film thus swings between the two affective poles of guilt and shame; as they part ways awkwardly, Sarvestani states, through her narrative voice-over: "A feeling of guilt can apparently push people in different directions. Shahin chose a path that to me was unthinkable. She is now a stranger to me although we were once so close. I feel utterly let down." By so thoroughly condemning the manner in which Shahin deals with her burden of guilt, Sarvestani subjects her to a merciless shaming.

The depiction of her disappointing reunion with Shahin makes for a disconcerting viewing experience because of Sarvestani's decision to tell the story of their meeting—and of her subsequent feelings of anger and betrayal—through what appear to be reenacted scenes. Reenactments, as Nichols (1991) has argued, draw our attention to how a particular event has been reconstructed for the camera (21); Sarvestani's deliberate and further shaming of her friend through these reenactments thus appears uncomfortably punitive. Sarvestani's motivation for making *My Stolen Revolution* was to come to terms with her own crushing sense of guilt at the deaths of her brother and her activist friends. But in her encounter with Shahin, the feeling of guilt that is the documentary's main engine comes into conflict with feelings of shame, particularly the shaming of others, in this case, of Shahin. This oscillation between guilt and shame creates a productive tension through the various and conflicting subject positions that emerge in Sarvestani's auto/biographical documentary.

Much has been written on shame in contemporary theory. The prominent American psychologist Silvan Tomkins, whose theorizations of affect are seen as central to the development of contemporary affect theory, has defined shame as "the most reflexive of affects" and "an inner torment, a sickness of the soul" (Sedgwick and Frank 1995, 136, 133). For Tomkins, however, feelings of shame encourage empathic identification with the shamed subject, thus inspiring and encouraging human connection. Indeed, in his view, shame encourages empathy, and empathic feelings are "a necessary condition for the experience of shame" (Sedgwick and Frank 1995, 162). Thus feeling shame can be seen as a precondition for moving outside of a Western European model of self-contained individualism, enabling communal attachments.[13]

Taking a contrary view to the positive representation of shame as challenging individualism and fostering a sense of community, Ruth Leys (2009) argues that the current focus on shame in contemporary theories, indeed, the overexposure of shame at the expense of theorizations of guilt, is a feature of contemporary affect theory that absolves the individual of responsibility.[14] Offering a persuasive argument that feelings of guilt emphasize individual responsibility and agency, while feelings of shame or shameful feelings emphasize interiority and the highlighting of personal difference, Leys (2009) claims:

> By common agreement, guilt concerns your actions, that is, what you do—or what you wish or fantasize you have done. . . . Shame, however, is held to concern not your actions but who you are, that is, deficiencies and inadequacies as a person as these are revealed to the shaming gaze of the other, a shift of focus from actions to the self that makes the question of personal identity of paramount importance. (11)

Leys's argument that theorizations of shame deflect notions of individual responsibility is particularly illuminating in relation to *My Stolen Revolution.*

While the film adopts guilt as its starting point (Sarvestani's sense of culpability in relation to the death of her brother and her escape from Iran during a time when many of her friends were arrested), it tilts towards a prioritization of shame: Sarvestani's disbelief and revulsion at Shahin's turn to religion is expressed through an almost ruthless shaming of her old friend. Here, shame works as an uncovering, an exposure of the humiliation to which Shahin has brought upon herself by reneging on her former atheistic beliefs and by assuming the faith of a theocratic government against which she once fought. Shahin is thus revealed as deficient in some way; she is shamed for who she *is;* for Sarvestani, it is Shahin's weakness of character that is the source of shame and indeed disgust. Shahin tries to explain that her overwhelming guilt about her instrumental role in recruiting so many young people to a movement that ultimately secured their death sentence led her to seek solace in religion. Her explanation is rejected by Sarvestani, but as Leys (2009) writes: "The current tendency to replace guilt with shame is an impulse to displace questions about our moral responsibility for what we do in favour of more ethically neutral or different questions about our personal attributes" (131). Although Sarvestani is herself wracked with guilt for having involved her brother in her political organization, and for having been able to leave Iran while her brother and friends were left behind to face execution, she rejects Shahin's explanation that she has turned to religion to help assuage her feelings of guilt. Instead, she expresses revulsion at what she sees as Shahin's (shameful) personality.

What makes this shaming noteworthy in the context of Sarvestani's search for absolution is that there appear to be two narratives—and two levels of shaming—unfolding in relation to Shahin: on the one hand, there is the story of Sarvestani and Shahin's reunion—and of Sarvestani's subsequent disillusionment at what she perceives to be the unforgivably altered politics of her friend. She expresses her disappointment by making her feel ashamed for this change. On the other hand, the story of this ill-fated reunion is retold and restaged through the lens of Sarvestani's camera. The documentary is filmed as though things are taking place in "real time," but documentary films do not offer a transparent lens on reality; they mediate between the event itself and the narration of the event. Through a careful framing of issues, documentaries restage and retell stories. Sarvestani, as the director—and the subject—of her auto/biographical documentary narrative, controls the story of their reunion with her camera. In Leys's (2009) words: "Shame is an emotion that is *routed through the eyes* and . . . the logic of shame is a *scene of exposure*" (126). Thus the fact that Shahin's shaming takes place in front of the camera makes this "scene of exposure" even more stark. Presumably (and rather astonishingly), Shahin has given her consent to be filmed and for her story to be represented by Sarvestani, a representation she must surely anticipate will not be a favorable one.

Shahin's concession to be represented on film in this way thus suggests a curious voluntary and public shaming of herself. From this perspective, then, Sarvestani's journey of self-reflexive critique and guilt in relation to the suffering and death of her brother begins to veer away from a politics of guilt and accountability, tilting instead toward a politics of shame that, to follow Leys's critique, detracts attention from individual responsibility and agency. At the risk of advancing a crude analysis of Sarvestani's reaction to Shahin, Sarvestani's harsh censure of her can be understood in the context of Sarvestani's own feelings of shame and guilt about having survived—and fled the country—while her brother and her friends were imprisoned, tortured, and later executed. Her severe judgment of Shahin can be understood therefore as a masking of her own anxieties at being implicated in what she perceives to be Shahin's betrayal of their former political views and years of activist work. By condemning her so thoroughly, Sarvestani distances herself from Shahin's tainted politics and perceived disloyalty to those who suffered and died in the name of their (at one time) shared political cause.

Turning away from Shahin and her disappointing narrative, the documentary shifts its focus to the testimonies and narratives of four other women whom Sarvestani knows from her revolutionary days: Azar Al-Kanaan, Parvaneh Aref, Soudabeh Ardavan, and Nazli Partovi. Sarvestani pays a visit to each of these women in their homes after her disheartening encounter with Shahin. Her first visit is with Nazli, who, as she shares her memories of prison, produces her prison-issued chador and blindfold. Claiming it as a rather disturbing keepsake, she also states that it still retains the smell of prison, as she has never washed it. Nazli's bubbly personality and irrepressible smile appear very much at odds with the memories she recounts, such as, for example, her description of being tortured for six hours and then subjected to a fake execution. After she tells her story, Sarvestani tries on Nazli's chador and blindfold, attempting to walk while asking such questions as: How could you see? Couldn't you lift the blindfold a bit? Who would notice? In response to Sarvestani's surprisingly naïve questions, Nazli gasps in disbelief, exclaiming that the revolutionary guards were watching them all the time so of course they couldn't raise their blindfolds. The scene is an uncomfortable one as Sarvestani's guilt at not having undergone Nazli's experience manifests itself in this moment through an almost gratuitous performance and an unwitting appropriation of Nazli's prison memories. The camera zooms in for a close-up of Nazli wearing her prison garb. With slow, purposeful movements, Nazli removes the blindfold and chador, and shakes her hair free as she stares straight into the lens of the camera. The symbolism of liberation from the oppressiveness of the veil and of her incarceration is a clear, if rather heavy-handed, one.

Sarvestani's attempts to work through her feelings of guilt about not having been in prison and subjected to torture results in the making of this documentary in which she creates a space for former political prisoners to narrate their traumatic experiences. Here, Sarvestani puts herself in the position of bearing witness to their individual traumas: Parvaneh was seventeen when she was arrested for distributing leaflets outside her school; reported to the authorities by her school principal, she spent nine years in prison. The torture she endured in prison left her with permanently damaged knees. Soudabeh depicts the psychological and physical conditions of prison through her artwork (much of it made surreptitiously in prison), for which she has in recent years received some international recognition. Azar, with whom Sarvestani identifies strongly because they are the same age and also have daughters of similar age, recounts her arrest when her daughter was only a year old. She describes the horror of having her one-year-old witness her subjection to torture, and of watching her child re-enact the role of the torturer/interrogator with her doll serving in the role of prisoner. Azar also shares with Sarvestani (and the camera) the terrorizing experience of being raped in prison, which she describes as exceeding the pain of any other form of torture.[15]

After having borne witness to the women's testimonies, Sarvestani returns home to Sweden but feels that she needs to hear more:

> I cannot stop thinking about the women I've now met. About their destinies, their lives. Meeting them was like coming home. All the customs I'm used to. The community. It's a long time since I felt so secure. They bore me back to the best days of my life, when all was bright. We looked on the future with great optimism. We had such energy, felt such joy. But that was before the mass arrests.

Deciding that she needs to see them all again, Sarvestani arranges a weekend gathering at her home in Stockholm so that the women can reunite and exchange their stories as a group. She also invites a fifth woman, Monireh Baradaran, of whom the other four have spoken in admiration, a woman who remains politically active against the Islamic regime from her home in Germany. Notably, Shahin is absent from this gathering, as Sarvestani deliberately rejects her, turning instead toward other friends in a desire for a kind of emotional cleansing and healing after the devastating reunion with her former mentor. Nevertheless, she also feels anxious about the gathering, remarking: "I realize that I lack an experience that the others have in common. . . . They have such powerful ties to each other. It makes me feel somewhat out of it." Despite feeling "out of it," Sarvestani assumes the role of willing and empathic witness as the women disclose their memories.

The five women gather in Sarvestani's Persian-style living room in Stockholm and are faced with the sudden appearance of Nazli in full prison garb. As the women gaze at her in surprise, Nazli explains that when she was released, she smuggled out her prison-issued chador and blindfold as a memory keepsake. Describing how she swapped chadors with that of her cellmate, Mina, so that they would remember each other, she also reveals that Mina was later executed. Sarvestani reflects:

> It's circumstance of that kind that makes my life different from theirs. The night the police broke into our house, I wasn't at home. It was me they were after. Two officers remained there, waiting for me to come home. My elder brother managed to get away from the house and warn me. That night, my brother Rostam and most of our comrades were arrested.

As Sarvestani bears witness to these women's chilling stories, she circles back to her own narrative, forcing herself to contend with the memories and the guilt she has kept at bay for thirty years.

With the exception of Soudabeh, the women all take turns wearing and then removing Nazli's chador and blindfold, as they stare defiantly into the camera, and slowly shake their hair free from the constraints of the prison garb. This spectacle of the women's donning—and tossing—of the unwashed prison chador and blindfold after disclosing their traumatic prison memories makes for an unsettling viewing experience. This symbolically laden gesture feels, uncomfortably, like an affected and manipulative visual strategy. The troubling feelings raised by these scenes underscore Nichols's (2001) critical question that, he states, is at the heart of all representative documentary: "'What responsibility do filmmakers have for the effect of their acts on the lives of those filmed?'" (6). Nichols's question about the politics of representation in documentary film is particularly apt in this documentary that uncovers these women's traumatic experiences in the face of an intrusive camera. While the recounting of traumatic memories to an empathetic listener is a crucial part of the healing process, through the presence of a willing "spectator-witness," as discussed in chapter 1, the theatrical donning of the prison garb by former political prisoners feels like a disconcerting manipulative visual strategy in the film.

These five women, however, gather and share their memories of prison, of torture, and of suffering, as well as their stories of friendship and of community building. These narratives help Sarvestani come to terms with her own memories and with her burden of guilt: "Since fleeing Iran, I have been running from my memories. During these days we've spent together,

I've been able to listen for the first time, daring to unleash my feelings. Their narratives could well have been accounts of my own life." Thus, by bearing witness to these women's at times horrifying, at times heartening, life narratives, Sarvestani finds the strength to face her own suffering and guilt. Through Baradaran, Sarvestani succeeds in meeting one of her brother's former cellmates, who now lives in Los Angeles. Requesting to remain anonymous, the former prisoner speaks of Rostam's last day and of the final moments before his execution. Emphasizing Rostam's pride, strength, and will to resist, even in the last few moments of his life, and despite the oppression and suffering to which he was subjected, he gives Sarvestani the gift of absolution. Recognizing that Rostam would probably have been executed regardless of whether or not she had turned herself in, Sarvestani releases herself from the guilt that has been weighing on her for the past thirty years: "Today I realize my brother would have been executed even if he had revealed my whereabouts. The killing was so systematic, so extensive. The oppression, the brutality, and the killings still go on today. The same regime is in power, the same atrocities are being committed now as then." The film ends poignantly with Rostam's favorite protest song, "Sar Oomad Zemestoon" (Winter has come to an end). This is a song with a complicated history, one that Upa Mesbahian explores in detail in a forthcoming book chapter. Based on the melody of an old Armenian love song, "Sari Siroun Yar" (Pretty Mountain Girl), the lyrics were rewritten in the early 1970s by Said Soltanpour, a member of the Cherikha-ye Fadaee Khalq (The People's Devoted Guerillas), a Marxist opposition group.[16] According to Mesbahian, Soltanpour wrote the song while in prison, where it circulated widely, becoming a popular protest song during the 1970s revolutionary period. Sar Oomad Zemestoon reemerged in the context of the 2009 protests in Iran as well as at gatherings in the diaspora; the metaphor of the end of winter and the birth of spring serves as richly evocative in the political contexts of both 1979 and 2009.

All three documentaries discussed in this chapter carry, at the heart of their stories, the traumatic rupture of the 1979 revolution. Sarvestani's auto/biographical journey is inextricable from her memories of revolutionary activism, which she revisits through an exploration of nostalgia and grief in *The Queen and I* and through her feelings of guilt and shame in *My Stolen Revolution*. Hers is a difficult transition from nostalgia to guilt and shame, and then finally, to absolution. In the end, the common feelings binding the three auto/biographical films discussed in this chapter are those of nostalgia for another time (real or imagined), guilt and shame (for having left), and empathy for those who were left behind to struggle and to suffer. Parhizgar and Sarvestani, as well as the subjects in their documentaries, look back upon the past with a longing to return to and retrieve their imagined future selves. Ultimately, the emotional work of navigating their respective feelings of guilt, shame, and nostalgia directs them to a more productive and hopeful space of empathy through the act of bearing witness to the suffering and pain of others.

· CHAPTER 4 ·

Repetitions of the Past

Marjane Satrapi and Intergenerational Memory

> *Memory is a means of "passing on," of sharing a social past that may have been obscured, thereby activating its potential for reshaping a future of and for other subjects. In sum, acts of personal remembering are fundamentally social and collective.*
>
> —Sidonie Smith and Julia Watson, *Reading Autobiography: A Guide for Interpreting Life Narratives*

THUS FAR, THIS BOOK HAS CONCERNED ITSELF with the concepts of memory, nostalgia, and trauma, each chapter addressing, in some way, the centrality of intergenerational witnessing in diasporic Iranian women's life narratives. This particular chapter considers the importance of intergenerational memory in Marjane Satrapi's graphic novels in English. Best known for her immensely popular autobiographical coming-of-age narratives, *Persepolis I: The Story of a Childhood* (2003) and *Persepolis II: The Story of a Return* (2004), Satrapi's work has been often compared to Art Spiegelman's *Maus I: A Survivor's Tale; My Father Bleeds History* (1986) and *Maus II: A Survivor's Tale; And Here My Troubles Began* (1991) and identified as part of the same genre: an autobiographical retelling of a traumatic moment in a personal, and public/national history.[1]

The *Persepolis* books have received universal praise by Western critics, and have been re-mediated into an animated motion picture, written and directed by Satrapi and Vincent Paronnaud (2007). Satrapi followed the *Persepolis* volumes with stories of her parents' and grandparents' generations collected in *Embroideries* (2005) and *Chicken with Plums* (2006), neither of which has received the same degree of critical attention as did the *Persepolis* volumes.

Chicken with Plums was adapted into a live-action film in 2011, codirected by Vincent Paronnaud and Satrapi, and featuring such celebrated stars as

Golshifteh Farahani, Isabella Rossellini, and Chiara Mastroianni. While the film received mostly positive reviews, the cinematic version of this story is less nuanced and complex than the comics version. The political context of 1953 is at the heart of the graphic novel, the love story of Nasser Ali and Irane functioning as a political allegory for the betrayal and disillusionment felt by Iranians who witnessed the overthrow of the democratically elected government of Mohamad Mossadegh. This specifically Iranian context is overshadowed in the film by a very European, specifically French, aesthetic (as an example, the only Iranian actor in the film is Golshifteh Farahani in the role of Irane). This muting of the political context makes it possible for audiences to focus on what might appear to be a universal story of star-crossed lovers. The film thus indulges in a nostalgia for an era when the ruling class in Iran emulated European aesthetic and cultural tastes; it does so without offering a critical view of the class politics that lay the groundwork for the immense cultural and social gap between the upper and the working classes in Iran, an economic and cultural division that eventually led to the revolution. This chapter will focus on *Embroideries* and *Chicken with Plums,* which extend Satrapi's autobiographical project through the development of complex intergenerational linkages reflected in the invocation of three generations of the Satrapi family, exploring how the autobiographical form overlaps with the recurring nature of the traumatic experience and traumatic memory.

Satrapi's four graphic novels present fertile ground for the study of the intersection of autobiography, memory, and trauma; her work can be situated in the company of a significant and growing body of diasporic Iranian women's life narratives. As we have seen, the outpouring of autobiographical expression by Iranian women in the diaspora illustrates how the traumatic effects of revolutionary rupture require a process of "working through" in autobiographical texts. Cathy Caruth (1995) has argued that trauma manifests itself through the "repeated possession of the one who experiences it" (4); the act of repetition through a process of continual departures from and returns to the site of trauma is thus integral to the traumatic experience. Borrowing Leigh Gilmore's (1998) formulation of the "serial autobiographer," this chapter considers Satrapi a writer and artist who understands "the project of self-representation to be open-ended, susceptible to repetition, extendible, even, perhaps, incapable of completion" (211). Satrapi's four autobiographical comics, or "autographics," can be seen as part of her larger auto/biographical project whose central concern is the trauma of revolution and the importance of bearing witness to the stories of others.[2]

The repetition of auto/biographical expression and the reemergence of trauma dovetail in productive ways in Satrapi's works. The site of trauma has been described often—and not without contention—as one of impossible articulation, but the sheer volume of diasporic Iranian women's texts about the postrevolutionary experience substantiates Wendy Hesford's (2011) claim that academic scholarship on trauma and human rights tends to focus on loss, absence, and suffering. She queries why scholarship on trauma continues to emphasize the inexpressibility of trauma when it has paradoxically produced so much writing and self-expression on the subject (Hesford 2011, 55). Indeed, Satrapi, as serial autobiographer, narrates her stories through the space of revolutionary trauma and loss, telling and retelling the stories of both personal and public traumas mediated through the voice and perspective of her autobiographical avatar, Marji.[3]

Understanding Satrapi's reiteration and repetition of herself as a serial autobiographer foregrounds two important and paradoxical features of contemporary diasporic Iranian women's life narratives: on the one hand, as Gillian Whitlock (2007) has argued, the proliferation of Muslim women's testimonials in the West, with their repetitive message of women's oppression in Muslim societies, reveal their possible co-optation as "soft weapons," illustrating how "the war on terror ripples in and through life narrative" (9). On the other hand, these narratives "can also be used to describe experiences of unbearable oppression and violence across a cultural divide" (55). In other words, while these autobiographical accounts sometimes participate in perpetuating negative representations of, in this case, Iran and Iranian women, these texts can also create possibilities for empathic connections, and for a humanization of a people and a place that has been vilified, in recent decades, in Western popular culture.

All four of Satrapi's "autographic" works are informed by the same concern she expresses in her introduction to *Persepolis: The Story of a Childhood.* In the preface to the English-language version, a text intended for a North American readership, Satrapi offers a pointed challenge to the West's representation of Iran as part of an "axis of evil."[4] Through the remembering and retelling of her own and her family's story, Satrapi's autographics gesture outward; in a deliberate effort to address and challenge a Western audience's preconceptions about Iran and Iranian culture, she turns personal stories into public discourse. At the same time, Satrapi's focus on intergenerational memory and history—particularly as represented by the emotional bonds Marji forges with her grandmother in all four books, and her uncle Anoosh in *Persepolis I,* and by her sympathetic representation of her great-uncle Nasser Ali in *Chicken with Plums*—suggests that intergenerational ties and memories become, for Marji, key sites of witnessing both personal and public/national traumas.[5]

Indeed, the presence of older generations, particularly that of her grandmother, in her narratives forces Marji to remain accountable for her actions in the present. In *Persepolis II,* for example, Marji's grandmother lashes out at her in anger and disgust for causing the arrest of a man she falsely accuses of sexual harassment in order to deflect the attention of the "morality police" from the heavy makeup she is wearing (a punishable offence under the Islamic Republic). Her grandmother reproaches her: "Have you forgotten who your grandfather was? He spent a third of his life in prison for having defended some innocents! And your Uncle Anoosh? Have you forgotten him too???! He gave his life for his ideas! What have I taught you? Hunh??? 'Integrity'!! Does this word mean anything to you?" (Satrapi 2004, 137). Shamed by the force of her grandmother's rebuke, Marji vows to always remember her words and the political sacrifices made by previous generations of the Satrapi family. This promise to always remember also serves as a constant reminder of what it means to be a socially responsible and ethical person.

Persepolis II ends with Marji visiting the grave of her grandfather and the final resting place of her uncle Anoosh, promising always to honor her family history. The panel depicting her at her uncle's grave is particularly powerful. He was among the thousands of leftist political prisoners executed in Evin in the 1980s and buried in unmarked graves.[6] In this panel, the long wall of Evin Prison is shaded black, as is Marji's small car parked behind the prison wall. Marji, also drawn in black, kneels in front of her bouquet of flowers, appearing small and vulnerable in the shadow of the infamous prison and in the shadow of her family's—and the nation's—memories. The stark whiteness of the ground—underneath which lie the bodies of political prisoners—the looming prison wall, and the small image of Marji kneeling at the site of their unidentified graves underscore the theme of intergenerational witnessing and the ethical imperative "to live within an upright attentiveness to traces of those who have inhabited times and places other than one's own" (Simon 2005, 133). Marji's diminutive figure in this panel thus serves as a visual reminder of Marji's conscious (and repeated) self-positioning within an intergenerational and familial network. Kimberly Wedeven Segall (2008) has observed that in *Persepolis*

I, "Satrapi visually depicts how stories of violation become part of a family's social fabric; indeed her memoir functions as a metaphor for collective loss" (38). Segall's observation about *Persepolis* could be extended to all of Satrapi's works and brings attention to how a sense of collective loss can be transformed into an awareness of the political responsibilities that accompany historical consciousness. Marji's sense of responsibility in remembering and narrating her family's past, a personal history that always remains intertwined with a public history, places her in the role of willing witness to private and public memory and to brutal historical events.

This will to remember manifests itself through the use of repetition in Satrapi's graphic novels. First, Satrapi's autobiographical avatar, Marji, is a recurring presence in all four of her texts; as Hillary Chute (2008) has remarked, "*Persepolis* proliferates selves on the page," an observation that could be made of all four of her graphic novels (97). Second, Satrapi reproduces and juxtaposes panels that at first glance appear identical, displaying slight differences, but upon closer examination reveal significant changes to the narrative. Central to this technique of repetition is the way in which memory is invoked through the visual medium of the graphic novel. Chute (2008) refers to the "retracing work of graphic narratives as ethical repetitions" of the past (93).[7] The remembering of the past through "a process of visualization" stresses the multiple and conflicting ways in which we can reinterpret the past through the present with a keen awareness of our future selves (Chute 2008, 93).[8]

The repeated appearance of Marji as autobiographical subject in Satrapi's works, and the juxtaposition of panels that appear identical but that, on rereading, reveal differences, function as a type of memory work that is key to a working through of trauma. In *Soft Weapons,* Whitlock (2007) contests "the idea that life narrative is a speaking cure for trauma that occurs according to the psychic need and personal recovery of the traumatized individual and outside of political constraints and opportunities" by invoking the role of the native informant to describe memoirs that are written with a Western readership in mind (165).[9] While the role of the native informant is certainly one to keep in mind, it is also worth remembering that repetition is integral to the traumatic experience, an experience that recurs through a retelling and reliving of the experience through narrative.

Connected to this notion of the belatedness and repetition of traumatic memory is the "serial autobiographer [who] returns to the scene because she has left a body there which requires further attention" (Gilmore 2001,

97). However, repetition is not just a personal working through or a reliving of trauma. The repetition and presence of the past articulated in life narratives can become a useful site for collective remembrance. Roger I. Simon (2005) has argued that "remembrance enacts possibilities for an ethical learning that impels us into a confrontation and reckoning not only with stories of the past but also with ourselves as we *are* (historically, existentially, socially) in the present" (135). Thus, the repeated incursion of the past, of a public and historical memory, into our present demands that we think in transformative ways about our place in the world and "evokes a persistent sense—*not of belonging, but of being in relation to*—of being claimed in relation to the experiences of others" (Simon 2005, 89). The overlapping of a public historical memory, which "moves remembrance beyond the boundaries of the singular corporal body" (88), and private familial memory structures all four of Satrapi's graphic novels.

Persepolis I and *II* are the most obviously autobiographical of Satrapi's works. Visually, the relationships between the images of her avatar, Marji, on the book covers and Satrapi's self-portrait on the dust jackets of her books suggest a conscious self-referentiality.[10] Although the cover of *Embroideries* features her glamorous grandmother in the prime of her youth, and the cover of *Chicken with Plums* depicts her musician uncle, both books display Satrapi's photograph on the dust jacket. Reading the relationship of the image on the covers against Satrapi's image underscores the self-referentiality in these texts and foregrounds Satrapi's subject position in her works. Whitlock (2008) has remarked that the "small blocky figure of Marji in the cutout on the cover of *Persepolis 1* is recalled in the ornately decorated sepia cover of *Embroideries,*" but the image on the latter cover is of Marji's grandmother (19). There are physical similarities, however, between the illustration and Satrapi's photograph, as the faces of grandmother and granddaughter are similar in shape, their heads tilted at similarly coy angles, with similar sardonic smiles. Satrapi draws her grandmother with a beauty mark similar to Marji's. This visual similarity stresses not only auto/biographical connection, as she appears to be mapping herself graphically onto her family past, but also the importance of intergenerational witnessing, the importance of bearing witness to the stories of those who come before us. In *Chicken with Plums,* in which Satrapi is almost entirely absent from the narrative, there is no obvious visual connection between the darkened image of her great-uncle on the book cover and her photograph. Yet the image of her great-uncle with his *tar* in a cutout on the front cover remains stylistically similar to her other three more self-consciously autobiographical books. The stories that Marji relays here are not her "own" experiences; however, they are part of her family's history and thus offer us some indication as to how Satrapi is redeploying autobiography to communal and familial ends in these extensions of her auto/biographical project. Here, she is also keeping her promise to her grandmother, at the end of *Persepolis II,* to "never forget" the history of her family, and by extension, her own personal history, and the history of her country.

Marji's "Proliferating Selves" in *Embroideries*

The repeated rearticulation of Marji as autobiographical subject in Satrapi's graphic novels invites us to consider this repetition of her autobiographical avatar through Gilmore's (1998) formulation of the subject-in-process as split between "the subject who writes and the subject in the text" (211). In Satrapi's case, this split becomes more complex since the subject(s) in her autographics are multiple. In the *Persepolis* books, Marji-as-child subject, Marji-as-adolescent subject, and Marji-as-adult subject all take turns as narrator. In *Embroideries,* (the adult) Marji occupies the position of "spectator-witness," and, in *Chicken with Plums,* Marji and her mother make only a cameo appearance, briefly interrupting the flow of the narrative. The interruption, however, comes at a significant point after an exchange between Nasser Ali and his favorite child, his daughter, Farzaneh, described by all as his "spitting image." The narrative then jumps to the present, where Marji and her mother visit a similarly depressed and world-weary Farzaneh just shortly before she dies of a heart attack. Here, Marji and her mother witness the end of another episode of the family's history that parallels and repeats Nasser Ali's own tragic end.

Though it has not received as much critical attention as the *Persepolis* books, *Embroideries* occupies an important place in Satrapi's oeuvre, especially when her four graphic novels are considered in terms of an extended autobiographical project, as well as the texts' relationship to the proliferation of diasporic women's autobiographical expression. The title of the book literally refers to reconstructive female genital surgery, the "embroidery" or stitching of the hymen so as to restore women's virginity in a culture that certainly at one time placed a high value on women's sexual inexperience. But it also refers to the interlacing of women's intimate stories with the public (and masculine) narratives of the state. The title can also be more broadly interpreted as the interweaving of Satrapi's autobiographical subject, Marji, with larger narratives pertaining to family and nation. In *Embroideries,* Marji is actively present as listener and facilitator for a lively and irreverent women's community that includes Marji's grandmother and mother and their close-knit circle of female friends and relatives.

In terms of page layout and composition, *Embroideries* is very different from *Persepolis;* there are no sequential panels in *Embroideries* producing series and so marking the passage of time. The stories in this text unfold during the men's afternoon siesta; thus, the women's narratives emerge out of a leisurely afternoon during which time slows down, enabling the sharing and exchange of women's memories. This slowing down of time is further reflected in the absence of page numbers in *Embroideries;* if a page numbering system is a marker of temporality, then temporal progress can be seen as briefly halted in the pages of this text. What is depicted here is literally "free" time, time liberated from such chronologizing markers as page numbers and panel borders.[11] A lined border around an image, referred to as a panel border, is a visual convention designed to separate moments and events from one another in comics narration. Their absence here liberates the image and produces the effects of events and experiences and stories interacting freely and flowing in and out of each other. In *Embroideries,* the pages of the book are taken over by Marji's mother, grandmother, and their circle of female relatives and friends. In fact, the women's "ventilations of the heart," the phrase used by Marji's grandmother to describe a robust and satisfying women's gossip session, and the images of the women themselves often compete for dominance of the page.

The prologue establishes the conditions for the women's conversation. The first page depicts Marji, her family members, and her friends seated around the dining room table engaged in postlunch chatter. Marji's grandmother, positioned at the center of the page, is complimented by her husband on her cooking, an acknowledgment of her domestic achievements to which she responds modestly, "Satrapi flatters me." Marji as narrator explains: "My grandmother called my grandfather Satrapi, never by his first name. She said one must respect one's husband." Here the text confirms the image we see: a demure Grandmother Satrapi basking in the glow of her husband's compliments. The next page depicts the women in the background carrying the lunch dishes to the kitchen in single file; in the foreground, the faces of Satrapi's grandfather and the top half of what appears to be her father's head are visible as the men leave the living room for an afternoon nap. Thus far, the representations of gender roles appear consistent with stereotypical representations of how the West imagines Muslim family dynamics. The conversation that unfolds within the subsequent pages of the book, however, undermines this representation.

While the women tidy the kitchen after lunch and settle themselves in the living room, Marji prepares the samovar and pours the tea; the page is filled with the faces of urbane, sophisticated women eager to begin the pleasant ritual of drinking tea and engaging in gossip. This scene is followed by an image of a needlepoint frame, with the title, "Embroideries," sewn on the canvas. The next page depicts a needle and thread, and the narrative begins in earnest. The pages of this book are filled with text; much of the dialogue is in speech bubbles, but there is a significant amount of dialogue and narration outside conventional speech bubbles and text boxes. The pages embody the joy of unrestrained speech as the words spill out onto the page. All the text in this book is in cursive handwriting—a stylistic device that not only emphasizes intimacy and informality but also adds to the sense that the narrative unfolding here is taking place outside of the usual graphic narrative structure: text boxes, frames, and panels.[12] The images of the canvas and of the needle and thread make a visual statement about the interconnectedness of stories, repeating once again the theme of weaving together intergenerational narratives.

Having prepared and poured the tea, and so fulfilling her duties as the youngest member in this gathering of women, Marji positions herself as witness to the narratives that unfold. One of the key elements of working through trauma is having a supportive environment in which one can bare one's emotional wounds to an empathic and active listener who, in her willingness to hear, enables the necessary articulatory process. Dori Laub (1992) observes: "Bearing witness to a trauma is, in fact, a process that includes the listener. For the testimonial process to take place, there needs to be a bonding, the intimate and total presence of an *other*—in the position of one who hears. Testimonies are not monologues; they cannot take place in solitude. The witnesses are talking *to somebody:* to somebody they have been waiting for for a long time" (70–71). Removing herself from the main subject of the narrative in *Embroideries* and *Chicken with Plums,* Marji adopts the position of the listener-spectator-witness. By serving in the role of active listener, she enables the articulation and expression of others' narratives. Although there is much ribald humor and fun in the pages of *Embroideries,* many of the stories that emerge are painful ones; in the background of the amusing tales lurk national and personal traumas that haunt these women's lives and affect their sometimes desperate attempts to leave Iran for Europe or the United States through sham marriages arranged for themselves or for their daughters. The stories also reveal the pressures that come with cultural expectations of women's premarital sexual inexperience and the radical steps some women take to feign their virginity on their wedding nights. One woman describes, for example, how, on the advice of Marji's feisty grandmother, she took a razor with her to bed in order to surreptitiously cut herself on the thigh, guaranteeing the appearance of a few drops of blood as proof of her virginity. In a moment of panic, however, she cuts her husband's testicles instead.

The book actually ends on a note of metaphorical castration; Grandfather Satrapi wakes up from his nap and wanders into the women's gossip session only to find himself berated by his wife, who orders him to return to sleep: "It's better for you," she says. Unlike on the first page of the book, she does not look the part of the demure wife with averted eyes, modestly deflecting her husband's compliments about her cooking. Here, she looks him directly in the eye, clearly irritated, and with her arms crossed. Chastened, her husband concurs and walks out of the room, past a long line of women engaged in lively conversation, their bodies and faces in shadow, rendering them indistinguishable from each other and thus emphasizing their collective strength. At the end of the line waits his wife, arms resolutely crossed over her chest, ensuring his expulsion from the women's space. This single file of forceful women reclaiming a space in which to speak freely and socialize without the presence of men is visually juxtaposed against the single file of women at the beginning of the book carrying the lunch dishes back to the kitchen. Placed alongside each other, these images work to produce a complex representation of gender relations in Iranian society, further illustrated by (Grandfather) Satrapi's wry remark on the final page of *Embroideries:* "When the snake gets old, the frog gets him by the balls." The book thus ends by undercutting the impression of women's subservience suggested by the image on the first page.

Throughout *Embroideries,* Marji is present but decentered from the narratives unfolding in the text. The stories are not directly about her, but include her in a broader sense as many of these narratives are about the lives of women to whom she is related or with whom she has a close friendship, suggesting how individual and collective identities are entwined with and shaped by intergenerational memories (Miller 2007; Segall 2008; Whitlock

2008). Marji thus serves as a key witness to their sometimes painful stories, asking questions and allowing the women to disclose their memories. *Embroideries,* then, at once invokes and evades Marji-as-Satrapi (the author). Visually, Marji's appearance in the text signals a self-referentiality that evokes Satrapi as endless or serial autobiographer. Notably, as her series of graphic novels progresses, Marji-as-autobiographical-subject is placed at a further remove from the narrative; in each text, she is further decentered from the events of the story. The repetition of herself in her texts, each time at a greater distance from the center of the narrative, from the autobiographical *Persepolis* to the more biographical *Embroideries* and *Chicken with Plums,* also suggests an awareness of and sensitivity to the "specificity of historical trauma" to which Dominick La Capra (2001) urges us to attend. La Capra (2001) argues that an "empathic unsettlement . . . involves a kind of virtual experience through which one puts oneself in the other's position while recognizing the difference of that position and hence not taking the other's place" (78). It thus depends upon "one's recognition that another's loss is not identical to one's own loss" (79).

The decentering of herself as autobiographical subject points to the complexity of Satrapi's works: her graphic novels are autobiographical, but always with an awareness of her and her family's place within a larger historical context. In interviews about the *Persepolis* books and movie, Satrapi has said repeatedly that her aim is to challenge dominant Western perceptions of Iranians as fanatical Muslims and as terrorists.[13] Indeed, her short introduction to *Persepolis: The Story of a Childhood* articulates these intentions very clearly. Satrapi offers a brief overview of the ancient history of the Persian civilization, then moves on to three critical moments in contemporary Iranian history: the 1953 CIA-backed coup that toppled the nationalist government of Prime Minister Mohammad Mossadegh; the 1979 Iranian revolution that overthrew the monarchical rule of Mohammad Reza Shah Pahlavi and established the Islamic Republic of Iran; and the 1980–88 Iran–Iraq war. These three historical moments constitute the national traumas around which Satrapi (inter)weaves her graphic narratives. In the last paragraph of her introduction in *Persepolis,* she states:

> Since [the 1979 revolution], this old and great civilization has been discussed mostly in connection with fundamentalism, fanaticism, and terrorism. As an Iranian who has lived more than half of my life in Iran, I know that this image is far from the truth.

> This is why writing *Persepolis* was so important to me. I believe that an entire nation should not be judged by the wrongdoings of a few extremists. I also don't want those Iranians who lost their lives in prison defending freedom, who died in the war against Iraq, who suffered under various repressive regimes, or who were forced to leave their families and flee their homeland to be forgotten. One can forgive but one should never forget. (Satrapi 2003, introduction)

This theme of remembering and not forgetting is the thread that runs through all four texts, articulating the imperative to collective and intergenerational witnessing. Satrapi's positioning of herself as witness to both the personal and the national traumas of an earlier generation is most clearly articulated in *Chicken with Plums,* a moving narrative that weaves together Satrapi's great-uncle's personal loss with that of a larger national loss.

Repetition and Memory in *Chicken with Plums*

Chicken with Plums chronicles the story of Satrapi's great-uncle, the musician Nasser Ali Khan, as he descends into depression and eventually commits suicide. His is the story of unfulfilled potential, as first his love affair, and then his music career, and finally his life are each cut short. The unfolding of this personal tragedy takes place at the forefront of the narrative while a national trauma—the 1953 CIA-backed coup deposing the popular government of Prime Minister Mohamad Mossadegh and ending the nation's hopes of economic self-determination and democracy—occupies the background. Marji is, for the most part, absent from this text, serving mainly as the unembodied narrative voice. But Marji and her mother do appear briefly in a visual sidenote to the story, thereby invoking the *Persepolis* books, as well as the recognizable and familiar presence of Marji and of her immediate family in all of Satrapi's works.

Satrapi's use of repetition is reflected in the repeated visual insertion of Marji as autobiographical subject in all four of her graphic novels. She also uses the strategy of repetition in her reproduction of the same panel at different places in the text; sometimes the panel is exactly the same but its repetition at a different point in the narrative invites conflicting interpretations of the same event. In other instances, the panel is reproduced with a slight alteration in the images, thus offering a quite different interpretation of the narrative.[14] In *Chicken with Plums,* the story is, at first glance, a simple one. It is about a man, Marji's uncle, Nasser Ali, and a woman, Irane, who love each other but whose families (specifically her father) forbid them from marrying each other. Nasser Ali is then forced to marry a woman whom he does not love. But this story also resonates at the national level: in 1953, a beloved, and democratically elected, national leader, Mohamad Mossadegh, is forcibly removed from power and replaced by a monarch, Mohamad Reza Pahlavi, supported by the British and American governments instead of by the Iranian people. But these private and public narratives are experienced and understood differently at different historical moments. For instance, a chance encounter in the street between former lovers or a moment of marital discord (both examples discussed in further detail below) are perceived in contrasting ways by the people involved. Using the strategy of repetition, Satrapi plays with the concepts of time and memory, illustrating how our identities in the present are closely invested in representations of the past.

Chicken with Plums relates the story of Nasser Ali Khan's broken *tar* (a classical Persian string instrument) and his ensuing depression from several different perspectives in a continuous folding of past memories into the present. Since memory is "not tied to the individual who experienced a given event" (Hodgkin and Radstone 2006, 27) but is continually reinterpreted and reimagined in a dynamic process across generations, the reasons for Nasser Ali Khan's depression, his troubled marriage and his search for the perfect *tar,* are offered to us from various standpoints. The story is thus repeated several times, but from different perspectives, demonstrating the mutability of memory and narrative.

Chicken with Plums is bookended by near-identical panels portraying mourners at Nasser Ali Khan's funeral. The introductory chapter concludes with a panel depicting the mourners at his gravesite with the following caption: "All those who had known him were present on that day" (Satrapi 2006, 18) (Figure 4). The significance of this comment becomes obvious at the end of the book when the panel is reproduced; this time, the figures of the mourners are blackened from head to toe with the exception of one woman, whom the reader will recognize as Nasser Ali Khan's former lover, Irane. She stands facing his gravesite, with a tear rolling down her cheek (Figure 5). Upon closer observation of the first appearance of this panel, what becomes clear is that it is Irane whose face is covered with a handkerchief, making her presence in the crowd of mourners easy to miss.

Figure 4. Funeral scene from Chicken with Plums. *Note Nasser Ali's wife in center. Irane appears behind her on the edge of the page with her face concealed. From* Chicken with Plums *by Marjane Satrapi. Translation copyright 2006 by Anjali Singh. Used by permission of Pantheon Books, an imprint of Knopf Doubleday Publishing Group, a division of Penguin Random House LLC. All rights reserved.*

Figure 5. Funeral scene from Chicken with Plums. *Note all figures silhouetted except for Irane. Also note the presence of Azrael, the Angel of Death. From* Chicken with Plums *by Marjane Satrapi. Translation copyright 2006 by Anjali Singh. Used by permission of Pantheon Books, an imprint of Knopf Doubleday Publishing Group, a division of Penguin Random House LLC. All rights reserved.*

The panel, in both instances, focuses on absence and loss, but the shading of the figures suggests an important difference. The first panel focuses on a communal and shared sense of loss among the gathering of mourners. The mourners are depicted standing in a semicircle around Nasser Ali's grave. His wife is at the center, positioned directly in front of his tombstone, clearly the principal grieving subject. Behind her is an older woman, looking somewhat irate, and behind her stands another woman who, in this visual iteration of the narrative, can be easily overlooked. Her face is covered with a handkerchief and she seems to blend into the background. But when the panel is reproduced at the end of the text, we recognize the woman as Irane, and here it is she who becomes the visual focal point, underscoring her centrality in Nasser Ali's emotional life. The elderly, cross-looking woman in the first panel is absent here; instead, Azrael, the Angel of Death, is situated next to Irane, looking at her quizzically. The next and final page depicts the solitary figure of the Angel of Death (in black) placed against a solid white page. The book thus concludes in an open-ended way, suggesting the possibility of Irane, too, dying of a broken heart.

The two illustrations of the mourners at Nasser Ali's gravesite further draw attention to the nuances of any narrative and the fact that the differences in detail often result in different versions. The importance of Irane's presence, but even more crucially of her absence, in Nasser Ali's life accounts for his total devastation when, many years after their relationship ends, they happen upon each other in the street and she claims not to remember him. *Chicken with Plums* begins with this chance meeting between Nasser Ali and Irane. This encounter opens the narrative and is then repeated—with a difference—at the end of the book. In the first panel of the original iteration of this scene, Nasser Ali is walking along the street (we later discover he is going to buy a replacement *tar* for the one his wife, Nahid, has broken in anger). He notices an elegant, older woman walking with her grandson; Nasser Ali approaches her and asks if her name is Irane. She acknowledges her name but does not acknowledge him. The last panel depicts Nasser Ali's profile in black watching Irane and her grandson recede into the distance (Figure 6). Irane's assertion that she does not remember him and his utter distress at her refusal to acknowledge their shared past illustrate how "memory always involves the deepest kind of emotional engagement" (Olney 1998, 373). Close to the end of the book, this incident is reproduced, but this time, the exchange is presented from Irane's perspective. After she tells Nasser Ali that she does not remember him, the next

Figure 6. First depiction of encounter between Nasser Ali and Irane. She does not recognize him; he is devastated. From Chicken with Plums *by Marjane Satrapi. Translation copyright 2006 by Anjali Singh. Used by permission of Pantheon Books, an imprint of Knopf Doubleday Publishing Group, a division of Penguin Random House LLC. All rights reserved.*

panel reveals a close-up of her anguished face, and of Nasser Ali walking away in the background. The last panel of that page shows Irane weeping and her grandson looking at her in confusion (Figure 7). In the first iteration of this scene, the panels have no borders, but they do in the second iteration.

Since borders help define and give order to the events in the narrative, the inclusion of them in the second iteration helps determine and fix the meaning of the encounter. This confirms and underscores the tragedy of the story as well: she does recognize him and still loves him but their separate courses have been set. Conflicting representations of the past serve as a reminder that memory is always dynamic and that "it is ever rewoven, constantly renewed or reconstructed, constantly evolving, a story and a work in progress" (Olney 1998, 244). But these contradictory narratives of the past also suggest that much is at stake when our memories contradict someone else's recollections of the same event: any challenge to our representation of the past affects our careful construction of ourselves in the present. If the happy memories of a past love sustain Nasser Ali in the present, allowing him to tolerate his present unhappy marriage, then the devastating thought that his memories were entirely fictional, that the love affair he remembers was not as extraordinary as he recalled, means these memories can no longer sustain him in the present as they had once done. In *Chicken with Plums,* in particular, Satrapi illustrates how our understanding of ourselves in the present remains contingent on our memories and our interpretation of the past.

The tension between conflicting and contrasting memories is further illustrated in the story of Nasser Ali Khan's marriage to and relationship with his wife, Nahid. These two figures have radically different recollections of key moments in their shared history, raising the question of how we remember the past and reminding us of memory's "profoundly constructive nature" (Olney 1998, 71). On the second day of his fast and at the height of his depression, Nahid brings her husband his favorite meal, chicken with plums, as a kind of peace offering. After reluctantly taking a mouthful, he promptly spits out his food in disgust, connecting his distaste for the meal with his loss of desire for all sensual and sensory experiences. Desperate to reconnect with him emotionally, Nahid evokes their long history together and their early courtship days. She reminds him that she has been in love with him since the age of eight and recalls their courtship with tenderness.

Her fond memories of their past, however, are interspliced with his memories, many of which are very much at odds with her nostalgic remembrances.

Figure 7. Second depiction of encounter between Nasser Ali and Irane. She has recognized him and weeps after they part ways. From Chicken with Plums *by Marjane Satrapi. Translation copyright 2006 by Anjali Singh. Used by permission of Pantheon Books, an imprint of Knopf Doubleday Publishing Group, a division of Penguin Random House LLC. All rights reserved.*

Nahid's pleasure in recalling her childhood crush on Nasser Ali Khan is juxtaposed with his recollection of using her as a means of conveying the love letters he wrote to his various girlfriends. And, while she remembers their courtship as a heady and romantic time, he remembers being forced by his mother into marrying her, a stable and dependable alternative to the glamorous Irane, with whom he was deeply in love and whose father objected to their marriage. The last panel in this sequence depicts their wedding day: the image shows an ecstatic Nahid in her white wedding dress, arm in arm with a visibly unhappy Nasser Ali, wearing black and against a black background, his head turned toward his mother, who had forced him into the unwanted marriage.

In all four of Satrapi's texts, the relationship between individual memory and trauma is interlaced with a larger national trauma. Memory, like trauma, works through repetition as traumatic memories return repeatedly, unbidden. Sidonie Smith and Julia Watson ([2001] 2010) have suggested that if we understand the act of "remembering not as an entirely privatized activity but as an activity situated in cultural politics, we can appreciate to what degree remembering is a collective activity" (25). The three historical moments Satrapi identifies in the introduction to *Persepolis I* are the 1953 coup d'état, the 1979 revolution, and the 1980–88 Iran–Iraq war. These are the national traumas that are entwined with the individual traumas of her family members. Throughout her works, the tragedies occurring at the level of the state and affecting a community of people are embodied through personal, individual traumas.

At the beginning of *Chicken with Plums,* when Nasser Ali is in the early stages of his depression, his friend Manuchehr comes to see him and makes an immediate connection between Nasser Ali's depression and the state of the nation. Manuchehr takes in his friend's disheveled appearance, remarking that he appears out of sorts, and concedes, "Although, how are you supposed to feel good with things as they are" (Satrapi 2006, 7). Here, Nasser Ali embodies the deteriorating state of the nation. Manuchehr makes note of this, and proceeds to launch into a monologue about the nation's lost hopes for a democratic and nationalist government since the events of 1953: "Do you remember the spring of '51? We were so enthusiastic . . . Our oil was nationalized. Mossadegh was our Prime Minister . . . / Two years of euphoria and wham! Mossadegh is in exile. The Americans and their allies own everything . . . / They think they're pumping our oil . . . In reality, it's our blood they're sucking . . . Are you listening?" Nasser Ali, deep in his own reveries, responds distractedly, "mmm, yes, yes" (Satrapi 2006, 8). In the next panel, Manuchehr looks at Nasser Ali's despondent face askance, and then Nasser Ali tells him: "Someone broke my Tar." Immediately, then, a connection is established between his broken *tar* (and, we later realize, its association with his old flame, Irane) and the lost future or potential of Iran as a democratic and sovereign nation. The breaking of this classical Iranian musical instrument signals a rupture with the past, not only at a personal level but also at the public and national level, suggesting a loss of Iran's cultural and political self-determination.

This connection between individual loss and national loss, between individual memory and national memory, exemplifies Hodgkin and Radstone's (2006) claim that "memory . . . both underpins and undermines the national narrative. . . . The question of how people remember their own stories, then, is intimately entwined with how they remember the national story" (170). The intertwining of private and public memory is a strategy Satrapi employs consistently and repeatedly in her works. In *Chicken with Plums,* when Abdi, Nasser Ali Khan's brother, attempts to rouse Nasser Ali out of his misery, the brothers begin reminiscing about the past, but these memories—like most memories depicted in this text—exist in contradictory tension with each other. Very quickly, the brothers move from personal reflections and childhood memories to Abdi's communist activities as a young man. Abdi was arrested and imprisoned for some time in his youth for his political activities, and this, according to Nasser Ali, both broke their mother's heart and depleted the family's wealth. Nasser Ali berates his brother for his communist beliefs: "Where were you, comrade, when Mossadegh was deposed?" His brother replies, "Mossadegh was pro-American," to which Nasser Ali responds, "Ha! Ha! Let me laugh! He was so 'pro-American' that he was chased out by the 'Americans.' Not to mention mom, who had to squander our family's entire fortune so that you could play at being a hero!" (Satrapi 2006, 36). There is an easy slippage in Nasser Ali Khan's retort from "Mossadegh" to "mom." The absence of a bridging sentence to signal a shift from the public to the personal suggests an almost interchangeable relationship between the individual and the state, or at the very least, a recognition of the ways in which national concerns and experiences fold into personal ones.

The memories of Nasser Ali and Abdi's childhood and young adulthood are still raw, and the traumatic memories of those years overlap with a national trauma: the interruption of a democratic government in Iran by external forces. The significance of this date, and its implications for the nation, is also evident in *Embroideries.* Amineh, one of the women who shares her tale of disappointed love, recalls her marriage to a man in 1953. The groom had been active in the communist movement but was forced to flee Iran for Germany after the coup d'état and the shah's return to power. Amineh describes her husband's dishonesty and betrayal of her, the details of her heartbreak, and her subsequent affair with a charming but married German man. Although the narrative focuses on Amineh's personal scars, the date 1953 resonates with the reader who has some familiarity with Iranian politics and history. Satrapi's graphic novels effectively and consistently position personal narratives at the forefront, conveying and relating national traumas through the lives of individuals. While the privileging of the micro level over the macro level is a popular feminist trope, this privileging of the private over the public also serves as a reminder that to "study memory in the context of the nation, then, is to engage very directly with the relations between individual and collective memory, between the subject and the state" (Hodgkin and Radstone 2006, 169). Indeed, the diasporic Iranian women's memoirs discussed in this book, and particularly in the next chapter, all narrate their personal stories as they overlap with public, national narratives.

The effects of the national traumas resulting from the coup of 1953, the revolution of 1979, and the war of 1980–88 repeat and reiterate themselves through the deaths of key figures in Satrapi's family: the depression and eventual suicide of her great-uncle is linked to the devastating aftermath of the 1953 coup; the murder of her uncle Anoosh occurs shortly after the 1979 revolution; and, finally, the war years further contribute to the deteriorating and dangerous conditions in postrevolutionary Iran, forcing Marji into exile. Satrapi's autobiographical avatar, Marji, appears in various iterations in her four graphic novels and reflects the effects of these national traumas, substantiating Sidonie Smith's (1998) claim that "historical memory is embodied in the very subjects that are its sites of remembering" (41). The intertwining of private memory and personal trauma with public memory and national trauma is thus repeatedly invoked in Satrapi's graphic works, calling attention to the fact that we cannot make sense of public, national traumas in isolation from personal ones.

Satrapi's repeated insertion of herself in her texts, and the continuous invocation of her extended family, suggests a recognition that to work through the traumatic experience—at both the public/national and the personal/familial levels—requires its repetition and reiteration within a collectivity. It also requires a willing and active listener-witness to make space for the stories that struggle to emerge. Nancy K. Miller (2007) has observed that in Satrapi's works, her bond with the women in her family, particularly with her mother and grandmother, offers "a fascinating twist on the late twentieth-century model of mother-daughter generations" (15). If the Western model of intergenerational memory and narrative highlights rifts between generations of mothers and daughters, Satrapi's narratives stress the importance of valuing the stories of previous generations of women. This emphasis on learning from and building on the knowledge of one's foremothers leads Miller (2007) to ask: "What happens to the mother-daughter plot when your mother is a dissident and a feminist, and your grandmother a nonconformist?" (17). Miller's question calls attention to one of the main arguments in this book: diasporic Iranian women's life narratives carry within them a profound commitment to remembering and honoring the past. Thus, by her own recognition, Miller's model of the mother-daughter plot that relies on a daughter's rejection of the maternal narrative does not apply here. The commitment to remember and to learn from the past, not to reject it, informs diasporic Iranian women's writing and their envisioning of themselves as empathic subjects. Like the other diasporic memoirists discussed in this monograph, Satrapi narrates personal family stories with a keen awareness of the ways in which events at the macro level are often reflected at the micro level, through the details of a family's stories. As the next chapter will discuss in further detail, at the heart of diasporic Iranian women's auto/biographical narratives is a collective commitment to come to terms with the historical past. Thus the folding over of past memories into the present impels the writer—and the reader—to remember and, more significantly, to transform the process of remembrance into a commitment to carry historical and personal memories into the future.

· CHAPTER 5 ·

Revolution, Nostalgia, and Memory in Diasporic Iranian Memoirs

In Iran your place becomes empty when you leave and stays empty as long as you are away. But what if the one who leaves forgets about his empty place? What if, by living so long in America or England or France, he starts to become part of those countries and no longer remembers his original home?

—Tara Bahrampour, *To See and See Again*

STRESSING THE FEELINGS OF LOSS that mark the condition of the exilic-diasporic subject, this quotation from Tara Bahrampour's (1999) memoir *To See and See Again: A Life in Iran and America* encapsulates the anxieties of cultural, emotional, and geographic displacement reflected in the life narratives produced by Iranian women in the diaspora.[1] These life narratives emphasize the importance of memory, and of a careful re-membering (in the sense of a piecing together) of personal stories of families and friends that have remained half told, lost in the frenzied shuffle between nations, between an Iran of their past and a (North) America, or Europe, of their present and future.

The Iranian expression "your place is empty," suggests Bahrampour (1999, 194), implies that the memory of a person remains alive in the hearts of those left behind and that the exilic subject can always find and reclaim her place again upon her return "home." But the anxieties that are part of the diasporic condition lead her to wonder what might happen if she forgets the sounds, the smells, the rhythm of life in her home country, and through this forgetting, lose a piece of her identity, her self? What happens to a person who by force of historical events leaves her home, never again to return? How does she preserve the memory of her personal and cultural history while managing to navigate a present reality: a new life in a foreign land?

Twenty years after the 1979 Iranian revolution, Gelareh Asayesh and Tara Bahrampour published autobiographical accounts of their childhoods in

Iran, narrating the impact of the revolution on their lives and their painful transitions to life in the diaspora. Published in 1999, Asayesh's *Saffron Sky: A Life between Iran and America* and Bahrampour's *To See and See Again: A Life In Iran and America* are at the forefront of what has now become a veritable phenomenon of diasporic Iranian women's autobiographical writing in English. Their memoirs are the first among a now substantial corpus of texts by a generation of diasporic Iranian women, many of whom experienced the 1979 revolution in pre- or early adolescence and who immigrated to the West with their families. Almost two decades after the publication of Bahrampour's and Asayesh's memoirs, there continues to be a significant number of auto/biographical narratives by diasporic Iranian women writing in English, and this output is matched by a seemingly insatiable market demand for such auto/biographical texts.[2]

This particular wave of Iranian memoirs is produced by a generation of authors whose childhood or early adolescence was interrupted by the 1979 revolution; thus, the predominant sentiment in these texts, nostalgia for a lost childhood, is deeply bound up with nostalgia for a lost (prerevolutionary) nation/home. Unlike the current generation of Iranian adolescents for whom the 1979 revolution represents a historical moment largely considered irrelevant to their present-day lives, the year 1979 figures prominently in diasporic memoirs by authors who experienced the revolution as children or as adolescents and whose lives underwent significant changes as a direct result. The memoirs produced by this particular generation of writers contain, at their core, a profound sense of the insurmountable and devastating effects of the revolution. This chapter takes a closer look at the twinning of private, familial memory with public memory in diasporic Iranian women's memoirs, positing that revolutionary rupture and trauma frames these writers' nostalgic recollections of Iran. The overlapping of private and public memory determines their relationships to their host country (in this particular instance, the United States) as well as their perceptions of their former home, (prerevolutionary) Iran.[3]

The memoirs discussed in the first half of this chapter—*To See and See Again; Saffron Sky;* Donia Bijan's (2011) *Maman's Homesick Pie: A Persian Heart in an American Kitchen;* Afschineh Latifi's (2005) *Even after All This Time: A Story of Love, Revolution, and Leaving Iran;* and Roya Hakakian's (2004) *Journey from the Land of No: A Girlhood Caught in Revolutionary Iran*—can be considered in terms of what Gillian Whitlock (2007) calls "generational" narratives produced by a generation of women who experienced the trauma of the revolution at "a critical moment of becoming in their personal histories" (164). As Whitlock (2007) observes: "The fact that it has taken almost three decades for a school of life narratives to emerge in English, and that they take the form of exilic writing, can be also attributed to the belatedness of traumatic memory and the place of these women in history: these memoirs are generational" (164). Too young to have participated in any of the political movements during the revolution, these writers have nevertheless felt the irrevocable impact of the revolution in their lives. This particular generation was old enough to recall, and later to feel nostalgic for, their lives before the revolution, but they were too young to have actually participated in the various revolutionary movements. They see the revolution as something that happened *to them,* and as a result, this particular generation battles with a sense of frustration over their lack of agency during a historical moment that had such a definitive and devastating impact on their lives. What binds these life narratives, then, is the shared experience and articulation of the revolution as a traumatic event, as an inflicted wound during a key period in the authors' personal development.

Understanding the revolution as trauma shows us the ways in which "trauma is not locatable in the simple violent or original event in an individual's past, but rather in the way that its very unassimilated nature—the way it was precisely *not known* in the first instance—returns to haunt the survivor later on" (Caruth 1996, 4). The very fact that the traumatic event is unassimilable at the moment of its occurrence explains the continued outpouring of autobiographies over three decades after the revolution. Further, this particular generation of writers, who experienced the revolution as children, began writing their memoirs at an age when they could process this trauma through the cathartic act of "scriptotherapy," a practice that Suzette Henke (2000) has argued renders the role of the analyst obsolete. These texts thus constitute what Kai Erikson (1995) has called a "gathering of the wounded," as they work through the experience of revolutionary trauma by sharing memories marked by revolutionary events (187). The loss of a familiar home, culture, and language are conveyed, in these texts, through nostalgia, a powerful affect that shapes—and sometimes scars—life in the diaspora.

Understanding the revolution as trauma, or as a radical rupture that severs the now-diasporic subject from her homeland, betrays, of course, the writer's social and cultural class. Some women belonging to the more traditional and often lower socioeconomic strata of society found the changes wrought by revolution enabling. The fact that women now outnumber men at Iranian universities, and that there is a significant population of highly educated and professional women in Iranian society today, has been noted in both scholarly and media publications about postrevolutionary Iranian society. However, for those women whose families were financially secure and who enjoyed high social standing in prerevolutionary Iran, the revolution represented a cataclysmic loss of a safe and privileged world. That particular generation, and social class, is inclined to understand the revolution as a calamitous event, and as a result, the autobiographical narratives by women from privileged backgrounds typically unfold in two discrete parts: life before the revolution (often celebratory and idealized) and life after the revolution (usually fraught and conflicted).

The second half of this chapter examines Azadeh Moaveni's (2006) *Lipstick Jihad: A Memoir of Growing Up Iranian in America and American in Iran* and her second memoir, *Honeymoon in Tehran: Two Years of Love and Danger in Iran* (2009). While in her first memoir Moaveni shares with Asayesh and Bahrampour, in particular, a powerful nostalgia for prerevolutionary Iran, hers is a nostalgia generated by and mediated through family narratives told in the diaspora. Moaveni's first memoir thus calls attention to the fact that "memory . . . is not tied to the individual who experienced a given event, but dispersed and transmitted to subsequent generations" (Hodgkin and Radstone 2006, 27). Moaveni's nostalgia for the "home" country, then, is mediated by what Marianne Hirsch (2001) has called "postmemory," which

> most specifically describes the relationship of children of survivors of cultural or collective trauma to the experiences of their parents, experiences that they "remember" only as the narratives and images with which they grew up, but that are so powerful, so monumental, as to constitute memories in their own right. (9)

As Hirsch describes it, then, postmemory is a very powerful type of memory that does not refer to or draw upon a person's actual past experiences; rather, it is a memory refracted through the lens of a preceding generation marked by trauma. Moaveni's second memoir, which chronicles her career in Iran as Middle East correspondent for *Time* magazine, her marriage to an Iranian, and the birth of her first child in Tehran, traces a trajectory coveted by many diasporics: a return "home" that affords her the chance to move out of the space of mediated nostalgia and lay claim to "authentic" experiences and memories of her own.

Perhaps in part because of their relative absence from the literary marketplace in the past, Iranian women's autobiographies have become phenomenally popular in North America and (perhaps to a lesser extent) in Western Europe. But these memoirs have not received the warmest of welcomes among scholars of Iranian culture and literature, some of whom have argued that these texts invite and encourage the Western imperial gaze, by offering readers a glimpse into the presumably "forbidden" world beneath the veil.[4] It is certainly worth noting that at least in North America the thirst for these autobiographies appears unquenchable; this prevailing interest in what Graham Huggan (2001) calls the "ethnic autobiography" invokes a history of the prurient "Western" desire to unveil the secrets of a feminized "East." These texts promise the Western reader access to the East, a promise that invokes a long history of colonial desire to unveil the simultaneously eroticized and abject Muslim woman. This colonial history of wanting to "know" and therefore to "own" the Orient needs to be understood as part of a civilizational discourse that categorizes nations along an axis of evolutionary development and provides "evidence" for foreign/imperial intervention. This civilizational discourse is also part of a narrative of universal human rights, and tell-all memoirs have to negotiate their ambivalent positioning between a genre of political engagement and human rights discourse and a kind of writing that Whitlock (2007) has called "a soft weapon," a type of propaganda.

On the one hand, the genre of the autobiography can render human the dehumanized and convey the fullness of voice and presence of those who have been denied their rights. But on the other hand, it can also be used as "a soft weapon because it is easily co-opted into propaganda. In modern democratic societies, propaganda is frequently not the violent and coercive imposition of ideas but a careful manipulation of information in the engineering of consent" (Whitlock 2007, 3). Any critical engagement with Iranian women's memoirs, then, needs to take into account their potential complicity with a neoimperial system of governance. These books, their publication, their marketing, and their popularity speak to their (possible) complicity with a system of knowledge production that markets and packages the exoticized and simultaneously reviled East for the consumption of the West. And by marketing the East in this way, as a place both inviting and threatening, these texts lend their implicit support for neocolonial intervention.

However, more can be said about these life narratives—and their popularity—than their putative complicity within a larger imperialist project. Leigh Gilmore (2001) has argued that the memoir has become the genre du jour in the West, a phenomenon she identifies as part of "the therapy-driven culture of confession" in which we currently live (2). The current surge in Iranian women's memoirs can be understood in terms of what, drawing on Gayatri Spivak's work, Gilmore (2001) identifies as the convergence of a "a 'culture of confession' and a culture of testimony" in contemporary Western society (2). Certainly, these memoirs can be considered in relation to our society's compulsive use of social media to document and broadcast the minutiae of our daily existence. But these texts also share the experience of the Iranian revolution, and the challenges of exilic life, as an emotional wound or radical rupture in the lives of their authors. These diasporic Iranian memoirs share a portrayal of the revolution as an individual and collective trauma, and all are driven by nostalgic memories of the prerevolutionary era. The dominant sentiments foregrounded in these memoirs are those of loss and mourning for another time and another place (prerevolutionary Iran) and another life (the one they would have led had the revolution not occurred). In the case of contemporary Iranian women's autobiographies, personal memoirs enter the political sphere by bringing to the fore questions of home and nation, identity and belonging. Indeed, diasporic Iranian women's memoirs demonstrate how public and political narratives in contemporary Iran have had a direct impact on, and are indeed closely intertwined with, personal narratives. These memoirs perform a range of functions, as I will explain in further detail below: some texts demand an audience to bear witness to the disclosure of traumatic memories, and this claiming of witnesses helps activate the process of emotional healing; some texts confirm a Western liberal notion of immigrant success through hard work and a willingness to adapt. All of these narratives, however, are imbued with a powerful sense of nostalgia.

Nostalgia and the Return "Home"

While both Asayesh's and Bahrampour's texts are marked by nostalgia and longing for a prerevolutionary Iran, filtered through idealized childhood memories, a significant difference between their narratives is captured by the use of prepositions in their respective book titles. While Bahrampour (1999) writes of "a life *in* Iran and America," situating herself as a more or less fluid border crosser who can live in either or both countries, Asayesh (1999) speaks of the pain of cultural dislocation and liminality as she lives "a life *between* Iran and America." Bahrampour is the child of an American mother and an Iranian father, and her memoir explores her bicultural identity, which predates the revolution: born in America, where she spends her early years, she reluctantly adapts to Iranian culture when her parents decide to relocate to Iran in the early 1970s. She then finds herself having to reacculturate to the United States when the family leaves Iran during the revolution. Asayesh, who was born and raised in Iran but leaves the country as a teenager with her parents during the revolution, shares her conflicted and troubled feelings about living in the space between cultures; her memoir offers a poignant meditation on diasporic existence. She turns her focus inward in her book, reflecting upon her relationship to Iran, to America, to her American husband, and to her children. *Saffron Sky* thus dwells on the fear of losing one's cultural identity and sense of self as a result of living in the diaspora.

Structured around the theme of departures and arrivals, leave-takings and homecomings, *Saffron Sky* begins with a chapter titled "The Return" in which Asayesh (1999) writes of going back to Iran after a fourteen-year absence and experiencing a return to Iranian culture through the senses:

> The taste of pomegranate juice, the sight of sheep on a city street, the way a pail is made . . . these are the details that define our lives. In forgetting them, I had forgotten my own face. Here in Mashad, little by little, I am restoring the contours of my identity. (22)

The second chapter, titled "Homecoming: America," underscores the irony of her homecoming to a place from which she feels dislocated. Indeed, the book is structured so as to emphasize the sense of "in-betweenness" to which the title draws attention. The book begins with "The Return" and "Homecoming: America"; these are followed by a central chapter titled "Homecoming: Iran." Both chapters on "homecoming" convey a sense of unease with the notion of claiming home in a single location. The book thus ends with an aptly titled chapter, "In Between," illustrating the quintessential diasporic condition: the inability or perhaps unwillingness to choose one side over the other, and the challenges of enduring "unhomeliness" everywhere.

This final chapter captures Asayesh's dilemma as an Iranian American: she is a product of both cultures and nationalities, but every occasion is marked by loss. Her experiences as a new parent, for instance, are tinged with apprehensions about the incursion of Americanness into her life and the attendant expulsion of her Iranian identity. Asayesh (1999) writes of her efforts to teach her daughter, Mina, how to speak Farsi, and of her panic when the child dilutes her vocabulary with English:

> Anxiety seizes me, for I know that language is the lifeblood of culture. Language is the self, reflected and clothed in nouns and verbs and adjectives. Without Farsi, the Iranian in Mina will shrivel up and die. Even as I think this, I know that my greatest fear is of my own inner shriveling, not Mina's. In guarding Mina's heritage, I guard my own, for they are linked. (213)

Asayesh's determination to enforce linguistic purity in her conversations with her daughter is her way of ensuring cultural continuity between her Iranian past and her American present; this desire is further expressed through a nostalgic longing for the Iran of her childhood, a childhood, and historical period, aborted by the rupture of revolution.

Scholars who work on nostalgia and memory have noted that the origin of the term *nostalgia* can be traced to a Swiss medical thesis published in 1688. The word comes "from the Greek *nostos,* to return home, and *algia,* a painful feeling," and the condition it described was diagnosed as "a debilitating, sometimes fatal, medical affliction" (Hirsch and Spitzer 2006, 82). The cure for the disease of nostalgia was generally understood to be a return to one's original homeland. Although nostalgia is no longer pathologized in the same way, its association with a lost homeland, or a sense of loss "of a more general and abstract type, including the yearning for a 'lost childhood,' for 'irretrievable youth,' for a vanished 'world of yesterday'" (Hirsch and Spitzer 2006, 82), continue to be associated with the term.

In her chapter titled "Childhood," about her childhood in Iran, Asayesh offers a nostalgic look back at a life filled with pleasure, one that is rich with family relationships and connections. This is a time and a place in her life during which she experiences a sense of wholeness that eludes her in America: "My life, my culture, fit me like my skin. It was as impossible then for me to comprehend a day when I would be a stranger to myself as it is now, looking back over the years, to comprehend my own innocence" (Asayesh 1999, 67). Her move to the United States, and her break from her Iranian girlhood and cultural traditions, her feeling of alienation from herself, is captured poignantly in the following chapter, titled "The Break." Here she recounts her experiences as a young girl, out on her first date with an American, who makes the bold decision to break the rules of acceptable (female) behavior by putting her arm around the young man's waist: "I can still remember, as if it were seared into the palm of my hand, the cool silk of his jacket, the forbidden heat of the body beneath. I can still remember the moment when I let go of that girl from Iran" (Asayesh 1999, 113). This final break with Iranianness coincides with a quintessential "loss of innocence" moment that signifies her departure from a "home" associated with childhood simplicity, coherence, and national belonging, into an "away-from-home" state equated with the confusing experiences of nascent adulthood, and severance from the original culture/nation.

The concept of "home" as both physical location and imaginative space has been addressed by theorists of the nation; their formulations of citizenship and belonging have been taken up by postcolonial and feminist scholars interested in questions of self and other, home and away, center and margin. This figuration of the nation as home has also been explored by scholars studying the culture of childhood who argue that the home/nation, often associated with the maternal, is frequently represented as the natural space of the child. Any transgression out of this space, any move "away" from "home," is marked by deep anxiety because it is the space of the unknown, a terrain laden with the anxieties of adolescence and entry into adulthood, and the accompanying loss of childhood innocence.

In point of fact, Asayesh's (1999) heartrending description of her sense of loss and dislocation upon arriving to America is deeply bound up with a mourning for the innocence of youth: "In America childhood seemed to end early, to be replaced by a cultivated cynicism that masked both vulnerability and immaturity. . . . Going to high school in America felt like a violation of my childhood, an abrupt and painful loss of innocence" (103). Her comments identify the place of exile as profoundly unnatural and disruptive to the organic wholeness of the state of childhood; exile corrupts and abridges what is perceived to be a pure experience and stage of life protected from the complex world outside the home.[5] While Asayesh explains the diasporic condition as a loss of childhood innocence and cultural belonging, an ambivalent location of self across national borders, her narrative also invokes an idealized representation of childhood and of the child's place within the home/nation. This nostalgic formulation and equation of childhood with memories of home and a sense of belonging is found in both Asayesh's and Bahrampour's texts; their poignant feelings of loss and deep nostalgia are bound up with a sense of the permanent loss of childhood and simultaneously of Iran-as-home. As they adapt to their new lives in the United States, they negotiate their own nostalgic childhood memories with the nostalgia of their parents' generation for an Iran left behind.

In *To See and See Again,* when Bahrampour (1999) announces to her parents that she is returning to Iran for a visit, her mother's response is swift and sharp: "She turns to me, trying to be calm, but there is a bitterness in her voice that I have never heard before. 'What are you looking for? Your childhood? You can't get that back'" (201). Her brusque reaction can be perhaps explained by an apprehension about the repercussions of what Bahrampour may be seeking; perhaps she fears that by revisiting the place of her childhood, Bahrampour is moving "away" from her current "home" and reclaiming a past and a cultural identity to which her (American) mother no longer has access. Her mother's anxiety about Bahrampour's decision takes on a heightened significance in light of the bureaucratic process she undergoes to have her passport reissued: "I must send nine hundred and eighty-seven dollars, the charge for separating my childhood passport from my mother's and issuing me a new, Islamic one" (Bahrampour 1999, 201). Thus her mother's apprehensions about Bahrampour's revisiting of her Iranian past can be understood through the symbolism of this separation. Bahrampour's nostalgia for her past life in Iran, and her desire to return to the place of an idealized childhood, therefore requires, paradoxically, a distancing from her mother.

Throughout her book, Bahrampour (1999) offers nostalgic anecdotes and remembrances of her childhood friends and of the games that they played. The book even ends with a poignant description of one of those games, which

> calls for four people to stand beside four trees in a wide-open square of grass. The fifth one stands in the center, and at a signal we run, trying to switch trees without the middle person getting there before us. The pattern is circular and endless. After each run, someone is always left floating in the middle of the lawn. The floater cries out and the rest of us pick a direction and run blindly until we hit a tree and whip our arms around it. We stop with a jerk, breathless, relieved to be holding on to the solid trunk. And then we look around to see where we are. (357)

By concluding with this description of a childhood game, the text reorients the reader back to an irretrievable past, but the game has ambivalence and unbelonging built into its very structure. The rules of the game require the participants to run blindly in the dark and then to orient themselves as quickly as possible; the game is thus both prophetic and symbolic of the scattering of Iranians around the globe. A key element of the game is the thrill of running around in the dark, not knowing where you will land, as you try and find secure footing. Once you have steadied yourself by holding on to what is in front of you, you open your eyes to discover where you have landed. Bahrampour seemed to enjoy this game precisely because of the feeling of not knowing where she was going or where she would find herself.

This acceptance and even embrace of the unknown manifests itself in Bahrampour's reflections on diasporic life. While Bahrampour's text, like Asayesh's, offers a nostalgic recollection of her idyllic childhood in Iran, her relationship to her diasporic identity is more accepting than Asayesh's, as suggested by the subtitle of her memoir, "A Life in Iran *and* America." The use of the coordinating conjunction "and" suggests an embrace of the two cultures rather than the fraught relationship implied by Asayesh's "between." Bahrampour's greater ease with occupying a fluid space of in-between is connected perhaps to being a product of two cultures, with an American mother and an Iranian father. Rather than feel out of place in either context, Bahrampour moves uninhibitedly across borders—performing the occasional social gaffe in Iranian contexts where the rules of social behavior are at times more prescribed than in American ones.

Like Asayesh, Bahrampour's recollections of her prerevolutionary childhood in Iran border on the idyllic, but she shows an awareness that her childhood experiences were not typical. During a reunion with an old friend from Iran, the daughter of American professors, she is initially startled to hear reference to herself as an expatriate but accepts the relative accuracy of the description:

> That day at breakfast Carla illustrated my own expatness with a story I hadn't remembered, an indication of how separate, at the age of four, we already felt from those around us. One day we begged to dress up like Iranian women, so Mama bought a length of black cloth and made us two little chadors. We draped them over our heads and squatted silently against a wall the way we had

> seen Iranian women do in the street. We already knew we would never wear chadors in our real lives; no matter how many dark, draped women we passed on the sidewalk, we would end up in minidresses and tights like our mothers. Ours was an expat game. You don't see children of immigrants to America dressing up as Americans for a day; they make sure to dress American every day. (Bahrampour 1999, 354)

Despite recognizing that her bicultural background set her apart from other Iranians, and that her performance of "Iranianness" only served to highlight her "Americanness," Bahrampour nevertheless claims Iran as her home, just as she also acknowledges America as home. At the same time, she is sensitive to the differences between her family's postrevolutionary exilic experience and that of other Iranians: "When we finally left, we were not immigrants to America either. Three of us had been born there; four of us spoke perfect American English. Landing in America, we went straight to Grandma and Grandpa's backyard swimming pool in the hills" (Bahrampour 1999, 355).

Bahrampour thus recognizes that she cannot uncomplicatedly claim a diasporic identity; although her parents were forced to choose one home over another, both places were equally home to them. At the same time, the transition to America was not entirely smooth, and she writes of the pain of displacement and dislocation filtered through the emotions of adolescence. Bahrampour (1999) recounts coming to terms with her Iranian identity as she embraces her American side, emphasizing the revolutionary trauma and sense of permanent loss experienced by Iranians of her generation, particularly those who were still in late childhood at the time of revolution:

> Strangely, [a sense of displacement] seems strongest in Iranians my own age. Those young enough to have adjusted to America but old enough to still remember Iran seem to have the most difficulty choosing their cultural allegiances, perhaps because they were too young to have made their own decisions about staying in Iran or leaving. (348)

The feeling of cultural alienation was heightened by the political climate in the United States in 1980; this was the time of the hostage crisis and overwhelming anti-Iranian sentiment in the United States. The yellow ribbons Americans pinned to their clothes and tied around trees signified support for American hostages in Iran, but they also worked as divisive symbols of true-blood American patriotism, bringing some members of society together, while excluding others. These ribbons were part of a visible campaign that drew clear lines in the sand, demarcating good from evil. This was also the time that the popular band Vince Vance and the Valiants released their song "Bomb Iran," to the tune of the famous Beach Boys song "Barbara Ann."[6] Many Iranians fleeing the trauma of revolution arrived in the United States only to suffer the trauma of American xenophobia during the hostage crisis.

Embracing Diaspora

Despite the numerous challenges they face upon their arrival in the West, most diasporic Iranian memoirs conclude with the authors' acceptance, even embrace, of their adopted country. Bijan's (2011) *Maman's Homesick Pie* is no exception. Her memoir, however, begins with the painful experience of loss. In this case, the loss is the accidental death of her mother, who is run over by a car. Bijan (2011) begins her narrative in her mother's kitchen, immersed in the melancholy task of packing away her belongings, when she discovers, to her amazement, a collection of American recipes: "Coleslaw, banana bread, carrot cake, macaroni and cheese" (4). Mystified by why her mother would want to learn these recipes, she muses: "Why had a woman so well versed in Persian cuisine, who had weathered a revolution, exile, and threats to her life and had built her family a new home through sheer will, felt pushed to the other side of belonging? Not one to be left out, she had seen a vital connection between food and belonging" (4). For Bijan, the story of revolution, exile, and diasporic identity can be told most effectively through the making and the consumption of food and the sharing of recipes. Each chapter in her auto/biographical story concludes with recipes that complement the narrative. For example, the book's introduction, in which we learn of her mother's death, concludes with instructions on how to steep "Persian Cardamom Tea" and bake "Orange Cardamom Cookies." Bijan thus begins her memoir by situating herself in her mother's "Persian" kitchen, a warm and communal space, as well as a place where the Persian tea, the lubricant of Iranian conversation and personal exchange, steeps.[7]

Having evoked the tea and cookies that are de rigueur in Iranian hospitality, her recollection begins in the same vein as other diasporic memoirs—by representing her Iranian childhood through a nostalgic and idealized lens: "The Tehran of my childhood was cosmopolitan and multicultural, bearing little resemblance to our Western notion of contemporary Iran—that of a fearful nation beneath the glare of clerics and Revolutionary Guards" (Bijan 2011, 9). Bijan represents prerevolutionary Iran as a tolerant and vibrant place of cultural difference, but what makes it "home" for Bijan, as for Asayesh, is primarily experienced through the senses. Recalling with vivid detail their sumptuous meals in Iran, Bijan (2011) writes:

> My parents nourished us with lavash bread from the oven wrapped around sheep's-milk cheese with fresh walnuts and just-picked tarragon, figs in season, buttery lamb shanks with fava beans and saffron-scented rice, cantaloupes spooned into chilled bowls and drizzled with rose water. They brought these to us as if for the first time. At times quarrelsome or tired, they were all enthusiasm when we were hungry. (24)

This first chapter, which describes a time of plenty and comfort in Iran, ends with recipes of her mother's Pomegranate Granita, Sour Cherry Upside-Down Cake, and Cardamom Cake. Already at this early point in the narrative, the recipes that Bijan shares suggest a blending of Iranian and Western traditions. (For instance, although sour cherries are very popular in Iran, upside-down cake is decidedly not a traditional Iranian dessert.)

Bijan continues the narrative of her family's journey from Iran to America through the discovery of new foods. Having arrived in the United States ahead of her parents, Bijan (2011) embarks upon a process of cultural assimilation and adaptation through an overindulgence in junk food:

> Thirty-six flavors of ice cream, thirty-six! Sundaes and milk shakes: small, medium, large? Large, of course! With or without whipped cream? With, with! Cereals, candy bars, treats made out of cereal and marshmallows, McDonald's hot apple pies! . . . I had to taste it all, and eventually I couldn't button my prize jeans. (53)

Her almost compulsive need to eat is Bijan's way of navigating a new culture and educating herself about a new world by tasting all that it has to offer. But if home, for both Bijan and Asayesh, is experienced through the senses and through sampling the delicate flavors of Iranian food, then the cheap ingredients and fast food Bijan consumes in America further highlight her separation from home and family. Filling herself with empty calories serves as a reminder to Bijan that she is not at home; it also becomes a way to fill the void of loneliness. When her parents finally join her in the United States, she is reassured by the comforting flavors and smells of which she had been deprived: "Our home smelled familiar again, of cardamom and mint, jasmine and rose water. California's bountiful Central Valley provided us with plenty of the ingredients, from figs to pomegranates, grape leaves, oranges and almonds, to cook Persian food" (Bijan 2011, 60). This story of the family's joyful reunion is experienced through her rediscovery of the pleasures of good food lovingly prepared; significantly, the chapter ends with her mother's Thanksgiving bread stuffing and persimmon parfait recipes. Although the American Thanksgiving meal is completely foreign to her mother, she embraces the tradition and menu with zeal upon her arrival in the country. Blending the familiar (Iranian) tastes and spices with the recipes and ingredients of her adopted country, Bijan's mother facilitates the family's entry into a new culture. Through its celebration of blended spices and recipes, Bijan's narrative upholds the liberal notion of the United States as an inviting land of opportunity for immigrants, at least for those who are willing to assimilate.

Pursuing her quest to learn about other cultures through food, Bijan relocates to Paris to study at Le Cordon Bleu (her account of her time in Paris is followed by such typical French recipes as duck à l'orange, galettes, and roast rabbit). Upon returning to America, she decides to blend French and Persian recipes, declaring:

> Paris, San Francisco, Tehran, all claim a part of me. As I looked out the window on the plane home from Paris, I thought about how the kitchens where I was shaped belong to all these places, and yet none claim to be the center. I'll always negotiate that in-between culture. And I'll always rely on the longing for these places, and I'll always be learning to move between them without falling through the gaps. (Bijan 2011, 203)

Like Bahrampour, Bijan is an ideal hybridized subject, taking pleasure in occupying the spaces *between* cultures; unlike Asayesh, for whom living in-between signifies loss and dislocation, Bijan transforms the feeling of longing into something tangible: the pleasure of a good meal.

For Bijan, home is not a particular physical location; home is created through the sharing of stories and food, through companionship and family ties. Her memoir begins in her mother's kitchen and ends in her own, in the company of her young son. Listening intently as she tells him stories of her family's life in Iran, he cracks walnuts with his grandmother's walnut cracker, to accompany his Iranian lunch of lavash bread, feta cheese, and mint: "It's still early, too early to go to school. And in the long stretch of these quiet mornings together—only his voice and mine, and the gurgle of the coffee machine, and his spoon tapping against a pale blue cup while I stir cocoa on the stove—I know I'm finally home" (Bijan 2011, 244). This final chapter ends with that most quintessential of American desserts: apple pie. The recipe, however, is her mother's version of this classic American dessert, one she taught herself to make in Iran at the request of the five-year-old Bijan, who saw it illustrated in a picture book. The hybridized apple pie, then, is a culinary testament to the family's willingness to embrace the tastes and the culture of their new home. The "homesickness" invoked by the title is one that can be overcome through the pleasures of food, and the blending of traditional Iranian flavors with American and/or French seasonings. *Maman's Homesick Pie,* which emphasizes the telling of stories and the preservation of memory, through nourishment and emotional sustenance, can thus be read as a model of a triumphant diasporic story.

The unequivocal celebration and embrace of diasporic identity is similarly echoed in Afschineh Latifi's (2005) *Even after All This Time.* Like *Maman's Homesick Pie,* Latifi's memoir begins with painful familial loss: in this case, the execution of her father, a colonel in the shah's army. The first chapter, "The Arrest," begins with her father's arrest in February 1979 by the revolutionary government, only one month after the departure of the shah. Accused of being an "enemy of God," he was sentenced to death for his assumed role in the infamous "Black Friday" shootings, which occurred on September 7, 1978, when demonstrators filled the streets in defiance of the martial law imposed by the shah's army. The crowd refused to disperse, and the army opened fire on revolutionaries, killing many protestors.[8] Despite the colonel's protestations of innocence, he was executed in May, only three months after his arrest.

Latifi's memoir recounts the story of her parents' lives, of their courtship and their marriage. Following the execution of her father, Latifi and her older sister move to Vienna to attend school, leaving their two younger brothers behind with their mother. From there, they move to the United States, enduring six years of hardship and separation from their mother and brothers until they are all successfully reunited in the United States. Theirs is a story of adversity and resilience; as with Bijan's memoir, the narrative adopts a Western liberal stance as it reasserts the rhetoric of opportunity and freedom available to (industrious) immigrants in America. In this text, there is no longing to return "home"; instead, when Latifi eventually does visit Iran briefly after a fifteen-year absence, her return to her American life comes as a relief: "I had seen enough. I was ready to go back" (Latifi 2005, 307). The last chapter, titled "Home," firmly locates Latifi and her family in the United States, and the book ends with an unequivocal embrace of the family's new home in America. In an effort to make her mother feel at home, Latifi orders roses from a "Persian greenhouse in Los Angeles" for her to plant on their new property: "Mom had tears in her eyes. It took her a long time to pull herself together. She planted vegetables that first summer, as well as all sorts of herbs" (317). The book ends on this symbolic note of immigrant adjustment and integration: the buying of land and the laying down of roots, but with an eye to incorporating the past into the present by planting Iranian roses, and herbs that will presumably be used in Iranian stews.

Like Latifi's *Even after All this Time,* Roya Hakakian's (2004) *Journey from the Land of No* also begins with a stark reference to violence in postrevolutionary Iran. Her book opens with this dedication: "Between 1982 and 1990 an unknown number of Iranian women political prisoners were raped on the eve of their executions by guards who alleged that killing a virgin was a sin in Islam. . . . This book is dedicated to the memory of those women" (ix). Immediately, then, Hakakian forces us into the role of witness to the atrocities that occurred at the height of revolutionary fervor and zeal in 1980s Iran.[9] For Hakakian, who worked at CBS's *60 Minutes,* another, more recent, violent event in Iranian history motivates her to write her memoir: the student protests of July 1999.[10]

David Unger, an editorial writer for the *New York Times,* contacts Hakakian for her views on the student protests, and soon begins prodding her to tell her own story. Initially reluctant to do so, Hakakian finally agrees to begin writing:

> When you have been a refugee, abandoned all your loves and belongings, your memories become your belongings. . . . When

> you have nothing left to guard, you guard your memories. You guard them with silence. . . . What you once witnessed is what biographers intended to write. But how much can biographers do if the witnesses are silent? (Hakakian 2004, 14)

Moved by the plight of the Iranian students, Hakakian recognizes that she can no longer nurse her memories in private. In fact, she sees herself as bearing a responsibility to make public her personal narrative as testimonial evidence in the face of continuing atrocities. Recognizing that she must break her silence, Hakakian begins to write, and as she does, she bears witness to the stories of those who have suffered in their resistance against the regime, just as David, and now the reader, bears witness to hers.

Her narrative begins and ends by stressing the importance of testimony and witnessing; before she makes the decision to write her memoir, Hakakian travels to Georgia on assignment for *60 Minutes* to interview the Reverend Jerry Cochran. Cochran, who was suffering from lung disease, attributed his disease to the hazardous tasks he was assigned while in the navy (Hakakian 2004, 16). During Hakakian's meeting with Cochran, she realizes that he had made numerous unsuccessful attempts to have his story heard, and this fact serves as a catalyst for the narration of her own memories of the revolution: "The feel of Jerry's firm grip as we shook hands still enveloped my hand, and his opening line kept playing in my mind: 'I have waited for years for you to come and hear my story.' So he had begun. And so I began" (18). Her meeting with Cochran persuades her of the power of storytelling and the importance of offering testimony in the face of continuing political and social injustice.

Like the other diasporic memoirs discussed in this chapter, Hakakian's story of childhood in Tehran tells of a happy time, although her narrative reveals that beneath the seemingly harmonious atmosphere in the country, there were whispers of discontent with the shah's regime. In her own family, her eldest brother is forced to leave Iran because his satirical drawings against the Pahlavi regime are attracting too much attention and his safety is becoming uncertain. Soon, the rumblings of revolution become louder, until the shah's regime is finally overthrown. Hakakian bookends her narrative with two maps of her Tehran neighborhood, one from 1978 and one from 1984, to show how the revolutionary narrative has overwritten a prerevolutionary one through the renaming of streets and boulevards.

The postrevolutionary move to rename Tehran streets can be read palimpsestically: by literally writing over the city's Pahlavi-era history, what emerges are the unresolved and deep-seated prejudices against racial, cultural, and class differences. For example, in Hakakian's text, the name *Johoud* emerges as a belated expression of the discrimination her father experienced as a Jewish child in an Iranian village; "Johoud" translates as Jew in Farsi, but for her family, "*Johoud* had only one meaning: a world, a word that Father buried before he left the village. There *Johoud* meant 'dirty'" (Hakakian 2004, 134). In response to the intense discrimination and ostracization he experienced as a child at school, his mother appealed to the district superintendent of the region, who put an immediate stop to the torment to which he was subjected. But years later, after the overthrow of the Pahlavi regime, Hakakian arrives home one day to see the word *Johoud* spray-painted on the wall of their home, and all the negative meanings the word had for her family and the Jewish community resurfaces: "Forty years later, there was *Johoud* again on the wall across from our door. It was punctuated by a strange sign. Not one I had ever seen: a plus sign gone awry, a dark reptile with four hungry claws" (135). For Hakakian, then, the nostalgia that she feels for what was, at one time, a happy childhood in a city with a substantial Jewish community is curbed by her memories of a growing anti-Jewish sentiment, and a shrinking Jewish population, in the aftermath of the revolution.

For Hakakian, two other ugly episodes stand out in her memory, together serving as unequivocal condemnations of the terror and oppression to which Hakakian, her family, and her friends were all subjected. The first is of the imprisonment and torture of her former neighbor, Bibi. Bibi, whom Hakakian had always admired for her intelligence and beauty, had become involved with the Mujahedin, one of the political opposition groups, and had been reported to the authorities by her school principal for distributing leaflets and disseminating political literature and ideas. The second incident is even more personal; Hakakian arrives home one day to see her father burning her treasured collection of literature, as well as her own notebooks. He destroys her books and her writings out of fear for her safety, realizing as he does so that if he must silence his daughter's voice in order for her to survive, it means they must leave the country (Hakakian 2004, 227).

Having watched her words consumed by flames over a decade earlier, Hakakian once more turns to writing as a way of bearing witness to her own painful memoires, as well as to the traumatic experiences of those whose suffering she was now witnessing from afar. Her book ends with an emphasis on the importance of telling stories: "And I am the lucky one, *escaped only to tell thee*" (Hakakian 2004, 233). Hakakian emphasizes the responsibility of the writer to bear witness to the suffering of others as a political imperative, an indisputable social responsibility, demonstrating, as Kay Schaffer and Sidonie Smith (2004) claim, that "acts of personal narrating can become projects of community building, organizational tools, and calls to action" (8). The diasporic memoirists discussed here—Asayesh, Bahrampour, Latifi, and Hakakian—all disclose painful personal and public memories, demonstrating that, as with other life narratives discussed above, these texts rely on a reader-witness willing to respond with empathy and generosity to accounts of loss and suffering.

Revolution and Postmemory

Azadeh Moaveni's relationship to Iran as she describes it first in *Lipstick Jihad: A Memoir of Growing Up Iranian in America and American in Iran* (2006) and then in *Honeymoon in Tehran: Two Years of Love and Danger in Iran* (2009) needs to be considered differently from the way other memoirists discussed in this chapter imagine their relationship to their homeland. While Moaveni's *Lipstick Jihad,* much like *Saffron Sky* and *To See and See Again,* is interwoven with nostalgic memories of Iran, Moaveni's longing for "home" precedes her visit to the country that she sees for the first time at age five. Her visit re-cements her nostalgia for an Iran mediated through an earlier generation's memories and yearning for an elusive homeland. While Asayesh, Bahrampour, and Hakakian mourn their carefully preserved memories of a prerevolutionary and idealized childhood in Iran, Moaveni's (2006) memoir begins with a critical self-awareness of her mediated relationship to her ancestral roots:

> I was born in Palo Alto, CA, into the lap of an Iranian diaspora community awash in nostalgia and longing for an Iran many thousands of miles away. As a girl, raised on the distorting myths of exile, I imagined myself a Persian princess, estranged from my homeland—a place of light, poetry, and nightingales—by a dark, evil force called the Revolution. I borrowed the plot from *Star Wars,* convinced it told Iran's story. (iv)

Keenly aware that her desire for Iran is shaped and mediated through what she repeatedly refers to as the "dusty" memories of her diasporic family and friends, Moaveni's nostalgia for Iran, or Persia, can be understood through Hirsch's (2001) "postmemory": "The relationship of children of survivors of cultural or collective trauma to the experiences of their parents, experiences that they 'remember' only as the narratives and images with which they grew up, but that are so powerful, so monumental, as to constitute memories in their own right" (9). While Hirsch uses the term to refer to the children of Holocaust survivors whose knowledge of an Eastern European home is mediated through the traumatic memories of their parents' generation, she recognizes its value in other cultural contexts, not limiting the term's applicability to survivors of the Holocaust.

The painful longing to return "home" defines and shapes the diasporic existence—whether the object of desire is an actual physical location where a person once resided or whether it is simply a place known and felt only through the imagination. Moaveni "inherits" a powerful longing for an idealized prerevolutionary Iran from her parents' generation and through the force of their nostalgia. This powerful affect is thus transmitted to the generation born in the diaspora by the preceding generation, which experienced the traumatic revolutionary years in Iran and lived through the backlash of the hostage crisis in the United States. This feeling of longing for a home that many diasporics have never themselves seen has been defined by Jennifer Delisle (2013) as "genealogical nostalgia: the affective drive to uncover, preserve, and record our family history and homeland—this notion of feeling a place 'in our bones,' despite never having seen it" (384). Moaveni's text illustrates the productive ways in which both the concept of postmemory and the concept of genealogical nostalgia can be applied to the particularities of a postrevolutionary Iranian context.

The memoirists discussed in this chapter all share an understanding of the diasporic experience as one shaped and defined through a sense of loss: a loss of childhood, a loss of cultural identity, and a loss of a (national) home. While Asayesh, Bahrampour, and Moaveni mourn the absence of a stable and knowable "home," other diasporic texts have described this experience in more positive terms, evoking descriptions of exile in celebratory terms as a state of "unbelonging." However, the overwhelming feelings of pain, loss, and longing that echo throughout all the life narratives discussed in this book suggest that the celebration of unbelonging requires generational distance as well as the security afforded by the privilege of social and economic class.

For Moaveni, her mediated nostalgia for Iran manifests itself through a longing for a childhood and a home to which she did not have access except during a brief visit to Tehran when she was five years old. She describes her memories of that trip through a nostalgic desire for a romanticized and idealized childhood experience: climbing mulberry trees in an "orchard . . . so dense that I could scramble from the limb of one tree to another, plucking the plump, red berries as I went along. . . . The trees stretched out as far as I could see, a glorious forest of mulberries, ripe for my picking" (Moaveni 2006, 3). This scene of idyllic childhood colors her understanding of her "Persianness" and shapes her relationship to a country that she has never physically inhabited but that occupies her imagination from childhood to adolescence in Northern California. It is this imaginative inhabiting of Iran that inspires her "return" to a country in which she has never lived and to write about that experience beginning with a chapter titled "Homecoming."

The chapter starts with Moaveni's relocation to Cairo as a Fulbright scholar to study Arabic; here she finds herself becoming increasingly preoccupied with thoughts of Iran, imagining what it might be like to be there instead of in Egypt. Particularly eloquent on the subject of nostalgia, Moaveni is both moving and astute on how nostalgia works particularly for Iranians in the diaspora. Having been "raised in the lap" of nostalgia, as she describes it in the first pages of *Lipstick Jihad,* she offers a compelling description and analysis of exile and diaspora. Moaveni describes, with poignancy, the emotional effects of living at a remove from one's country of origin. While nostalgia is a powerful affect, it can often be *felt* as a vague and overwhelming emotion, but Moaveni (2006) offers a remarkably incisive description of both the intensity of the feelings and of their source:

> Originating from a troubled country, but growing up outside it, came with many complications. Worst of all, at least on a personal level, was that you grew up assuming everything about you was related to that place, but you never got to test that out, since the place was unstable and sort of dangerous, and you never actually went there. You spent a lot of time watching movies about the place, crying in dark theaters, and feeling sad for your poor country. Most of that time, you were actually feeling sorry for yourself, but since your country was legitimately in serious trouble, you didn't realize it. . . . That, really, was why I wanted to

> go to Iran. To see whether the ties that bound me were real, or flimsy threads of inherited nostalgia. (32–33)

However perceptive her description of the stresses and tensions of diasporic life, what also emerges from the description above is Moaveni's at times reproachful view of diasporic Iranians whom she characterizes as jealously guarding stale memories of a prerevolutionary era and indulging their nostalgia for an Iran of their imagination. This tension between disparaging the nostalgia felt by diasporics while at the same time validating the intensity and pain of their nostalgic feelings is one that runs through both of Moaveni's memoirs but is particularly evident in *Lipstick Jihad.* For Moaveni, nostalgia is a negative affect: it encourages an ossified relationship with the country of origin and hinders a complex and comprehensive understanding of and engagement with the country's contemporary politics, society, and culture.

In her first memoir, Moaveni recounts her decision to move to Tehran in 2000, at the age of twenty-four, as a Middle East correspondent for *Time* magazine. Throughout her memoir, she shares her conflicted feelings about her self-positioning as an Iranian. Acutely aware that her relationship to Iran until this moment has been mediated through the memories of a wounded, diasporic generation that has glorified and glamorized the prerevolutionary era and vilified the postrevolutionary period, she writes in self-deprecating fashion: "Iran, as it turned out, was not the Death Star, but a country where people voted, picked their noses, and ate French fries" (Moaveni 2006, iv). Moaveni's "rootless nostalgia," a nostalgia generated through postmemory and genealogical nostalgia, propels her "home" to Iran (Hirsch and Spitzer 2006, 85). The idea of "going home" to a place that is mostly foreign to her illustrates how the condition of exile, a persistent longing to return to the home country, is here conjoined with the effects of a national trauma.

Trauma, as Cathy Caruth (1995) has described it, is an event experienced "belatedly, in its repeated possession of the one who experiences it" (4). It is indeed this very belatedness of the traumatic experience that gives rise to the concept of postmemory, according to Hirsch (2001): "Perhaps it is *only* in subsequent generations that trauma can be witnessed and worked through, by those who were not there to live it but who received its effects, belatedly, through the narratives, actions and symptoms of the previous generation" (12). Delisle (2013) understands the force of genealogical nostalgia in a similar vein; the desire for a home one has never seen but feels "in one's bones" is a desire that emerges belatedly through subsequent generations of exiles and diasporics (384). Trauma and memory, then, are at the heart of the Iranian exilic-diasporic experience, both of which are experienced belatedly through the profusion of life narratives that have flourished in the North American literary marketplace.

The painful memories of exilic displacement and of revolutionary trauma inform Moaveni's personal narrative. Recognizing that she carries the burden of inherited nostalgia, Moaveni decides to return to the home of her imagination and confront her feelings in the very place that serves as the object of her nostalgia. Upon her arrival in Iran, Moaveni relishes the warm welcome she receives from her family and describes, with genuine emotion, the experience of sitting in her grandfather's kitchen: "The kitchen smelled like summer, and I sat on a barstool at the island in the center, enchanted with the abundance and the knowledge that generations of my ancestors had eaten this precise sort of apple, exactly those peaches" (Moaveni 2006, 46). In this moving description of her reconnection with a personal (and larger, national/cultural) history, which until now had only existed as part of a carefully preserved family lore, Moaveni romanticizes her ancestral connections to Iran and perpetuates the nostalgic narrative of cultural origins.

Here, Moaveni taps into a "memory" that is deep-seated, a memory belonging to generations of her ancestors with whom she reconnects through the sensory experience of taste. Gelareh Asayesh (1999) narrates a similar experience of having arrived "home" through the sensory experience of taste; for her, the taste of pomegranate juice transports her back to a familiar world and a familiar time when the experience of "home" was uncomplicated, and to a time when she felt whole, rather than divided between cultural identities (22). Donia Bijan's (2011) entire narrative constructs "home" through the kitchens in which she has tasted Iranian, French, and American cultures, but it is her mother's Iranian kitchen that resonates with her at the most profound level.

For many diasporics, the romance of what R. Radhakrishnan calls the "quest for origins" is difficult to avoid, but as Radhakrishnan (2003) cautions: "Feeling deracinated in the diaspora can be painful, but the politics of origins cannot be the remedy" (128). Radhakrishnan's concern about the search and the claiming of one's cultural origins arises in response to the tendency for some diasporics to resort to parochial nationalist positions, disparaging other histories or nations in an effort to assert one's own.

Moaveni's sometimes harsh criticisms of the diasporic Iranian community in North America, which she sees as particularly out of touch with the real Iran, occasionally run the risk of setting up a hierarchy of "better" (or more "authentic") Iranians in tune with the country and "inferior" Iranians who are seen as "out of touch" with their country and their culture.

Thus, despite her often sensitive and affecting descriptions of how nostalgia shapes the life and emotions of the diasporic subject, Moaveni also reveals herself to be, at times, a surprisingly unforgiving critic of diasporic Iranians and their nostalgic relationship to an Iran to which they cannot or will not return. Quoting a friend with whom she engages in numerous conversations on the subject of nostalgia and diaspora, and who often berates Moaveni herself for looking at Iran through a nostalgic lens, she writes: "If you are a nostalgic lover of Iran, he said, you love your own remembrance of the past, the passions in your own life that are intertwined with Iran. If you love Iran realistically, you do so *despite* its flaws, because an affection that can't look its object in the face is a selfish one" (Moaveni 2006, 45).

Indeed, much of *Lipstick Jihad* is preoccupied with the subject of nostalgia, which Moaveni connects, at times in unsettling ways, to the topic of loyalty: loyalty to one's origins and to one's place of birth. Turning a critical lens on herself, her aunt, and her cousin, who all went to Iran under the spell of nostalgia for an Iran about which they all fantasized, Moaveni (2006) writes:

> All of us, Khaleh Zahra, Kimia, and I, had arrived in Tehran as Iranians of the imagination. We had Iranian identities, but they were formed by our memories and the Farsi-speaking parts of our soul—the part that responded, with years of accumulated references, when someone said "love" to us in Farsi, our first language of affection. But we could not navigate the Tehran of today, or share in the collective consciousness of the Iranians who never left. (86)

Bound up with the politics of Iranian diaspora and nostalgia is thus the question of loyalty: those who left Iran during or shortly after the revolution are depicted as having abandoned the nation in the face of adversity. Those who stayed behind suffered through the immediate and bloody aftermath of the postrevolutionary period and the eight-year Iran–Iraq war. So much has happened to the country and to its inhabitants post-1979 that those who left the country and who live abroad are portrayed as unable to understand the realities of contemporary Iran. One of the problems with this position is that it also raises, albeit perhaps inadvertently, the question of authenticity: those who live abroad are Iranians of the imagination; those who stayed behind and suffered through the war and the policies of the Islamic Republic are the "real" Iranians.[11] For Moaveni, this question of authenticity and belonging, of authentic and inauthentic Iranianness, is the personal conflict with which she struggles continuously in terms of her own relationship to Iran, and it is one that surfaces repeatedly in both of her memoirs. In *Lipstick Jihad,* she describes visiting California and attending a gathering of Iranian friends and family with her mother. In this instance, she tempers her inclination to dismiss Californian Iranians whom she has previously described as disconnected from the real Iran, acknowledging instead:

> Iran existed here, in the interior intimacy and rhythm of our lives. This enclave in California felt as much home as did the strange world of Tehran, the homeland itself, where our Iranian relatives lived as strangers. I resigned myself to never saying goodbye, because I now realized that I would perpetually exist in each world feeling the tug of the other. The yearning, which I must embrace and stop assaulting, was a perpetual reminder of the truth, that I was whole, but composed of both. (Moaveni 2006, 243)

Recognizing that working within the framework of authenticity presents its challenges, Moaveni concedes that the concept of belonging is itself a slippery one and that even in Iran young people feel displaced from the culture and society in which they live.[12] *Lipstick Jihad* ends with this thoughtful observation about belonging and nostalgia, diaspora and home:

> We were all displaced, whether internally, on the streets of Tehran, captives in living rooms, strangers in our own country, or externally, in exile, sitting in this New York bar, foreigners in a foreign country, at home together. At least for now, there would be no revolution that returned Iran to us, and we would remain adrift. But the bridge between Iran and the past, Iran and the future, between exile and homeland, existed at those tables—in kitchens, in bars, in Tehran or Manhattan—where we forgot about the

> world outside. Iran had been disfigured, and we carried its scraps in our pockets, and when we assembled, we laid them out, and were home. (Moaveni 2006, 246)

A defining feature of most diasporic narratives is an embrace of the ambiguous, ambivalent space of the border. But in the memoirs discussed in this chapter, the diasporic experience is described mostly through the trauma of revolution and the loss of childhood, home, and cultural identity. Asayesh, in particular, and on occasion, Moaveni, are less interested in celebrating the state of "unbelonging," to which writers such as Bahrampour, Bijan, and Latifi appear to have reconciled themselves. Asayesh's (1999) efforts to reproduce Iranian culture on a small scale—by renovating a room in her house in the traditional Iranian style, by ensuring that her American husband and her children speak Farsi, by returning regularly to Iran for long visits with her family—are indicative of her efforts to bring her understanding of "home" into her experience of "away." Through these efforts, she re-creates, on a small scale, a version of Iranian culture and identity for her and her children to inhabit within their own domestic space in the United States. Rather than celebrating a diasporic "border" identity, then, both Asayesh and Moaveni make attempts to lay claim to an elusive but locatable Iranian identity.

In her second memoir, Moaveni (2009) recounts her decision to live, work, marry, and have a child in Iran; unlike her first memoir, *Honeymoon in Tehran* recalibrates Moaveni's identity as legitimately Iranian. Her successful attempt to "return" offers her the possibility of accessing an authentic Iranianness no longer available to the population of nostalgic Iranians living in the diaspora. Her return, however, is short-lived: eventually, she is forced to leave Iran, this time with her husband and small child, as it becomes increasingly evident that she cannot work safely as a journalist in Iran. Their decision to leave is an intensely conflicted one for her and prompts Moaveni to raise once again the questions of diasporic existence and disloyalty: "Indeed, Arash and I were joining the great stream of educated Iranians who each year abandoned (yes, abandoned) their country for better jobs and better futures abroad" (Moaveni 2009, 315–16). Moaveni's feelings of guilt over her decision to leave Iran are shared in many of the narratives discussed throughout this book; the feeling of guilt (and accompanying shame) about leaving the country tends to transform itself into an anxiety about belonging: How can one stake a claim in a country one leaves behind?

A critical diasporic cultural politics focuses on a creative tension between the home and the host country, interrogating the concept of the nation-state, and celebrating a border space that facilitates fluid cultural identities.[13] But for diasporic Iranians, particularly for the generation that lived through that tumultuous period in Iranian history, the wounds of revolution remain relatively fresh. Diasporic Iranian life narratives continue to explore a powerful sense of collective loss in response to the 1979 revolution. Thus the revolution, as recounted in these memoirs, can be understood as both rupture and possibility, positioning diasporic Iranian women writers as key witnesses to testimonial narratives of loss and suffering.

Testimonial Life Narratives

My argument in this book has hinged on the claim that the overwhelming production of diasporic Iranian life narratives over the past (almost) two decades has been motivated by a nostalgic reflection and remembrance of prerevolutionary Iran. Alongside and, at times, intertwined with these nostalgic narratives is an articulation for human rights in testimonial accounts of suffering. Many of the published memoirs discussed in this book have had notable market success, with a wide readership interested in the genre. For some, particularly a non-Iranian readership, part of their interest in these memoirs emerges from a desire to learn more about an unfamiliar place, Iran, a country that circulates in mainstream media as both mysterious and menacing. For diasporic Iranians, these narratives may reflect their nostalgic longing for "home" or depict their own traumatic experiences of postrevolutionary Iran, and it is the *familiarity* of these accounts that captures their interest. In this monograph, I have suggested that diasporic Iranian life narratives should be understood as part of the "memoir boom." And in my discussion of these narratives (in the form of memoir, film, and online disclosures), I have questioned their reach: Which ones have the most affective impact? And why? Which ones have succeeded in securing an empathic response from a wider audience? Conversely, which narratives languish in obscurity, unsuccessful in their attempts to claim willing witnesses?

In an attempt to answer these questions, I turn to two testimonial narratives published in response to the state crackdown on protestors in June 2009. Both narratives have been well received by critics in the West but have had different experiences in terms of their market success and circulation: Afsaneh Moqadam's (2010) *Death to the Dictator: A Young Man Casts a Vote in Iran's 2009 Election and Pays a Devastating Price* and Amir and Khalil's (2011) *Zahra's Paradise*. *Death to the Dictator* was published pseudonymously while *Zahra's Paradise* was published under partial anonymity as the authors reveal their first names but not their surnames. Both texts share the same narrative premise: the disappearance of a young man in the aftermath of the June 2009 protests in Tehran. In *Death to the Dictator,* the narrative is focalized through the perspective of Mohsen Abbaspour, a young man who is arrested after his participation in the protests. He is tortured and raped in prison but is eventually released. In *Zahra's Paradise,* the narrative is told from the point of view of Hassan Alavi, whose younger brother, Mehdi, disappears on June 15, three days after the election, and at the height of the protests. After much searching and investigation, Hassan and his mother finally learn that Mehdi has been killed in prison.

These texts are part of a genre of testimonial literature that straddles the border of auto/biography and testimony. Anne Cubilié (2005) makes this distinction between the two: "Over the past several decades, testimonial literature has begun to develop as a distinct genre of literature, neither memoir nor autobiography, that addresses the specifically located moments of violence directed toward isolatable groups of people that have periodically occurred across the globe" (190). Cubilié's depiction of testimonial literature as different from memoir or autobiography, however, does not fully take into account the more elastic and very useful term *life narrative,* which Sidonie Smith and Julia Watson ([2001] 2010) have defined as including "autobiographical acts of any sort" (4).[1] In their work on human rights narratives and life writing, Kay Schaffer and Sidonie Smith (2004) blur the lines between the two genres:

> We are using the term "life narrative" in its broadest sense, as an umbrella term that encompasses the extensive array and diverse modes as its starting point. These modes can range from oral or written testimony that unfold as retrospective, ethnography, confession, memoir, testimonio, letters, journals, recorded oral history; to autobiographical and semiautobiographical fiction that adheres to some invocation of historical events or persons. (7)

Schaffer and Smith, then, do not mark as clear a distinction between testimony and autobiography as does Cubilié above; for Schaffer and Smith, these texts can be situated within a looser, more expansive genre in which testimonial writings and life narratives overlap.

Death to the Dictator and *Zahra's Paradise* are both examples of testimonial writing that draw on the genre of life writing. Both make truth claims as they attest to be based on eyewitness accounts and reports from "on the ground" activists. Their narratives thus call on the reader-spectator to bear witness to accounts of imprisonment, torture, and suffering. Ann Kaplan's (2005) definition of "witnessing" as "prompting an ethical response that will perhaps transform the way someone views the world, or thinks about justice" is a useful consideration in the context of readers' engagement with these testimonial narratives (123). Testimonial narratives such as *Death to the Dictator* and *Zahra's Paradise* make an emotional demand on the reader-spectator-witness: to allow herself to be affected by, and to serve as witness to, testimonial narratives that seek an empathic audience.

On the surface, then, these two texts are not that different from one another. *Death to the Dictator,* the title of which is taken from one of the protestors' chants during the protests of 2009, is a fictionalized memoir told in the third person from Mohsen's perspective. Published under a female pseudonym, the story is nevertheless narrated from his point of view. After enduring weeks of imprisonment, torture, and rape, Mohsen is finally released but is a broken man. *Zahra's Paradise* narrates the story of the disappearance of Mehdi from the perspective of his brother, Hassan. Like Mohsen in *Death to the Dictator,* Mehdi also disappears as a direct result of his participation in the protests. However, unlike Mohsen, Mehdi does not return home; he dies in prison.

One of the major differences between these texts has been their circulation and reception. The two narratives tell a similar story; both are engaging but emotionally demanding reading experiences. However, while *Zahra's Paradise* achieved enormous market success, *Death to the Dictator* has not circulated as widely as *Zahra's Paradise* or as some other diasporic Iranian life narratives and testimonials (such as, for example, *Prisoner of Tehran,* whose author has attained almost celebrity status internationally but particularly in Canada—where she currently resides).[2] In 2011, however, *Death to the Dictator* was shortlisted for the Orwell prize, which, according to its website, is "Britain's most prestigious prize for political writing."[3] Despite such accolades and high praise in the world of journalism and politics, a quick glance at its Amazon sales rankings—an admittedly flawed, but still useful, index of a book's market success—demonstrates *Death to the Dictator*'s comparatively small impact: as of August 2015, Marina Nemat's *Prisoner of Tehran,* which has been in print for approximately eight years, is ranked at 71,938 and *Zahra's Paradise* at a very respectable 122,494. *Death to the Dictator,* however, barely manages a place in the top 2,000,000 books Amazon offers for sale.

There are perhaps a number of things that work against the possibility of empathic engagement with *Death to the Dictator,* and therefore its successful circulation for a general, popular readership: the pseudonymous status of the author; the anonymity of the narrative style of the third person, which tends to be above the action rather than in it; and even the uncertainty for the reader about the gender of the author. This causes us to question what we as readers demand affectively from victims of torture and oppression before we are willing to share empathy with them. It is an unfortunate trade-off: the use of a pseudonym affords protection for the individual but seems to disbar them from the full embrace of empathy. The lack of affective impact in the popular context raises the question of the authentic truth of the narrative. For Julie Rak (2013), a memoir by an "ordinary" or marginal figure appeals to a mainstream audience through

> identification (the protagonists of the story are seen to be ordinary like themselves), dis-identification with the event (the event did not happen to all or most of the readers), and an attachment to the protagonist through the account's veracity (the event's status as a "true story" makes the protagonist into something heroic). (184)

How might this process of identification with the author be complicated when the author is pseudonymous? Does the genre of life narrative (by ordinary people) necessitate a verifiable author in order to elicit a widespread and far-reaching empathic response? In his groundbreaking (and oft-critiqued) essay on the "autobiographical pact," Philippe Lejeune ([1975] 1989) has gone so far as to say that

> the author of an autobiography *cannot be* anonymous. If the disappearance of the author's name is due to an accidental phenomenon . . . there are two possibilities: either the narrator states his name someplace in the text, and an elementary historical study lets us know if this has to do with a real person, given that by definition an autobiography recounts a dated and situated story; or else the narrator-protagonist does not give his name, and we are dealing with a . . . simple fiction. If the anonymity is intentional (a published text), the reader is in a state of legitimate mistrust. (19, emphasis added)

Thus, for Lejeune, the anonymity of the author puts in jeopardy the public's confidence and trust in the "truth" of the narrative. But what can one do when anonymity or the concealment of an author's identity is required in order to protect the safety of the author, when it is in fact a necessary condition for the articulation of the story? In other words, in order for the narrative to become visible, the author must render herself invisible, as a safeguard against potential political consequences. In this instance, the truth of the narrative must be verified through other means.

On a recent radio broadcast of *The Takeaway,* with John Hockenberry, Roger Cohen and Azadeh Moaveni, both of whom worked as reporters in Iran, emphasize the veracity of the story. Hockenberry (2010) begins the interview by stating: "Let's look at this from the perspective of journalism for a moment because this is a work of journalism but by an anonymous author. You know the author and you've established these claims that are in the book?" Categorizing the text as a work of journalism, Hockenberry attempts to validate its status as a truthful document. After framing the discussion as an example of journalism (and therefore as a verifiably truthful document), he turns to Cohen and asks him to confirm that he knows the author and can attest to the truth of the story. Cohen is emphatic in his response:

> Yes, I know the author. And the author is a very good journalist and excellent writer. And yes, I'm convinced that all that's related in the book is accurate. Not only because I know this person but also because I lived some of those days in Tehran and I saw the violent, raging state into which the Islamic Republic veered, alas, in the immediate aftermath of the tumultuous June 12 election. (Hockenberry 2010)

Hockenberry's question and Cohen's categorically positive response draw attention to one of the key questions that the genres of memoir and testimony raise: the imperative of attesting to their legitimacy as "true" stories.[4]

On the subject of testimonial literatures and affective witnessing, Gillian Whitlock (2007) observes: "Testimony is a political act that works on the emotions, and as a carrier of affect; it shapes how emotions move and shift relationally" (86). But what kind of affective response can be elicited by a testimonial narrative when it is published pseudonymously? This is a question worth returning to in the context of memoirs: in order for life narrative to generate an empathic response, does the story need to be associated with a known—or at least named, and therefore knowable—person?[5] Lejeune ([1975] 1989) has argued that the autobiographical genre relies on authors attesting to the truth of their narratives, and on readers' willingness to believe the authors' truth claims. As Rak (2013) remarks, memoirs by marginal or "ordinary" people rely on the veracity of their story in order to become popular. The success of the narrative hinges on its verifiability as truth; this requirement for truth, however, is not as important for memoirs penned by famous people whose stories hold appeal for readers regardless of their truth value, or for fiction writing.[6] But something has to compel the reader to read a story by unknown or "ordinary" persons such as themselves. The appeal of the memoir by "ordinary people" is to see someone like themselves in "extraordinary" circumstances; this, according to Rak (2013), explains why so many of these stories are about surviving traumatic events (184).

Thus the truth claim of a testimonial narrative or a memoir, or a narrative that combines elements of both genres, is important to its success. But verifying the truth of a story becomes more difficult, as we have already seen, if the writer's identity is not disclosed. Thus, the question of whose story receives more attention and attracts more sympathy, and whose traumatic experience gets witnessed, can be addressed with an attention to the politics of visibility. If the person is "ordinary" and remains unidentified, but their story is sensational, how do we ensure the truth of their narrative? Cohen is unequivocal in his assertion both on *The Takeaway* radio interview (Hockenberry 2010) and in an op-ed in the *New York Times* that *Death to the Dictator* is based on true events: "I know the author, who agreed that the true identity of Ms. Moqadam be revealed to me. The author is reliable, knowledgeable and assiduous. After speaking to the author, I have no doubt the events related in the book took place as described" (Cohen 2010). The appeal of *Death to the Dictator* is that it relates the story of one man, and through him, the experiences of many young Iranians during the protests. Therefore, the character of Mohsen can be based on the actual experiences of one person for whom the name Mohsen acts as a pseudonym. But Mohsen can also be a composite of many Iranians, reflecting the experiences of "hundreds, not thousands," as Cohen also claims. This narrative crosses generic borders: classified as both memoir and news reportage, it functions as an eyewitness account of the state crackdown on protestors in 2009. Whether Mohsen is based on a real person to whom these horrific events actually occurred or whether he is a composite character of all the brutalized victims of the 2009 protests, the story's credibility—and its status as "truth"—is attested to by journalists who have lived and worked in Iran. Nevertheless, assurances from reliable respected journalists such as Cohen and Moaveni do not succeed in bridging the emotional distance created between a pseudonymous author and the reader. While the reporter can assert the legitimacy or the veracity of the story, she cannot create the site on which to make the necessary empathic connection. The book has received positive reviews and high praise from well-reputed newspaper publications such as the *New York Times,* the *Guardian,* and the *LA Times.* Moaveni has called it "the modern sequel to Ryszard Kapuscinkski's 'Shah of Shahs,'" claiming that it is a text people will be reading in twenty years' time to get an insight into Iranian society and politics (Moaveni 2010).[7]

We return to the question, then, of whether a narrative, no matter how powerful, has trouble affecting a reader if the author's identity remains unknown. In order to inspire empathic engagement, Hesford (2011) argues, testimonial narratives require their subject to come into full view. The history of human rights, as she notes, has been "a history of selective and differential visibility, which has positioned certain bodies, populations, and nations as objects of recognition and granted others the power and means to look and to confer recognition. As this history suggests, struggles for recognition are also struggles for visibility" (Hesford 2011, 30). Whose narrative coheres and circulates as one worth hearing, and which subject comes into full view as a wholly recognizable human whose violated rights must be addressed, are questions that need to be at the fore of discussions about testimonial literatures. The issue with *Death to the Dictator* is not only its visibility but also its accessibility; the barriers that protect the identity of the author guaranteeing anonymity and protection also create barriers to the intimate connection empathetic readers seek with the author as part of the emotional process of bearing witness. In the context of his analysis of the James Frey controversy, Paul John Eakin (2008) observes that "the reception of memoir is contractual: readers expect autobiographers to exhibit some basic respect for the truth of their lives" (20). This idea of the autobiographical "contract" originates with Lejeune ([1975] 1989), who has argued that there is an "autobiographical pact" between the author and the reader; the reader approaches the text with an expectation that there is a connection between the author of the text and the narrator of the text, and that the subject of the autobiography can be said to have a real-life correlative.

Following Lejeune's formulation, then, the reader must be able to have confidence in the truth of the narrative and the truth of the author-narrator's existence and identity.

How, then, can we make sense of the difference between the circulation of these two texts, both of which were published without disclosing their authors' identities? As mentioned above, Amir and Khalil's (2011) *Zahra's Paradise* tells a story very similar to that of *Death to the Dictator;* the narrative takes place during the same brief historical period: the aftermath of the June 2009 protests. In this text, a young man, Mehdi, is arrested, like Mohsen, for his participation in the protests, but unlike Mohsen, he is killed in prison. This graphic narrative was initially published as a Web comic in serialized form. Unlike *Death to the Dictator,* this narrative immediately became popular and circulated widely on the Internet and has since been translated into fifteen languages ("Iran's 'Zahra'" 2013); in 2011, it was published in the form of a graphic novel. Initially choosing to publish the text under only their first names, the authors of *Zahra's Paradise* have since revealed their identities. The most visible and outspoken of the two is Amir, who identifies himself as an Iranian American human rights activist. His partner, Khalil, has been somewhat less visible, but he, too, has given interviews about his work on the comic ("'Zahra's Paradise'" 2011). While the disclosure of the authors' full names has likely only sustained the book's popularity, the astounding success of *Zahra's Paradise* happened *before* the identities of the authors became known. So, what might account for the difference in reception between these two texts? Like *Death to the Dictator, Zahra's Paradise* creates a distancing effect between the object of empathy and the reader, as Mehdi's story is not told through him but through his brother; however, the latter met with resounding success while the former had limited popular circulation. I suggest here that the difference can be explained at least in part by the medium in which the narratives are told.

The published memoir, in the form of a testimonial, requires a name to authenticate the narrative, so that the author and, by extension, the author's narrative, can be identified, recognized, and rendered visible. In the case of *Zahra's Paradise,* the medium is a graphic and visual form, and if, as Hesford (2011) says, the history of human rights is one of visibility, then what better medium than comics to depict human rights abuses and traumatic experiences? Indeed, part of the reason for the success of *Zahra's Paradise* is its blending of two visual mediums, comics and photography, with the genre of testimony. The cover of the book is an illustration of the outstretched arm of a protestor holding a cell phone and taking a photograph of the tower in Azadi Square, the site of the postpresidential election protests. Immediately, then, through this illustration, the narrative signals to us that this is a work of testimonial witnessing. Each chapter begins with what looks to be an image seen from within the camera lens, thus conveying to us the immediacy of the event and the sense that this is eyewitness testimony.[8]

The visual form, then, foregrounds the fact that we are *witnessing* an articulation of the demand for human rights in two mediums: in the form of comics and through the lens of the (cell-phone) camera. Here, once again, as we saw in relation to Satrapi's works, we are experiencing a "double witnessing."[9] As readers, we are witnessing the witnessing as we see the events unfold through the eyes of the narrator, Hassan, who is the main witness to, and documenter of, human rights abuses. The immediacy of the comics form as a visual medium puts pressure on the reader as witness since it is more difficult to turn away from graphic and visual depictions of trauma than it is to disengage emotionally from a published "conventional" memoir, particularly if the text is published pseudonymously or under (partial) anonymity.

The prologue of *Zahra's Paradise,* titled "Premonition," depicts a brutal story: it begins in Evin, but not in the notorious prison; here, Evin refers to a picturesque neighborhood in northern Tehran known for its hiking trails and beautiful scenery. A young boy plays with a dog and her new pups until a menacing-looking man arrives and begins rather ominously digging a ditch. He grabs the pups, throws them in a gunny sack, and gives their growling mother a vicious kick to the head. Taking a spade, he viciously beats the puppies to death and throws the gunny sack into a stream. The caption beneath the image of the sack floating in the stream states: "Now you too are in the stream." The next five panels show the gunny sack as it floats away; the captions read, in sequential order: "Touched by all that's still and waiting"; "A lost generation"; "buried inside the eye of this blog." The last panel depicts the sack filled with puppies sinking to the bottom of the water, with the final caption: "Zahra's Paradise" (Figure 8).[10]

The images in this text are searing: they draw the reader, as spectator-witness, into the text: "Now you too are in the stream." "You" in this sentence refers to the young people in Iran at the mercy of an oppressive government. But it is also a direct call to the reader to enter fully into the narrative as witness. This can be done more easily because the medium is

Figure 8. First depiction of puppies in gunny sack thrown in stream, sinking to the bottom of the water. From Zahra's Paradise. *Copyright 2011 by Amir and Khalil. Reprinted by permission of First Second, an imprint of Roaring Brook Press. All rights reserved.*

a visual one, despite the fact that the authors do not fully disclose their identities. What *Zahra's Paradise* makes *visible* to us is a narrative of terror and human rights abuses conveyed through a double visual experience: through the media of photography and drawing in comics. Thierry Groensteen (2007) argues that the visual medium of comics requires work on the part of the reader to pay close attention to the whole range of visual elements and graphic features they offer, as well as to their spatial arrangement on the page and throughout the book. His concept of "arthrology"—as a way of thinking about the relation of graphic elements across the physical space of comics—is extremely constructive in the context of *Zahra's Paradise* in particular; he coins the term *arthrology* from the Greek word *arthron,* meaning articulation (Groensteen 2007, 21). The comics medium draws our attention to, and so obliges us to consider, the relationship of similar or "rhyming" visual elements—for example, panels and images—across the narrative. For Groensteen, there are two types of arthrology: restricted and general. Restricted arthrology refers to the sequential relationship of panels and the images in them; general arthrology refers to the relation of images and panels across the book (Groensteen 2007, 22).

The concept of general arthrology offers a particularly productive approach to *Zahra's Paradise,* as it allows for a reading and analysis of certain images that repeatedly surface throughout the book in very different contexts. For example, the first chapter ends with an image of a gunny sack full of puppies sinking beneath the water. That image is repeated twice. First, it appears in the middle of the narrative when the mistress of a prison official discovers the truth about the nature of her lover's job—that he is responsible for the beating and murder of prisoners. Running away from him, she comes to a bridge, where she tears off the necklace from around her neck, a necklace that he once gave her and that she now realizes was taken from a prisoner's corpse. The last panel on that page shows the necklace plunging to the bottom of the water in a visual echo of the sinking puppies (Figure 9).

The next iteration of this image of the sinking necklace (and, by extension, the "rhyming" image of the drowning puppies) occurs when Hassan, Mehdi's brother, manages to hack into Evin Prison's records and look through the documents relating to personal belongings removed from the corpses of murdered prisoners: he comes across Mehdi's beloved custom-made silver Zidane necklace.[11] Here the image of the sinking gunny sack carrying the beaten newborn pups is reproduced, showing them sinking

Figure 9. Necklace sinking in water in visual echo of puppies in gunny sack. From Zahra's Paradise. *Copyright 2011 by Amir and Khalil. Reprinted by permission of First Second, an imprint of Roaring Brook Press.*

to the bottom of the water at the same time that it recalls the rhymed image of the sinking necklace connecting ideas of the hierarchical and unequal nature of power and of the potential for its abuse, in different contexts (Amir and Khalil 2011, 190).

Reading and analyzing the visual echoes here offer an example of the effectiveness of the testimonial narrative in graphic form: recognizing and reading the linkages between the metaphor of the sinking (innocent and vulnerable) puppies at the whim of an arbitrary yet terrifying brutality with the capture of young protestors who find themselves captured and thrown into the back of a truck create a powerful critique of the arbitrary exercise of power that led to an atmosphere of anxiety and terror in the aftermath of the 2009 protests. Here the visual parallel is made explicitly through the use of "restricted arthrology," as the panels are arranged in a deliberate sequence so that the reader can make a direct link between the images and is compelled to respond affectively (Amir and Khalil 2011, 27).

There are other powerful visual examples of "general arthrology" in the book—for example, in the illustration of doors, which figure prominently throughout the text. The numerous visual references to doors form a connecting thread throughout *Zahra's Paradise.* At the beginning of the narrative, Hassan dreams that he senses his brother, Mehdi, behind a door. He opens it and Mehdi walks back into their lives (Amir and Khalil 2011, 31). As the search for his brother becomes more and more complicated and confusing, the doors in his dreams multiply. Hassan dreams that he opens one door only to find himself in a strange space with many staircases leading up and back down, and with many doors at strange angles. This panel takes up the entire page and illustrates the labyrinthine Iranian bureaucratic system with which he has to contend. After discovering that his brother is buried in an unmarked grave in Zahra's Paradise, and after the panel showing the sinking puppies (Figure 8), the next page shows just a closed door on a large blank space and Hassan leaning forward with his head resting on his knees (Figure 10). At the end of the narrative, Hassan has to leave the country, his life at risk now for having hacked into Evin Prison's records. The door is thus reproduced again on the very last page of the book, but this time, it is open, and through the open door, we can see the sun shining on the flowers and butterflies.

There are other powerful visual echoes throughout the book that draw our attention to the urgency of the act of witnessing: as Groensteen (2007) has argued, the visual repetition and echoes matter because the story is

Figure 10. A devastated Hassan after he hacks into prison records and discovers that his brother, Mehdi, has been killed. All doors have been closed to him. From Zahra's Paradise. *Copyright 2011 by Amir and Khalil. Reprinted by permission of First Second, an imprint of Roaring Brook Press. All rights reserved.*

being told in what is primarily a visual medium. This story asks us very literally to bear witness and to remember. Throughout the narrative, we see cell phones being used and photographs being taken; the visual witnessing works on numerous levels: the graphic form itself, the cell-phone cameras it depicts recording events, and the role of the reader as witness to the witness in the story (Hassan). The other echoes in the book include the narrative of Neda, whose death and whose iconic photograph circulated on Facebook (see chapter 1) and is reproduced in the book. Indeed, Neda's image surfaces twice: first, her bloodied face is shown in the pages of a book in the coroner's office (Amir and Khalil 2011, 86); and second, the narrative includes the iconic image of her dying on the street, followed by the unveiled photograph of her that circulated on Facebook (177).

These visual echoes in *Zahra's Paradise,* then, refer to the narrative in the text (drowning puppies and student arrests) but also reach beyond the text to events that received a significant amount of attention on the news and social media in the months following the contested presidential election. Thus the powerful impact of *Zahra's Paradise* has a great deal to do with its use of the visual medium. This is a medium that creates emotional intimacy and a sense of urgency, making it difficult for the reader to look away. The graphic form thus creates an imperative to witness the testimonial narrative. While I do not want to suggest that the visual text creates more opportunities for empathic engagement than a written one, it appears that when the "autobiographical pact" comes under question, the visual narrative succeeds more readily in producing the sought-after affective response. In the absence of a known autobiographical "I" in a pseudonymous or (partially) anonymous life narrative, the powerful formal qualities of the visual text produce an affective response in the reader that counters the expectation (or perhaps even the requirement) that the author disclose her name.

In examining the range of genres in which diasporic Iranians choose to narrate their autobiographical experiences, this book hopes to have succeeded in making the reader reflect on what, in Anne Cubilié's (2005) words, "we are willing to do as witnesses to the witnesses" (3). Diasporic Iranian life narratives seek to elicit an empathic response from readers willing to hear, to know, and to respond to accounts of trauma, of testimony, of memory. The questions, then, with which we are left to contend as readers are: Which narratives do we choose to engage with? Which narratives do we allow to affect us and which ones do we choose to ignore?

Acknowledgments

SOME OF THE WORK FOR THIS BOOK was completed during a sabbatical year in France. It seemed fitting to spend the year writing about cultural dislocation and revolutionary trauma from the site of my own experience of cultural and personal dislocation. Paris was the first city in which I resided as an émigré. Over thirty years later, I returned with my own family to revisit and reside in a place that, for me, recalled vivid memories of postrevolutionary nostalgia and loss. It was a rejuvenating year in the midst of a community of friends—old and new. This project has been generously supported by a SSHRC Standard Research Grant, which allowed me to hire a group of smart and conscientious research assistants, all of whom have gone on to bigger and better things and some of whom have established themselves now as emerging scholars in their own right: Anna Candido, Eva Hellreich-Newby, Nazli Kamvari, Golbarg Rekabtalaei, Sara Saljoughi, and Meghan Somerville. I am grateful to Nina Hoeschele for her meticulous work in preparing the manuscript for publication and for the indexing. At Ryerson University, I have had the good fortune of working in a very supportive environment: my thanks and appreciation to the office of the Arts for support of this project with a Faculty of Arts Small Projects Grant. My thanks to Lorraine Janzen and Michael Finn, whose detailed and helpful feedback on a very early proposal for this project set me on the right path. I would also like to thank Irene Gammel and the Modern Literature Research and Culture Centre for support and assistance in preparing high-resolution images for chapter 4 and the Conclusion. I am grateful to Brian Schiff of the American University of Paris (AUP) for his kind support while I was in Paris. My thanks also to the wonderful librarians at the AUP, Isabelle Dupuy-Ilorente and Michael Stoepel, for their help in locating research material. Our own librarian at Ryerson University, Val Lem, is a gem in the Faculty of Arts, always and tirelessly going out of his way to help faculty with their research projects. The American Library in Paris was my writing home for the year; I thank them for providing me with a welcoming space in which to think and to write.

I had the opportunity to present various versions of this material in different venues and benefited from the feedback of participants at numerous international conferences and symposiums. I am deeply grateful to Julie Rak and Shahla Talebi for their thoughtful and helpful comments on chapter 2. Sarah Brophy and Janice Hladki provided valuable comments on a much earlier iteration of chapter 4. I would be remiss if I did not mention the extensive feedback I received on my work from Gillian Whitlock, whose scholarship I find inspirational. All of the suggestions I received have helped improve this book; any weaknesses are, of course, my own.

Golkou Parhizgar generously sent me her documentary film *Round-Trip,* and Kristen M. Fitzpatrick of *Women Make Movies* made Nahid Persson Sarvestani's *My Stolen Revolution* available to me before it was possible to purchase a DVD copy. Paula B. Slater gave me permission to reproduce photographs of her two Neda sculptures, and Amir Soltani helped me secure permissions to reproduce panels from *Zahra's Paradise.* I thank them all for their kindness and generosity.

At the University of Minnesota Press, Richard Morrison was an initial supporter of this project; after he moved on to another position, I was fortunate to work with Danielle M. Kasprzak and Anne Carter, for whose immeasurable support and patience throughout this process I am most thankful. I am very grateful to Sheila McMahon and Scott Mueller for their careful copyediting and proofreading, and to the various departments at the University of Minnesota Press whose hard work made the publication of this book possible, from the editorial and production teams to the marketing department.

This book has been in process for a very long time, interrupted over the years by various personal and professional commitments. My friend, colleague, and husband, Andrew O'Malley, is, I imagine, the happiest of all to see the end of this journey. He has served as sounding board and interlocutor, providing invaluable critical feedback on the manuscript even as he worked on meeting his own writing commitments while simultaneously taking on the lion's share of the work at home. Our children, Safianna and Cyrus, have been extremely patient with me as they, too, tolerated the extent to which this project took me away from our family time. Without their love and support, this project would remain as yet unfinished.

Notes

Introduction

1. See Cathy Caruth (1995, 1996), Dominick La Capra (2001), and Ann Kaplan (2005) for their works on trauma and on the importance of having a willing and empathic witness to enable the healing process for the traumatized subject. Human Rights scholars such as Wendy Hesford (2011), Sharon Sliwinski (2011), and Anne Cubilié (2005) also emphasize the crucial role of the spectator-witness in recognizing the humanity of another; the viewer has to be willing to extend to the suffering and traumatized subject the recognition of sameness, of equality, and of humanity.

2. See Julie Rak (2013) for her analysis of the publishing industry's pivotal role in the "memoir boom."

3. Sidonie Smith and Julia Watson ([2001] 2010) use the term *auto/biography* to describe the "interrelatedness" of autobiography and biography (256).

4. Farzaneh Milani has published an article about the remarkable shift from a virtual absence of Iranian life narratives to an outright explosion of such narratives in the diaspora, stating: "In view of my evolving perspectives and the outburst of intimate revelations by women writers and bloggers inside and outside Iran, I now question my earlier assertions that life narratives are cultural and literary misfits in Iran" (Milani 2013, 145).

5. See Babak Elahi's "Translating the Self: Language and Identity in Iranian American Women's Memoirs" (2006) and "Fake Farsi: Formulaic Flexibility in Iranian American Women's Memoir" (2008) for insightful analyses of how cultural identity and displacement are conveyed through language in (diasporic) Iranian women's memoirs.

6. The exceptions here are the memoirs of Firoozeh Dumas, whose quirky, self-deprecating, and culturally appeasing *Funny in Farsi* (2003) and *Laughing without an Accent* (2008) have circulated with great success in Farsi translation in Iran. These memoirs approach both Iranian and American cultures with affection, offering an overall positive view of both cultures while also gently poking fun at both equally. While most of the other contemporary memoirs focus on loss and longing, trauma and grief, Dumas represents her diasporic experience through the lens of humor, acceptance, and celebration. This conciliatory and nonthreatening approach to both cultures likely accounts for its popularity in both countries.

7. Many scholars have pointed out the inadequacy of terms such as *West* and *East* and some have introduced compelling alternatives such as *North and South* or *two-thirds world* to underscore the inequitable distribution of economic resources in the world. While I recognize the value of those terms and the inadequacy of the generalizing and vague terms *West* and *East,* I continue to use them, for the time being, in my own work since none of the other terms resonate as much in terms of evoking economic, social, and cultural power. The *West* covers a very large and diverse part of the globe; in this study, I use it to refer to North America, England, and Australia.

8. Persis Karim has also been actively involved in promoting and facilitating the growth of a diasporic Iranian literary community. She is the coeditor of two anthologies on Iranian American writing, *A World Between: Poems, Short Stories, and Essays by Iranian-Americans* with Mohammad Mehdi Khorrami (1999) and *Tremors: New Fiction by Iranian Americans* with Anita Amirrezvani (2013); and the (sole) editor of *Let Me Tell You Where I've Been: New Writing By Women of the Iranian Diaspora* (2006).

9. In "Towards a Theory of Iranian American Life Writing," Amy Motlagh (2008), while recognizing these texts as diasporic literatures, reclaims them as part of an ethnic American writing tradition: "Critics hoping to understand these works must position them not only within diasporic debates, but also within the ongoing conversation about autobiographical genres in American letters, and the American dialogues about selfhood and ethnicity that have developed with this tradition" (19). Motlagh is making a welcome and important intervention here by addressing some of the forceful denunciations of these texts as imperialist, and by trying to change the terms of the acrimonious debate by focusing our attention on the literary history of memoir writing. However, placing these texts within an ethnic American writing tradition means that we risk losing sight of the explosion of memoir writing by diasporic Iranians across the globe.

10. The term *ethnic literatures* strikes me as specific to an American context: the notion that a body of literature can be subsumed under the category of "American," but with a difference, so therefore "ethnic" seems particular to the assimilationist immigration policy of the United States. In Canada, for instance, diasporic literatures are reflective of a multicultural policy that (at least officially, if not always in practice) fosters and encourages the preservation of immigrant cultures and languages alongside a "Canadian identity," a notion often subject to scrutiny and debate. In European countries, where there is no pretense of celebrating multiculturalism, diasporic literatures appear to exist alongside the literary tradition of the host nation. For these reasons, it makes sense to me to consider diasporic Iranian literatures as part of a global phenomenon rather than being designated as part of American "ethnic literature." Not only are the particularities of the diasporic Iranian experience lost under the designation of "American ethnic" literature, but

what becomes of the literature produced by Iranians who live in the diaspora—but not in the United States?

11. This generation has also been referred to as the "Burnt Generation." See chapter 1 for Arash Hejazi's (2011) reference to this generation (with whom he identifies) in *The Gaze of the Gazelle.*

12. Some titles, in order of their publication, are: Firoozeh Dumas (2003), *Funny in Farsi: A Memoir of Growing Up Iranian in America;* Farideh Goldin (2003), *Wedding Song: Memoirs of an Iranian Jewish Woman;* Marjane Satrapi, *Persepolis: The Story of a Childhood* (2003) and *Persepolis 2: The Story of a Return* (2004); Roya Hakakian (2004), *Journey from the Land of No: A Girlhood Caught in Revolutionary Iran;* Afschineh Latifi (2005), *Even after All This Time: A Story of Love, Revolution, and Leaving Iran;* Azadeh Moaveni (2006), *Lipstick Jihad: A Memoir of Growing Up Iranian in America and American in Iran;* Nahid Rachlin (2006), *Persian Girls: A Memoir;* Shirin Ebadi (with Azadeh Moaveni) (2006), *Iran Awakening: From Prison to Peace Prize, One Woman's Struggle at the Crossroads of History;* Davar Ardalan (2007), *My Name Is Iran: A Memoir;* Firoozeh Dumas (2008), *Laughing without an Accent: Adventures of an Iranian American at Home and Abroad;* Azadeh Moaveni (2009), *Honeymoon in Tehran: Two Years of Love and Danger in Iran;* Shappi Khorsandi (2009), *A Beginner's Guide to Acting English.*

13. Gillian Whitlock (2007) has called these narratives "generational," as they are written by a generation of women for whom the trauma of the revolution took place at a key moment of personal development (164). These texts are also part of the "Burnt Generation" mentioned above.

14. This initially negative reaction has been tempered in scholarly circles as a growing number of scholars are looking at these memoirs from different perspectives. In addition to Elahi, Karim, and Motlagh mentioned above, there are now several more who are publishing in the field. See, for example, Sharareh Frouzesh's (2011) "The Politics of Appropriation: Writing, Responsibility, and the Specter of the Native Informant," Manijeh Nasrabadi's (2011) "In Search of Iran: Resistant Melancholia in Iranian American Memoirs of Return," Karim Mattar's (2012) "Rereading the 'Rogue State': The Politics of Gender in Anglophone Iranian Literature," and Marie Ostby's (2013) "De-Censoring an Iranian-American 'Memoir': Authorship and Synchronicity in Shahriar Mandanipour's *Censoring an Iranian Love Story.*" See also Sanaz Fotouhi's (2014) *The Literature of the Iranian Diaspora: Meaning and Identity since the Islamic Revolution* and Daniel Grassian's (2013) *Iranian and Diasporic Literature in the 21st Century: A Critical Study.*

15. Azar Nafisi's (2003) *New York Times* best seller, *Reading Lolita in Tehran,* came under sharp criticism by scholars such as Hamid Dabashi (2006) and Fatemeh Keshavarz (2007), among others. See Amy Motlagh's (2011) "Autobiography and Authority in the Writings of the Iranian Diaspora" for her critique of the anti-imperialist approach to diasporic Iranian life writings. Also, chapter 5, "Revolution,

Nostalgia, and Memory in Diasporic Iranian Memoirs," briefly addresses the negative responses to Nafisi's *Reading Lolita in Tehran*.

16. In an otherwise excellent (and much-lauded) article on Marjane Satrapi in which she offers a nuanced analysis of diasporic Iranian cultural identity and expression, Amy Malek (2006) makes several references to the importance of diasporic Iranian writers moving out of what she perceives to be the restricted space of the memoir into a more culturally rich and rewarding space of "exile cultural production": "One can only hope that these memoirs will both inspire an opening of *literary* genres to Iranian and Iranian-descendant authors, as well as provide a catalyst for further creative productions of culture by the second and third generations" (368, emphasis added).

17. See Ben Yagoda's (2009) *Memoir: A History* and Thomas Couser's (2012) *Memoir: An Introduction* for more on the historical prejudices against the genre.

18. Amy Motlagh (2008) proposes that the wave of what she calls "Iranian American" memoir writing can be traced back to Najmeh Najafi's 1953 text, *Persia Is My Heart*. However, she makes this claim based on understanding these writings as part of ethnic American literature. See Motlagh (2008, 18–19).

19. See, for example, Sattareh Farman Farmaian's (1992) *Daughter of Persia: A Woman's Journey from Her Father's Harem through the Islamic Revolution* and Cherry Mosteshar's (1995) *Unveiled: Love and Death among the Ayatollahs*.

20. Shusha Guppy's famous and celebrated *Persian Love Songs and Mystic Chants* (1971) emerged out of her work with Prévert.

21. Her husband, from whom she eventually divorced, was the writer and explorer Nicholas Guppy, who himself came from a long line of explorers and inventors. The guppy fish is in fact named after one of his ancestors who "discovered" it.

22. The idea of the transmission of affect is one that I borrow from Teresa Brennan (2004). Her understanding of affect contests the notion that we are self-contained individuals, that we can "control" and contain our emotional reactions. For Brennan, the model of emotional containment is inherited from a European Enlightenment conception of the individual, but she argues that affects travel, and that the emotional energies or mood of one person can be *felt* by another. See the discussion in chapter 1 of the circulation of affect in social media in response to the coverage of the postpresidential election protests in Iran for an example of how affect gets transmitted.

23. There is a third date that lies in the shadows behind 1979 and 2009: the 1988 massacre of political prisoners in Evin Prison. Many of the life narratives discussed here make reference to that terrible event. See especially chapters 2 and 3 for a more detailed treatment of this subject.

24. The terms *Green Movement* or *Green Wave* refer to a political movement responding to the 2009 presidential elections in Iran. Presidential hopeful Mir Hossein Mousavi made public appearances wearing a green shawl or scarf, thus

successfully branding his campaign while deliberating invoking a connection to the Prophet Muhammad. After the disputed election results, Mousavi's supporters and other protestors spilled out onto the streets draped in green, now the color of protest against the regime, as well as a symbol of hope and change for the future. There are numerous books on Iran's Green Movement; some titles include *The People Reloaded: The Green Movement and the Struggle for Iran's Future* (Hashemi and Postel 2010), *Iran: From Theocracy to the Green Movement* (Nabavi 2012), and *Iran, the Green Movement and the USA: The Fox and the Paradox* (Dabashi 2010). Negar Mottahedeh's *#iranelection: Hashtag Solidarity and the Transformation of Online Life* (2015) was released while this book was in the editing stage.

25. *Autobiographical avatar* is Gillian Whitlock's (2006) term used to describe the visual manifestation of the auto/biographical narrator in comics.

1. Claiming Neda

1. See, for example, Sharon Sliwinski's (2011) *Human Rights in Camera,* Wendy Hesford's (2011) *Spectacular Rhetorics: Human Rights Visions, Recognitions, Feminisms,* and John Tulloch and R. Warwick Blood's (2012) *Icons of War and Terror: Media Images in an Age of International Risk.*

2. Remarkably, this same heady excitement colored Western media responses to the Tunisian and Egyptian uprisings in 2011. As with Iran's so-called Twitter revolution, these proclamations made by pundits in the West were quickly undermined when the protests were managed and suppressed through government force.

3. See Elham Gheytanchi's (2010) "Symbols, Signs, and Slogans of the Demonstrations in Iran" for her analysis of how information about the street protests was transmitted online. See also Babak Rahimi's (2011) "Affinities of Dissent: Cyberspace, Performative Networks and the Iranian Green Movement" for his views on the possibilities of online political activism through the mobilization of dissent and affect.

4. See Paul John Eakin's (2008) discussion of Neisser's term *the extended self* in chapter 1 of *Living Autobiographically.*

5. The frenzy and compulsion to name the young woman in the video led to a case of mistaken identity with tragic consequences, the details of which are addressed in further detail later in this chapter.

6. Iconic images, according to Robert Hariman and John Louis Lucaites (2007), are those that "are reproduced widely and placed prominently in both public and private settings, and . . . used to orient the individual within a context of collective identity, obligation, and power. . . . They have more than documentary value, for they bear witness to something that exceeds words" (1).

7. Similarly, Wendy S. Hesford (2011) writes: "Although the United States, with its strict refugee laws, has granted asylum to few of the world's refugees, the

Afghan girl has become a symbol of American charity and compassion—a representation that rests on the narrative configuration of the girl refugee as a deserving victim in need of rescue, and on the familiar dualism of tradition and modernity—intended to champion human rights within the framework of Western liberation" (1–2). Indeed, Neda's story has been taken up in similar ways. Seen as a "deserving victim," her love of travel, clothes, and music pits her commitment to modernity against tradition.

8. Many sources claim that Neda was *Time*'s Person of the Year, but in fact the person of the year was the U.S. Federal Reserve chair Ben Bernanke. Neda was included on the list of "people who mattered" in 2009 (see the complete list at http://content.time.com/time/specials/packages/completelist/0,29569,1946375,00.html).

9. I am grateful to Paula Slater for generously providing me with high-resolution photographs of her Neda sculptures. These can also be viewed online at http://www.PaulaSlater.com.

10. Some of her most heavily criticized roles have included the terrorist Dina Araz in the television series *24* and Zahra in the brazenly manipulative film *The Stoning of Soraya M* (2008). Aghdashloo has recently published her own memoir, *The Alley of Love and Yellow Jasmines* (2013).

11. Azar Nafisi's writings, particularly her wildly successful memoir *Reading Lolita in Tehran* (2003), came under severe attack by diasporic Iranian academics who see her as providing fodder to neoconservative politicians in the United States interested in supporting "regime change" in Iran; indeed, many critics have noted her close professional ties to such politicians. The most outspoken of her critics has been Columbia University's Hamid Dabashi (2006), who published a scathing opinion piece on Nafisi's memoir and of her political connections in *Al-Ahram Weekly:* "Native Informers and the Making of the American Empire."

12. See the description of this event in Abbas Milani's (2011) biography, *The Shah.*

13. Hermanson's current website features her artwork, including her portrait of Neda. The updated caption next to the portrait reads: "During a protest in Iran, Neda was shot and killed. Her brutal death was shared over social media, and she has become a symbol of the Iranian protest movement" (Hermanson n.d.). This caption reveals a change from Hermanson's intensely personal reaction to Neda's death in 2009 to a more dispassionate description on her current website. The change in tone reflects the emotional trajectory of many people who were caught up with the images coming out of Iran that summer. Neda's death resonated powerfully around the globe, eliciting personal identification with what she came to represent in popular discourse: an "everywoman" who was struck down in the prime of her life and in her struggle for freedom. Over the course of time, her death is still seen as a tragedy but the intense personal identification with Neda has attenuated.

14. As discussed at further length in chapter 5, the proliferation of diasporic Iranian memoirs shows how narratives about traumatic experiences emerge belatedly; thus temporal and emotional distance are both key to the successful articulation of narratives about trauma.

15. The martyrdom of Imam Hussain in Karbala, Iraq, in 680 AD holds a powerful place in Iranian cultural and religious contexts, and was used effectively during the 1978 revolutionary protests to portray the religious leader Ayatollah Khomeini in a fight for justice against the shah, who was cast in the role of the tyrannical caliph Yazid. See Mahr (2009).

16. See chapter 2 for a more in-depth exploration of this question in relation to prison memoirs.

17. The Islamic Republic adopted a similar strategy in an effort to rewrite the story of Neda Agha-Soltan. Shortly after the shooting, they re-created the scene of her death, bringing her music teacher (who was with her at the time she died) to retrace his steps and to assert in the face of the cameras that her death was caused by outside forces. The government then went on to accuse CNN and BBC of masterminding Neda's death. When that approach did not work, the government turned to Neda Soltani and tried to pressure her into making a statement that she was the real Neda and that the Neda whose death was circulating on YouTube had never existed.

2. Human Rights, Humanitarianism, and Empathic Witnessing

1. Diasporic Iranian men have also begun publishing accounts of their imprisonment in postrevolutionary Iran, including, most recently, Houshang Asadi's (2010) *Letters to My Torturer: Love, Revolution and Imprisonment in Iran,* Maziar Bahari's (2011) *Then They Came for Me: A Family's Story of Love, Captivity, and Survival,* and Jafar Yaghoobi's (2011) *Let Us Water the Flowers: The Memoir of a Political Prisoner in Iran.* These are not isolated examples of prison writings by Iranian men. Bozorg Alavi, a prominent literary figure and Marxist activist, pioneered the genre of prison writing in Iran, as Ervand Abrahamian (1999) has observed: "Iran has a rich genre of prison literature going back to the 1940s. The genre began in 1942 when Bozorg Alavi, a young Marxist writer just released from prison, published two best-sellers entitled *Prison Scrap Papers* and *The Fifty-three*" (14). The tradition of political prison memoirs in Farsi by mostly leftist writers has continued to the present day; some of these texts are now available online by the Abdorrahman Boroumand Foundation (n.d.) based in Washington, D.C. (http://www.iranrights.org) and on Shahrzad Mojab's (n.d.) University of Toronto website, Political Prisoners: The Art of Resistance in the Middle East (http://womenpoliticalprisoners.com). However, this chapter focuses on the more recent phenomenon of prison writing published in English by Iranian women in the

diaspora. These texts have, for the most part, commanded more public attention and interest in the West than their (Farsi) predecessors for reasons that I will discuss in this chapter.

2. See Richard Ashby Wilson and Richard D. Brown's (2009) "Introduction" in their edited volume, *Humanitarianism and Suffering: The Mobilization of Empathy,* and Thomas Laqueur's (2009) article "Mourning, Pity, and the Work of Narrative in the Making of 'Humanity'" in that same collection for a historical overview of the development of the humanitarian narrative.

3. David G. Chandler (2011) marks a distinction between the development of a "new humanitarian" discourse, one that has become increasingly politicized as NGOs "have been integrated into policymaking forums," and the older humanitarianism, which actively distanced itself from politics and partisanship, operating on a principle of neutrality (678). This "new humanitarianism" advocated by NGOs since the end of the Cold War, argues Chandler (2011), has facilitated the development of a new form of "military humanitarianism."

4. According to Sophia A. McClennen and Joseph R. Slaughter (2009): "Human rights are under threat everywhere, especially when the language of human rights is used to justify their violation. It should be remembered, for instance, that the arguments to invade Afghanistan after the World Trade Center terrorist attacks were framed from the start by a dual rhetoric of retaliatory pay back and generous humanitarianism" (2).

5. According to Marjorie Garber (2004), "*Sympathy* remained historically a condition of equality or affinity, whether between the body and the soul, between two bodily organs, or, increasingly, between persons with similar feelings, inclinations, and temperaments. *Sympathy*'s roots are Greek and Latin: it literally translates as 'having a fellow feeling,' from *sym* plus *pathos,* 'suffering together.' . . . Empathy, we might note, is a modern word, although it has a Greek analogue. Coined in the early years of the twentieth century . . . it has come to denote the power of projecting one's personality into the object of contemplation" (23–24). Because *empathy* does not assume commonality, suggesting, rather, a willingness on the part of one person to place herself in the place of another, I find it a more useful term than *sympathy,* which suggests a prioritization of samenesss over difference.

6. One of the most popular examples of the Puritan captivity narrative is Mary Rowlandson's 1682 *The Soveraignty and Goodness of God, Together with the Faithfulness of His Promises Displayed; Being a Narrative of the Captivity and Restauration of Mrs. Mary Rowlandson,* also published under the shorter title *A True History of the Captivity and Restoration of Mrs. Mary Rowlandson.* Upon its publication, it quickly became a best seller, "printing four times (three times in New England and once in London)" (Potter 2003, 153). For more on the development of Puritan captivity narratives, see Vaughan and Clark (1981).

7. For foundational works on the literature of "contact," see Peter Hulme's (1986) *Colonial Encounters: Europe and the Native Caribbean, 1492–1797,* Dean MacCannell's (1992) *Empty Meeting Grounds: The Tourist Papers,* and Mary Louise Pratt's (1992) *Imperial Eyes: Travel Writing and Transculturation.*

8. Farzaneh Milani (2011) makes this careful distinction: "On the surface, women's prison memoirs and hostage narratives share certain commonalities. Born out of a desire to refuse erasure, both categories cathartically recount traumatic experiences and share personal tales of survival and liberation. Both genres present gripping tales, a form of protest against imposed stillness and invisibility. Underneath the seeming similarities, however, the two genres are as different as pomegranates and dates. Whereas prison memoirs are often an eloquent testimony to women's agency, courage, and defiance, hostage narratives trivialize or contradict, in impact, if not in intent, women's attempts at subversion, resistance, and self-assertion. Though prison memoirs depict fiery protagonists who have inserted their agency and voice in the public discourse, hostage narratives revolve around helpless, voiceless, and powerless victims" (228).

9. Although the Puritan captivity narrative does not explicitly address questions of sexuality, the unarticulated danger in these narratives is the ever-present threat of the European woman's rape by the native other. The theme of captivity (with a frisson of sexual danger) is more explicitly present in Harlequin romances and particularly the "desert romance" that plays on the attraction/repulsion dynamic between the European/white woman and her (racialized) captor. For more on the desert romance, see Jarmakani (2011).

10. I have discussed this tension between the domesticated, familiar, and absolute other in relation to journalists Alexandra Avakian and Christiane Amanpour in chapter 2 of *Rethinking Global Sisterhood* (Naghibi 2007).

11. While the Seven Stories Press website does not have prepared book club questions for *Camelia,* the press highlighted it as a good "book club pick" in November 2012 (see http://www.sevenstories.com/reading-group-picks/book-club-picks-november-2012/).

12. Canada Reads is a national competition sponsored by the Canadian Broadcasting Corporation (CBC) in which a select group of books is presented to the public and, after several rounds of discussion, debating, and voting, one book is chosen as the one that all of Canada should read. In early 2012, Nemat's book was on the list of four finalists, but after controversial comments made by one of the judges regarding the veracity of her tale, her book was voted out of the competition in the first round.

13. The most serious of attacks against Marina Nemat by members of leftist groups in Canada, many of whom are former political prisoners, is that by virtue of her (forced) marriage to her interrogator, and the small privileges she was allowed

in prison, she revealed herself as a *tavvab,* a collaborator with an oppressive system responsible for the imprisonment, torture, and murder of countless Iranian political prisoners. Thus Nemat's aligning of herself with murdered political prisoners such as the Iranian Canadian Zahra Kazemi, who was raped and tortured to death in Evin in 2003, and the circulation of Nemat's story's as the *ur-text* of human suffering and individual triumph against state oppression is particularly difficult to bear for former political prisoners, many of whom were tormented by *tavvabs* in prison. Similarly, Entekhabi-Fard (2007) is hard-pressed to find sympathy among her former Iranian colleagues and associates as she admits, at the very least, to feigning collaboration with prison officials. Most egregiously, however, she admits to initiating a bizarre romantic relationship with her interrogator, a relationship that ultimately secured her freedom.

14. "There is not only among torturers but even among people appalled by acts of torture and sympathetic to those hurt, a covert disdain for confession. This disdain is one of many manifestations of how inaccessible the reality of physical pain is to anyone not immediately experiencing it. The nature of confession is falsified by an idiom built on the word 'betrayal': in confession, one betrays oneself and all those aspects of the world—friend, family, country, cause—that the self is made up of" (Scarry 1985, 29).

15. See chapter 1 for a discussion of Neda as an iconic figure of the 2009 post-presidential elections in Iran and the use of her image and her name in diasporic Iranian autobiographical expressions.

16. Robert Hillman's (2007) liberal politics and the performance of compassion and tolerance for the immigrant other that they foster brings to mind Wendy Brown's (2006) counsel that "tolerance as a term of justice . . . sustains a status of outsiderness for those it manages by incorporating" (28).

17. I borrow this formulation from Anne Cubilié (2005), who asks of us to move beyond merely "witnessing"; she poses the question of what we are willing to do *after* we have served as "witnesses to the witnesses" (of genocide, of torture, of suffering). See "Witness and Testimony: Ethics, Trauma, Speech, and Paradox," in Cubilié 2005.

18. For more on the mass killings of leftist political prisoners in 1988, see Ervan Abrahamian's (1999) *Tortured Confessions: Prisons and Public Recantations in Modern Iran,* Reza Afshari's (2001) *Human Rights in Iran: The Abuse of Cultural Relativism,* and *The Massacre of Political Prisoners in Iran, 1988* (Robertson 2010), a report published by the Abdorrahman Boroumand Foundation.

19. The most well known of such cases in recent Iranian history include Maziar Bahari, Haleh Esfandiari, Ramin Jahanbegloo, and Roxana Saberi—all of whom were able to secure their release and their freedom after high-profile humanitarian campaigns.

3. Feeling Nostalgic, Feeling Guilty

1. See chapter 5 for further discussion of how class determines authors' representation of the Iranian revolution as traumatic.

2. Gillian Whitlock (2007) also makes this argument in *Soft Weapons: Autobiography in Transit* (164). See also chapter 5 for more on the development of diasporic Iranian women's life narratives as a belated expression of revolutionary trauma.

3. For more on the historical development of nostalgia as both physiological and psychological disease, see Svetlana Boym's (2001) comprehensive *The Future of Nostalgia* and Andreea Deciu Ritivoi's (2002) *Yesterday's Self: Nostalgia and the Immigrant Identity.*

4. See chapter 2 on prison narratives for further discussion of the mass executions of Iranian political prisoners in the 1980s. The second half of this chapter, which discusses Nahid Persson's (2013) *My Stolen Revolution,* also focuses on testimonials by former political prisoners in 1980s Iran.

5. There is a growing body of writing by and about the "children of Evin." Sahar Delijani's (2013) best-selling *Children of the Jacaranda Tree* is a moving, fictional account about the children of Iranian political prisoners in the 1980s. Although this is a work of fiction, the story draws on her own experiences as the child of former political prisoners. *Children of the Jacaranda Tree* is one of the first—of what promises to be many more—narratives of children bearing witness to their parents' traumatic prison experiences. The stark collection of memoirs *We Lived to Tell* (Agah, Mehr, and Parsi, 2007), discussed in chapter 2, also offers painful accounts of the experiences of political prisoners and of their children in Evin. Azar Al-Kanaan, a former political prisoner in 1980s Iran featured in Sarvestani's (2013) *My Stolen Revolution,* has become an outspoken witness at human rights tribunals about Iran. For Al-Kanaan, one of the most traumatic memories of her imprisonment was having her young daughter with her in prison and knowing that she was forced into witnessing the torture of her mother (as well as that of other prisoners).

6. See chapter 1 for a more detailed discussion of the June 2009 protests. In the period leading up to the election, there was a strong sense of optimism that a change in political leadership would usher in the reforms for which Iranian youth were clamoring: a more open and democratic political system, and a more positive relationship with the West. As discussed in chapter 1, this reference to "change" was also alluded to by the Obama-style "hope" posters that demonstrators later used to protest both the results of the election and the government crackdown on angry voters.

7. See chapter 5 for further elaboration of the concept of mediated or inherited nostalgia through Marianne Hirsch's (2001) term *postmemory.*

8. Persson does not mention which of her films was deemed objectionable by the government, but both *Prostitution behind the Veil* (2004), which explores the seedy and poverty-stricken side of contemporary Iranian society, and *Four Wives—One Man* (2007), which examines the practice of polygamy (officially permitted by the government), cast a critical lens on the subordinate position of poor women in postrevolutionary Iran.

9. See chapter 1 for further discussion of how nostalgia was transmitted among diasporic Iranians in the aftermath of the contested Iranian presidential election results of June 2009, and particularly in reaction to the death of Neda.

10. The process of filming *The Queen and I* (2008) ignites a desire in Persson to confront her emotions, specifically her feelings of guilt and shame, with respect to the death of her brother, Rostam. These fraught emotions provide the impetus for the making of her next documentary, *My Stolen Revolution* (2013), which I will discuss in further detail below.

11. See the pseudonymously published *Death to the Dictator: A Young Man Casts a Vote in Iran's 2009 Presidential Election and Pays a Devastating Price* (Moqadam 2010) and the documentary film *The Green Wave* (2010) by Ali Samadi Ahadi for moving accounts of both the feeling of optimism before the June elections and the devastating repercussions of the postelection protests for young activists in Iran.

12. See chapter 1 for a more detailed analysis of the proliferation of life narratives by diasporic Iranians in response to the June 2009 protests, and particularly in response to the viral video of Neda's death.

13. Teresa Brennan (2004) has made this observation about the transmission of affects in general, stating that "the transmission of affect means that we are not self-contained in terms of our energies" (6).

14. Ruth Leys stakes a strong stance against contemporary understandings of affect in literary criticism and queer theories. For Leys (2009), the problem with an understanding of affect through the works of Silvan Tomkins and Eve Sedgwick is their inclination to represent affects as "nonintentional states" (135). This approach, Leys argues, removes the centrality of the object to which one is reacting (such as the death of a parent, or in this case, the traumatic effects of revolution). Contemporary affect theory suggests that affects lie dormant and that objects serve as triggers for what is already inherent, and would eventually emerge (Leys 2009, 135).

15. Azar Al-Kanaan has elsewhere given interviews, initially under the pseudonym of Nina Aghdam, about being raped in prison. Since 2009, however, she has become more outspoken on the issue of rape in the prisons of the Islamic Republic. In a disturbing interview posted on YouTube in which she speaks about her traumatic experiences, the male interviewer, whom we do not see but whose voice we hear, devotes the first minute and a half pressuring her to reveal her real name until she finally relents. This unsettling interview offers another example of how shame works to uncover and to expose the other. In the glare of the camera, Al-Kanaan

reveals both her face and her name as she narrates the most traumatizing episode of her life ("Interview" 2009). This uncomfortable exchange also exemplifies Nichols's claim about the hierarchical nature of the interview (Nichols 1991, 50).

16. My thanks to Upa Mesbahian for generously sharing with me her research on this topic. For a thorough exploration of the history of this song, see her forthcoming chapter "From Romance to Protest: The Folklorisation of an Armenian Song in Iran" in *"You Say You Want a Revolution": Protest Music in the Second Half of the Twentieth Century,* edited by Luca Levi Sala.

4. Repetitions of the Past

1. See Marianne Hirsch's (2011) analysis of postmemory and personal and collective trauma in *Maus I* and *Maus II.*

2. "Autographics," a combination of "autobiography" and "comics," was coined by Gillian Whitlock "to draw attention to the specific conjunctions of visual and verbal text in this genre of autobiography, and also to the subject positions that narrators negotiate in and through comics—features of discursive frameworks that Leigh Gilmore discusses in terms of 'autobiographics'" (Whitlock 2006, 966).

3. Gillian Whitlock (2006) uses the term *autobiographical avatar* to describe Marji and Art (from Spiegelman's *Maus*) as autobiographical subject and narrator in their graphic novels (971). Sidonie Smith and Julia Watson ([2001] 2010) also describe this term, in the context of graphic auto/biographies, in their revised edition of *Reading Autobiography* (170). See also Leigh Gilmore (2011) for her discussion of the child witness and the imperative of witnessing trauma in *Persepolis.*

4. The *Persepolis* books were originally published in French in four volumes, by the French publisher L'Association, between the years 2000 and 2003 and were very well received in France, but her *global* popularity arose after the translation of her works into English. Julie Rak offers a compelling analysis of the differences (with respect to the marketing and the packaging of her work) between the French-language version and the English-language version of the comics. See her chapter "Exceptionally Public: Marjane Satrapi's *Persepolis I: The Story of a Childhood* and James Frey's *A Million Little Pieces*" in Rak 2013.

5. Comics and graphic novels are a particularly powerful medium for the act of witnessing for several reasons: the use of an avatar, in this case, Marji, who is a visually represented figure whose witnessing of events in the book doubles the effect. She witnesses events and the reader witnesses her witnessing.

6. Chapters 2 and 3 explore this period of Iranian history (the 1980s), during which thousands of political prisoners in Evin were executed.

7. Hillary Chute's (2008) use of the term *ethical* in this context addresses the politics of visibility in graphic narratives. See "The Texture of Retracing" (Chute 2008) for her full discussion of this point.

8. Scholars have made this point in relation to the recording of home movies that present (usually happy) memories as a way of managing and securing future representations of oneself. In other words, at the very moment of recording the present, we are keenly aware of preserving our memories in very specific ways, determining how our future selves will interpret and remember the present-past. Thus the visual recording and retracing of the past in the graphic narrative and in the home video share a similar investment and impulse to preserve the future past in (very) prescribed ways. For scholarship on home videos, see, for example, James Moran's (2002) *There's No Place Like Home Video,* Marsha Orgeron and Devin Orgeron's (2007) "Familial Pursuits, Editorial Acts: Documentaries after the Age of Home Video," and José Van Dijck's (2008) "Future Memories: The Construction of Cinematic Hindsight."

9. *Native informant* is a term that Gayatri Spivak (1999) coined to describe the ethically comprised and complicit position of a colonized subject within a colonial system of power. The role of the native informant is to explain the culture of the colonized to the colonizing power in exchange for a privileged status. For a full discussion of her use of this term, see *A Critique of Postcolonial Reason: Toward a History of the Vanishing Present* (Spivak 1999). Hamid Dabashi (2006) famously referred to Azar Nafisi as a "native informer" after the publication of *Reading Lolita in Tehran.* See "Native Informers and the Making of the American Empire" (Dabashi 2006).

10. See Nima Naghibi and Andrew O'Malley (2005) for further discussion of the visual relationship between the front cover and back flap of the *Persepolis* books.

11. Gillian Whitlock (2008) has also commented on how Satrapi's graphic choices disrupt the usual conventions of temporality in *Embroideries.* See "From Tehran to Tehrangeles" (Whitlock 2008).

12. In "From Tehran to Tehrangeles," Whitlock (2008) observes, in reference to *Embroideries:* "The dialogue balloons capture gossip and innuendo in mobile and changing forms across the pages of the text; often large and filled with handwritten script, Satrapi suggests the drama and pleasure of this shared communion of speaking and listening amongst women by shifting the shape and relations amongst the balloons" (20). In fact, Satrapi at times completely eschews the conventions of speech balloons and boxes for narrator's text, which has the further effect of dissolving not only the conventions for designating who the speaker is but also the conventional separation of text and image itself.

13. Examples include *Believer* magazine's interview with Satrapi (Bearman 2006) and an interview about the film version of *Persepolis* on Moviefone (Davis 2007). Satrapi also speaks about humanizing Iranians through animated film (as opposed to "live action") in an interview in one of the "extras" on the *Persepolis* DVD.

14. Thierry Groensteen (2007), in *The System of Comics,* argues that the fragmented and visual nature of the comics "language" requires the reader to consider

graphic features or patterns that echo or "rhyme" across a given work. When a reader notices repeated panels or other graphic elements, she is forced to compare them and consider their relation to one another; this reading process he refers to as an "arthrology": a bringing together of similar visual features from across a book that articulates them and draws out narrative resonances (Groensteen 2007, 21–23).

5. Revolution, Nostalgia, and Memory in Diasporic Iranian Memoirs

1. In their introduction to the special issue on "Iranian Diaspora" in *Comparative Studies of South Asia, Africa and the Middle East,* Persis Karim and Babak Elahi (2011) trace a detailed and useful trajectory of the terms *exile, immigrant,* and *diaspora.* Recognizing what they identify as the "critical tensions" among these various terms, they use the term *diaspora* "partly because of the critical questions it engenders and partly to invoke a term that suggests Iranians' continuing migration out of Iran because of the political situation inside that nation" (Karim and Elahi 2011, 381). *Exile,* for Karim and Elahi (2011), invokes an "urgency" that emerges out of rupture and discontinuity, whereas the term *diaspora* "situates Iran and Iranian culture in the continuum of more global diasporic consciousness" (384). In this chapter, I use the terms *exile* and *diaspora* interchangeably but rely more on the term *diaspora;* although I recognize that *exile* suggests rupture and discontinuity more so than *diaspora,* it is also important to note that the feeling of exilic alienation cannot be separated neatly from the diasporic experience.

2. A handful of examples include Davar Ardalan's (2007) *My Name is Iran: A Memoir,* Jasmin Darznik's (2011) *The Good Daughter: A Memoir of My Mother's Hidden Life,* Firoozeh Dumas's (2003) *Funny in Farsi: A Memoir of Growing Up Iranian in America,* Firoozeh Dumas's (2008) *Laughing without an Accent: Adventures of an Iranian American at Home and Abroad,* Farideh Goldin's (2003) *Wedding Song: Memoirs of an Iranian Jewish Woman,* Nahid Rachlin's (2006) *Persian Girls: A Memoir,* and Nesta Ramazani's (2002) *The Dance of the Rose and the Nightingale.*

3. Nancy K. Miller (2000) has argued that "memoir writing . . . participates in an important form of collective memorialisation, providing building blocks to a more fully shared national narrative" (424). Her observation can be applied to the diasporic Iranian context as these memoirs share a collective impulse to remember and to memorialize not just the authors' personal experiences at the micro level but also the larger national narrative of pre- and postrevolutionary Iran. See "'But enough about me, what do you think of my memoir?'" (Miller 2000).

4. See Niki Akhavan et al.'s (2007) "A Genre in the Service of Empire," Roxana Bahramitash's (2005) "The War on Terror, Feminist Orientalism, and Orientalist Feminism: Case Studies of Two North American Bestsellers," Catherine Burwell's (2007) "Reading Lolita in Times of War: Women's Book Clubs and the Politics of Reception," Hamid Dabashi's (2006) "Native Informers and the Making of the

American Empire," Anne Donadey and Huma Ahmed-Ghosh's (2008) "Why Americans Love Azar Nafisi's *Reading Lolita in Tehran,*" Fatemeh Keshavarz's (2007) *Jasmine and Stars: Reading More than Lolita in Tehran,* and Negar Mottahedeh's (2004) "Off the Grid: Reading Iranian Memoirs in Our Time of Total War." See also references to Nafisi in Nima Naghibi and Andrew O'Malley's (2005) "Estranging the Familiar: 'East' and 'West' in Satrapi's *Persepolis*" and Nima Naghibi's (2007) *Rethinking Global Sisterhood: Western Feminism and Iran.*

5. See Mavis Reimer's (2008) edited collection *Home Words: Discourses of Children's Literature in Canada* for various conceptualizations of home and childhood in Canadian children's literature.

6. This ugly chapter in American history reared its head again when the Republican presidential candidate Senator John McCain made a glib reference to the song "Bomb Iran" on a campaign stop in South Carolina in April 2007. In response to an irate audience member who wanted to know what he was going to do regarding the "obvious" Iranian "threat," McCain's response was to sing "Bomb Iran." His offhand allusion to this inflammatory song was posted on YouTube and attracted much criticism.

7. Marjane Satrapi's (2005) *Embroideries* also begins with the pouring of tea in preparation and anticipation of the free and uninhibited women's conversation that unfolds within its pages. See chapter 4 for a more detailed discussion of this text.

8. According to Abbas Milani (2011), about ten thousand people opposing the regime had congregated in Jaleh Square; the shah's soldiers tried to get the demonstrators to leave but eventually used tear gas and began firing into the crowd: "The city was suddenly awash with rumors of 'thousands killed' by soldiers. According to the foreign embassies, the actual number was anywhere from a dozen to 300" (389). Nikki R. Keddie (1981) has claimed that the number of people killed in Jaleh Square "probably numbered from 500 to 900, though both higher and lower figures are given" (250).

9. See chapters 2 and 3 for an analysis of the prison narratives that document the events of this period in Iran.

10. A horrifying story that emerged from those protests was that of a young student, Ahmad Batebi, who became famous after the *Economist* published a picture of him holding up the bloodied T-shirt of one of his friends. This photograph attracted global attention; like the iconic image of Neda (discussed in chapter 1), the photograph of the young and photogenic Batebi circulated, unbeknownst to him, as an icon of the student resistance movement. As a result of this attention, Batebi was arrested and sentenced to death. His death sentence was then changed to fifteen years. After nine years of imprisonment and torture, Batebi was temporarily released for medical treatment, during which time he managed to escape the country.

11. The question of authenticity continues to haunt debates and discussions in the diasporic Iranian community all the time. The crisis point for many Iranians

around their authentic connections to Iran emerged in the social media narratives around the 2009 protests and the death of Neda. See chapter 1 for an analysis of the crisis in diasporic Iranian engagement with Iranians on the ground.

12. This feeling of unbelonging even in one's own country is a concept explored in Golkou Parhizgar's (2010) documentary *Round-Trip,* in which many young Iranians express their feeling of discontent and alienation with the Iranian regime. See chapter 3 for more on this. Roya Hakakian (2004) also writes about the state of being in exile in one's home country. Writing about her favorite teacher, who gives her students hope through her classes on literature, she states: "Mrs. Arman gave us courage to face a bitter fact: We were in exile in our own city. We were girls, living in a female ghetto. Instead of yellow armbands, we wore the sign of our inferiority on our heads. We switched sidewalks when we saw men approaching. Beaches, family parks, movie theaters had all been segregated" (Hakakian 2004, 212).

13. See Nasrin Rahimieh's (2007) "Border Crossing" for a poignant exploration of the politics and poetics of the "in-between," as she theorizes her own border crossings from Iran, to the United States, to Canada, and back to the United States, where she currently resides. Her analysis grapples with the critical questions of citizenship and belonging, trauma and memory, which preoccupies the current generation of Iranian diasporic women writers.

Conclusion

1. In making the distinction between testimony, memoir, and autobiography, Cubilié (2005) writes: "Unlike traditional autobiography or memoir, which relies on the 'I' of authorial experience, testimonial by its very act undermines the distinct claim of individualism. Instead, testimonial replaces the absolute, authorial 'I' with an authorial voice that retains the individuality of the author's experience while also disclaiming the singularity of that experience, claiming that the story that the author tells is the same story that could be told by any of the other people who shared the same experience" (190). Not all memoirs use the authorial "I," however, and the term *life narrative* is broad enough to encompass auto/biographical elements.

2. See chapter 2 for more on the success and controversy of *Prisoner of Tehran* (2007) and on the negative reactions toward its author, Marina Nemat.

3. See http://theorwellprize.co.uk.

4. The most (in)famous incident to highlight the necessity of truth-telling in memoir writing is the James Frey controversy. After initially endorsing and celebrating his memoir, *A Million Little Pieces,* Oprah Winfrey then subjected him to a public shaming on her show for embellishing the "truth." See Julie Rak (2013) for her analysis of the Frey–Winfrey episode and the public demand for "truth-telling" in memoir and auto/biography.

5. My thanks to Azadeh Moaveni for drawing my attention to the importance of *Death to the Dictator* as a testimonial narrative. The question regarding the impact of a pseudonymously authored text came out of a discussion I had with her at a stimulating conference on "Life Narratives of Muslim Women in the Middle East and South Asia" hosted by Farzaneh Milani at the University of Virginia.

6. Rather than relying on the empathic response of the reader, the celebrity memoir relies instead on the curiosity of the reader *to want to know* the private details of a public life; the success of the celebrity memoir, then, is in part determined by its willingness to disclose salacious details about the lives of the famous and by the prurient interest on the part of readers to learn about them.

7. Moaveni makes this observation in her radio interview with John Hockenberry (2010).

8. This is an effective technique deployed in Alison Bechdel's (2006) *Fun Home: A Family Tragicomic,* where each chapter starts with a drawing of a family photograph, lending the photograph's privileged aura of truthfulness and transparency to the comics medium. I am grateful to Andrew O'Malley for this observation.

9. See chapter 4 for a discussion of the autobiographical avatar as witness in Satrapi's comics.

10. This is a particularly poignant image, and the comparisons between the young Iranian protestors and the vulnerable puppies are made all the more explicit since "Zahra's Paradise" is also the name of the largest cemetery in Tehran.

11. Mehdi was an avid soccer fan, and for his birthday, his mother had a silver necklace with a soccer ball made for him, engraved with the name of his favorite soccer player, Zinedine Zidane.

Bibliography

Abdorrahman Boroumand Foundation. n.d. Human Rights & Democracy for Iran. http://www.iranrights.org.

Abrahamian, Ervand. 1999. *Tortured Confessions: Prisons and Public Recantations in Modern Iran.* Berkeley: University of California Press.

AFP. 2009. "Slain Neda is 'One of My Daughters,' Shah's Son Says." June 22. http://www.rezapahlavi.org/details_article.php?&article=370.

Afshari, Reza. 2001. *Human Rights in Iran: The Abuse of Cultural Relativism.* Philadelphia: University of Pennsylvania Press.

Agah, Azadeh, Sousan Mehr, and Shadi Parsi. 2007. *We Lived to Tell: Political Prison Memoirs of Iranian Women.* Toronto: McGilligan Books.

Aghdashloo, Shohreh. 2013. *The Alley of Love and Yellow Jasmines.* New York: Harper.

Ahadi, Ali Samadi. 2010. *The Green Wave.* Germany: Dreamer Joint Venture Filmproduction. DVD.

Ahmed, Sara. 2004. *The Cultural Politics of Emotion.* New York: Routledge.

Akhavan, Niki, et al. 2007. "A Genre in the Service of Empire." *ZNet,* February 2. https://zcomm.org/znetarticle/a-genre-in-the-service-of-empire-by-niki-akhavan-golbarg-bashi-mana-kia-and-sima-shakhsari-na-gb-and-mk-ss.

Amir and Khalil. 2011. *Zahra's Paradise.* New York: First Second Books.

Anderson, Chris. 2009. "Q&A with Clay Shirky on Twitter and Iran." *TEDBlog,* June 16. http://blog.ted.com/2009/06/16/qa_with_clay_sh.

Anderson, Linda. 2001. *Autobiography.* London: Routledge.

Anderst, Leah. 2013. "'I've spent a lot of time looking at these images': The 'Viewing I' in Contemporary Autobiographical Documentary." *a/b: Auto/Biography Studies* 28, no. 2 (Winter): 212–41.

Appadurai, Arjun. 1996. *Modernity at Large: Cultural Dimensions of Globalization.* Minneapolis: University of Minnesota Press.

Ardalan, Davar. 2007. *My Name Is Iran: A Memoir.* New York: Henry Holt.

Asadi, Houshang. 2010. *Letters to My Torturer: Love, Revolution and Imprisonment in Iran.* Oxford: Oneworld Publications.

Asayesh, Gelareh. 1999. *Saffron Sky: A Life between Iran and America.* Boston: Beacon Press.

Assmann, Aleida, and Corinna Assmann. 2010. "Neda—The Global Career of an Icon." In *Memory in a Global Age: Discourses, Practices and Trajectories,* edited by Aleida Assman and Sebastian Conrad, 225–44. Basingstoke: Palgrave Macmillan.

Bahari, Maziar, with Aimee Molloy. 2011. *Then They Came for Me: A Family's Story of Love, Captivity, and Survival.* New York: Random House.

Bahramitash, Roxana. 2005. "The War on Terror, Feminist Orientalism, and Orientalist Feminism: Case Studies of Two North American Bestsellers." *Critique: Critical Middle Eastern Studies* 14, no. 2 (Summer): 221–35.

Bahrampour, Tara. 1999. *To See and See Again: A Life in Iran and America.* New York: Farrar, Straus and Giroux.

Bearman, Joshuah. 2006. "Marjane Satrapi." *Believer,* August. http://www.believermag.com/issues/200608/?read=interview_satrapi.

Bechdel, Alison. 2006. *Fun Home: A Family Tragicomic.* Boston: Houghton Mifflin Harcourt.

Berlant, Lauren. 2004. "Introduction: Compassion (and Withholding)." In *Compassion: The Culture and Politics of an Emotion,* 1–13. New York: Routledge.

Beverley, John. 2004. *Testimonio: On the Politics of Truth.* Minneapolis: University of Minnesota Press.

Bijan, Donia. 2011. *Maman's Homesick Pie: A Persian Heart in an American Kitchen.* Chapel Hill, N.C.: Algonquin Books.

Boym, Svetlana. 2001. *The Future of Nostalgia.* New York: Basic Books.

———. 2011. "Off-Modern Homecoming in Art and Theory." In *Rites of Return: Diaspora Poetics and the Politics of Memory,* edited by Marianne Hirsch and Nancy K. Miller, 151–65. New York: Columbia University Press.

Brennan, Teresa. 2004. *The Transmission of Affect.* Ithaca, N.Y.: Cornell University Press.

Brown, Wendy. 2006. *Regulating Aversion: Tolerance in the Age of Identity and Empire.* Princeton, N.J.: Princeton University Press.

Burwell, Catherine. 2007. "Reading Lolita in Times of War: Women's Book Clubs and the Politics of Reception." *Intercultural Education* 18, no. 4 (October): 281–96.

Butler, Judith. 2004. *Precarious Life: The Powers of Mourning and Violence.* London: Verso.

Caruth, Cathy, ed. 1995. *Trauma: Explorations in Memory.* Baltimore, Md.: Johns Hopkins University Press.

———. 1996. *Unclaimed Experience: Trauma, Narrative, and History.* Baltimore, Md.: Johns Hopkins University Press.

Chandler, David G. 2011. "The Road to Military Humanitarianism: How the Human Rights NGOs Shaped a New Humanitarian Agenda." *Human Rights Quarterly* 23, no. 3 (August): 678–700.

Chute, Hillary. 2008. "The Texture of Retracing in Marjane Satrapi's *Persepolis.*" *WSQ: Women's Studies Quarterly* 36, no. 1/2 (Spring–Summer): 92–110.

Clifford, James. 1994. "Diasporas." *Cultural Anthropology* 9, no. 3 (August): 302–38.

Cohen, Roger. 2010. "Hell in the Islamic Republic." *New York Times,* May 27.

Couser, Thomas G. 2012. *Memoir: An Introduction.* Oxford: Oxford University Press.

Cubilié, Anne. 2005. *Women Witnessing Terror: Testimony and Cultural Politics of Human Rights.* New York: Fordham University Press.

Cvetkovich, Ann. 2012. *Depression: A Public Feeling.* Durham, N.C.: Duke University Press.

Dabashi, Hamid. 2006. "Native Informers and the Making of the American Empire." *Al-Ahram Weekly,* no. 797, June 1–7. http://weekly.ahram.org.eg/2006/797/special.htm.

———. 2010. *Iran, the Green Movement and the USA: The Fox and the Paradox.* New York: Zed Books.

Darznik, Jasmin. 2011. *The Good Daughter: A Memoir of My Mother's Hidden Life.* New York: Grand Central Publishing.

Davis, Erik. 2007. "Interview: 'Persepolis' Writer-Directors Marjane Satrapi and Vincent Paronnaud." *Moviefone,* December 29. http://news.moviefone.com/2007/12/29/interview-persepolis-writer-directors-marjane-satrapi-and-vin.

Dehghan, Saeed Kamali. 2010. "The Day I Fled Iran in Terror and Left My Family Behind—A Journalist's Story." *Observer,* June 13. http://www.theguardian.com/world/2010/jun/13/saeed-dehghan-iran-exile.

Delijani, Sahar. 2013. *Children of the Jacaranda Tree.* New York: Atria Books.

Delisle, Jennifer Bowering. 2013. "'Iraq in My Bones': Second-Generation Memory in the Age of Global Media." *Biography* 36, no. 2 (Spring): 376–91.

Donadey, Anne, and Huma Ahmed-Ghosh. 2008. "Why Americans Love Azar Nafisi's *Reading Lolita in Tehran.*" *Signs: Journal of Women in Culture and Society* 33, no. 3: 623–46.

Dumas, Firoozeh. 2003. *Funny in Farsi: A Memoir of Growing Up Iranian in America.* New York: Villard.

———. 2008. *Laughing without an Accent: Adventures of an Iranian American at Home and Abroad.* New York: Villard.

Eakin, Paul John. 2008. *Living Autobiographically: How We Create Identity in Narrative.* Ithaca, N.Y.: Cornell University Press.

Ebadi, Shirin, with Azadeh Moaveni. 2006. *Iran Awakening: From Prison to Peace Prize; One Woman's Struggle at the Crossroads of History.* Toronto: Alfred A. Knopf Canada.

Elahi, Babak. 2006. "Translating the Self: Language and Identity in Iranian American Women's Memoirs." *Iranian Studies* 39, no. 4 (December): 461–80.

———. 2008. "Fake Farsi: Formulaic Flexibility in Iranian American Women's Memoir." *MELUS* 33, no. 2 (Summer): 37–54.

Entekhabi-Fard, Camelia. 2007. *Camelia, Save Yourself by Telling the Truth: A Memoir of Iran.* Translated by George Mürer. New York: Seven Stories Press.

Erikson, Kai. 1995. "Notes on Trauma and Community." In *Trauma: Explorations in Memory,* edited by Cathy Caruth, 183–99. Baltimore, M.D.: Johns Hopkins University Press.

Esfandiari, Haleh. 2009. *My Prison, My Home: One Woman's Story of Captivity in Iran.* New York: HarperCollins.

Farmaian, Sattareh Farman, with Dona Munker. 1992. *Daughter of Persia: A Woman's Journey from Her Father's Harem through the Islamic Revolution.* New York: Anchor Books.

Fotouhi, Sanaz. 2014. *The Literature of the Iranian Diaspora: Meaning and Identity since the Islamic Revolution.* New York: I.B. Tauris.

Frouzesh, Sharareh. 2011. "The Politics of Appropriation: Writing, Responsibility, and the Specter of the Native Informant." *Yearbook of Comparative Literature* 57: 252–68.

Garber, Marjorie. 2004. "Compassion." In *Compassion: The Culture and Politics of an Emotion,* edited by Lauren Berlant, 15–28. New York: Routledge.

Ghahramani, Zarah, with Robert Hillman. 2008. *My Life as a Traitor.* New York: Farrar, Straus and Giroux.

Gheytanchi, Elham. 2010. "Symbols, Signs, and Slogans of the Demonstrations in Iran." In *Media, Power, and Politics in the Digital Age: The 2009 Presidential Election Uprising in Iran,* edited by Yahya R. Kamalipour, 251–64. Lanham, Md.: Rowman and Littlefield.

Ghosh, Bobby. 2009. "People Who Mattered: Neda Agha-Soltan." *Time.* http://content.time.com/time/specials/packages/article/0,28804,1946375_1946333_1946305,00.html.

Gilmore, Leigh. 1998. "Endless Autobiography? Jamaica Kincaid and Serial Autobiography." In *Postcolonialism and Autobiography,* edited by Alfred Hornung and Ernstpeter Ruhe, 211–32. Amsterdam: Rodopi.

———. 2001. *The Limits of Autobiography: Trauma and Testimony.* Ithaca, N.Y.: Cornell University Press.

———. 2011. "Witnessing Persepolis: Comics, Trauma, and Childhood Testimony." In *Graphic Subjects: Critical Essays on Autobiography and Graphic Novels,* edited by Michael A. Chaney, 157–63. Madison: University of Wisconsin Press.

Goldin, Farideh. 2003. *Wedding Song: Memoirs of an Iranian Jewish Woman.* Lebanon, N.H.: Brandeis University Press.

Grassian, Daniel. 2013. *Iranian and Diasporic Literature in the 21st Century: A Critical Study.* Jefferson, N.C.: McFarland.

Groensteen, Thierry. 2007. *The System of Comics.* Jackson: University Press of Mississippi.

Guppy, Shusha. 1988. *The Blindfold Horse: Memories of a Persian Childhood.* London: Minerva.

———. 1991. *A Girl in Paris.* London: Minerva.

———. 1993. *Persian Love Songs and Mystic Chants.* New York: Lyrichord Discs. CD.

Hakakian, Roya. 2004. *Journey from the Land of No: A Girlhood Caught in Revolutionary Iran.* New York: Crown.

Hariman, Robert, and John Louis Lucaites. 2007. *No Caption Needed: Iconic Photographs, Public Culture, and Liberal Democracy.* Chicago: University of Chicago Press.

Hashemi, Nader, and Danny Postel, eds. 2010. *The People Reloaded: The Green Movement and the Struggle for Iran's Future.* Brooklyn, N.Y.: Melville House.

Hejazi, Arash. 2011. *The Gaze of the Gazelle: The Story of a Generation.* London: Seagull Books.

Henke, Suzette. 2000. *Shattered Subjects: Trauma and Testimony in Women's Life-Writing.* New York: St. Martin's.

Hermanson, Bri. 2009. "Neda Agha-Soltan." June 26. http://brihermanson.blogspot.ca/2009/06/neda-agha-soltan.html.

———. n.d. "Portraits: Neda Agha-Soltan." http://www.bhermanson.com/portraits/neda-agha-soltan#sthash.b4c7NZFY.dpu.

Hesford, Wendy. 2011. *Spectacular Rhetorics: Human Rights Visions, Recognitions, Feminisms.* Durham, N.C.: Duke University Press.

Hillman, Robert. 2007. "Looking for Peace, Not Pity." *Sydney Morning Herald,* February 17. http://www.smh.com.au/articles/2007/02/16/1171405446876.html.

Hirsch, Marianne. 2001. "Surviving Images: Holocaust Photographs and the Work of Postmemory." *Yale Journal of Criticism* 14, no. 1 (Spring): 5–37.

———. 2011. "Mourning and Postmemory." In *Graphic Subjects: Critical Essays on Autobiography and Graphic Novels,* edited by Michael A. Chaney, 17–44. Madison: University of Wisconsin Press.

Hirsch, Marianne, and Nancy K. Miller. 2011. "Introduction." In *Rites of Return: Diaspora Poetics and the Politics of Memory,* 1–20. New York: Columbia University Press.

Hirsch, Marianne, and Leo Spitzer. 2006. "We Would Not Have Come without You." In *Memory, History, Nation: Contested Pasts,* edited by Katharine Hodgkin and Susanna Radstone, 79–95. New Brunswick, N.J.: Transaction.

Hockenberry, John. 2010. "The Writing of 'Death to the Dictator!'" Interview of Roger Cohen and Azadeh Moaveni. *Takeaway,* July 22. http://www.thetakeaway.org/story/88768-writing-death-dictator.

Hodgkin, Katharine, and Susanna Radstone. 2006. *Memory, History, Nation: Contested Pasts.* New Brunswick, N.J.: Transaction.

Huggan, Graham. 2001. *The Post-Colonial Exotic: Marketing the Margins.* London: Routledge.

Hulme, Peter. 1986. *Colonial Encounters: Europe and the Native Caribbean, 1492–1797.* London: Routledge.

"Interview with an Iranian Woman Who Has Been Tortured and Raped in Iran's Prisons (Subtitled)." 2009. YouTube video, posted by "niko05766," August 13. http://www.youtube.com/watch?v=wAQsRmioHzU.

"Iran's 'Zahra' Tells Alternate Tale of Presidential Campaign." 2013. Narrated by Peter Kenyon. All Things Considered. *NPR,* May 20. http://www.npr.org/blogs/parallels/2013/05/20/185558815/irans-zahra-tells-alternate-tale-of-presidential-campaign.

"IRIB Television Cover Up about Taraneh Mousavi." 2009. YouTube video, posted by "mahnazjoon84," August 12. https://www.youtube.com/watch?v=KrobOWdeWo8.

Jarmakani, Amira. 2011. "Desiring the Big Bad Blade: Racing the Sheikh in Desert Romances." *American Quarterly* 63, no. 4 (December): 895–928.

Kaplan, Ann. 2005. *Trauma Culture: The Politics of Terror and Loss in Media and Literature.* New Brunswick, N.J.: Rutgers University Press.

Karim, Persis M., ed. 2006. *Let Me Tell You Where I've Been: New Writing by Women of the Iranian Diaspora.* Fayetteville: University of Arkansas Press.

Karim, Persis M., and Anita Amirrezvani. 2013. *Tremors: New Fiction by Iranian Americans.* Fayetteville: University of Arkansas Press.

Karim, Persis M., and Babak Elahi. 2011. "Introduction: Iranian Diaspora." Special issue, *Comparative Studies of South Asia, Africa and the Middle East* 31, no 2: 381–87.

Karim, Persis M., and Mohammad Mehdi Khorrami, eds. 1999. *A World Between: Poems, Short Stories, and Essays by Iranian-Americans.* New York: George Braziller.

Karim, Persis M., and Nasrin Rahimieh. 2008. "Writing Iranian Americans into the American Literature Canon." Special issue, *MELUS* 33, no. 2 (Summer): 7–16.

Keddie, Nikki R. 1981. *Roots of Revolution: An Interpretive History of Modern Iran.* New Haven, Conn.: Yale University Press.

Keshavarz, Fatemeh. 2007. *Jasmine and Stars: Reading More than Lolita in Tehran.* Chapel Hill: University of North Carolina Press.

"khanvadeh shahzadeh reza pahlavi dar tazahorat Washington D C." 2009. YouTube video, posted by "Ahoogorizans kanal," June 28. https://www.youtube.com/watch?v=97wocoHoyYQ.

Khorsandi, Shappi. 2009. *A Beginner's Guide to Acting English.* London: Ebury Press.

La Capra, Dominick. 2001. *Writing History, Writing Trauma.* Baltimore, Md.: Johns Hopkins University Press.

Landsberg, Allison. 2004. *Prosthetic Memory.* New York: Columbia University Press.

Laqueur, Thomas. 2009. "Mourning, Pity, and the Work of Narrative in the Making of 'Humanity.'" In *Humanitarianism and Suffering: The Mobilization of Empathy,* edited by Richard Ashby Wilson and Richard D. Brown, 31–57. Cambridge: Cambridge University Press.

Latifi, Afschineh. 2005. *Even after All This Time: A Story of Love, Revolution, and Leaving Iran.* New York: HarperCollins.

Laub, Dori. 1992. "Bearing Witness, or the Vicissitudes of Listening." In *Testimony: Crises of Witnessing in Literature, Psychoanalysis, and History,* edited by Shoshana Felman and Dori Laub, 57–75. New York: Routledge.

Lejeune, Philippe. (1975) 1989. "The Autobiographical Pact." In *On Autobiography,* translated by Katherine Leary, 3–30. Minneapolis: University of Minnesota Press.

Leys, Ruth. 2009. *From Guilt to Shame: Auschwitz and After.* Princeton, N.J.: Princeton University Press.

MacCannell, Dean. 1992. *Empty Meeting Grounds: The Tourist Papers.* London: Routledge.

Mahmoody, Betty, with William Hoffer. 1987. *Not without My Daughter.* St. Martin's.

Mahr, Krista. 2009. "Top 10 Heroes: 2. Neda Agha-Soltan." *Time,* December 8. http://content.time.com/time/specials/packages/article/0,28804,1945379_1944701_1944705,00.html.

Malek, Amy. 2006. "Memoir as Iranian Exile Cultural Production: A Case Study of Marjane Satrapi's *Persepolis* Series." *Iranian Studies* 39, no. 3 (September): 353–80.

Massumi, Brian. 1995. "The Autonomy of Affect." In "The Politics of Systems and Environments," part 2. Special issue, *Cultural Critique* 31 (September): 83–110.

Mattar, Karim. 2012. "Rereading the 'Rogue State': The Politics of Gender in Anglophone Iranian Literature." *Interventions* 14, no. 4: 551–68.

McClennen, Sophia A., and Joseph R. Slaughter. 2009. "Introducing Human Rights and Literary Forms; or, the Vehicles and Vocabularies of Human Rights." *Comparative Literature Studies* 46, no. 1: 1–19.

Mesbahian, Upa. Forthcoming. "From Romance to Protest: The Folklorisation of an Armenian Song in Iran." In *"You Say You Want a Revolution": Protest Music in the Second Half of the Twentieth Century,* edited by Luca Levi Sala. Turnhout, Belgium: Brepols.

Milani, Abbas. 2011. *The Shah.* New York: Palgrave Macmillan.

Milani, Farzaneh. 1992. *Veils and Words: The Emerging Voices of Iranian Women Writers.* London: I. B. Tauris.

———. 2011. *Words Not Swords.* Syracuse: Syracuse University Press.

———. 2013. "Iranian Women's Life Narratives." *Journal of Women's History* 25, no. 2 (Summer): 130–52.

Milbank, Dana. 2009. "Washington Sketch: The Shah's Son Offers His Services to Iran." *Washington Post,* June 23. http://www.washingtonpost.com/wp-dyn/content/article/2009/06/22/AR2009062202625.html.

Miller, Nancy K. 2000. "'But enough about me, what do you think of my memoir?'" *The Yale Journal of Criticism* 13, no. 2 (Fall): 421–36.

———. 2007. "Out of the Family: Generations of Women in Marjane Satrapi's *Persepolis*." *Life Writing* 4, no. 1 (April): 13–29.

Moaveni, Azadeh. 2006. *Lipstick Jihad: A Memoir of Growing Up Iranian in America and American in Iran.* New York: Public Affairs.

———. 2009. *Honeymoon in Tehran: Two Years of Love and Danger in Iran.* New York: Random House.

———. 2010. "Tehran in Chains." *New York Times,* July 16.

Modleski, Tania. 1982. *Loving with a Vengeance: Mass-Produced Fantasies for Women.* New York: Routledge.

Mojab, Shahrzad. 2007. "Introduction: Years of Solitude, Years of Defiance: Women Political Prisoners in Iran." In *We Lived to Tell: Political Prison Memoirs of Iranian Women,* edited by Azadeh Agah, Sousan Mehr, and Shadi Parsi, 7–18. Toronto: McGilligan Books.

———. n.d. Political Prisoners: The Art of Resistance in the Middle East. http://womenpoliticalprisoners.com.

Moqadam, Afsaneh. 2010. *Death to the Dictator: A Young Man Casts a Vote in Iran's 2009 Election and Pays a Devastating Price.* New York: Farrar, Straus and Giroux.

Moran, James. 2002. *There's No Place Like Home Video.* Minneapolis: University of Minnesota Press.

Morrison, Aimée. 2014. "Facebook and Coaxed Affordances." In *Identity Technologies: Constructing the Self Online,* edited by Anna Poletti and Julie Rak, 112–31. Madison: University of Wisconsin Press.

Mosteshar, Cherry. 1995. *Unveiled: Love and Death among the Ayatollahs.* London: Hodder and Stoughton.

Motlagh, Amy. 2008. "Towards a Theory of Iranian American Life Writing." In *Iranian American Literature.* Special issue, *MELUS* 33, no. 2 (Summer): 17–36.

———. 2011. "Autobiography and Authority in the Writings of the Iranian Diaspora." *Comparative Studies of South Asia, Africa and the Middle East* 31, no. 2: 411–24.

Mottahedeh, Negar. 2004. "Off the Grid: Reading Iranian Memoirs in Our Time of Total War." *Middle Eastern Report Online,* September. http://www.merip.org/mero/interventions/grid.

———. 2015. *#iranelection: Hashtag Solidarity and the Transformation of Online Life.* Stanford: Stanford University Press.

Nabavi, Negin. 2012. *Iran: From Theocracy to the Green Movement.* New York: Palgrave Macmillan.

Nafisi, Azar. 2003. *Reading Lolita in Tehran.* New York: Random House.

Naghibi, Nima. 2007. *Rethinking Global Sisterhood: Western Feminism and Iran.* Minneapolis: University of Minnesota Press.

Naghibi, Nima, and Andrew O'Malley. 2005. "Estranging the Familiar: 'East' and 'West' in Satrapi's *Persepolis*." *English Studies in Canada* 31, no. 2/3 (June/September): 223–47.

Najafi, Najmeh. 1953. *Persia Is My Heart*. New York: Harper and Brothers.

Nasrabadi, Manijeh. 2011. "In Search of Iran: Resistant Melancholia in Iranian American Memoirs of Return." *Comparative Studies of South Asia, Africa and the Middle East* 31, no. 2: 487–97.

Nemat, Marina. 2007. *Prisoner of Tehran: A Memoir*. Toronto: Viking Canada.

———. 2010. *After Tehran: A Life Reclaimed*. Toronto: Viking Canada.

Nichols, Bill. 1991. *Representing Reality*. Bloomington: Indiana University Press.

———. 2001. *Introduction to Documentary*. Bloomington: Indiana University Press.

Olney, James. 1998. *Memory and Narrative: The Weave of Life-Writing*. Chicago: University of Chicago Press.

Orgeron, Marsha, and Devin Orgeron. 2007. "Familial Pursuits, Editorial Acts: Documentaries after the Age of Home Video." *Velvet Light Trap* 60 (Fall): 47–62.

Ostby, Marie. 2013. "De-Censoring an Iranian-American 'Memoir': Authorship and Synchronicity in Shahriar Mandanipour's *Censoring an Iranian Love Story*." *Iranian Studies: Journal of the International Society for Iranian Studies* 46, no. 1 (January): 73–93.

Panah, Hamid Yazdan. 2013. "The Legacy of Neda Agha Soltan." *Near East Observatory*, January 23. http://neobservatory.org/near-east-observations/the-legacy-of-neda-agha-soltan.

Parhizgar, Golkou, dir. 2010. *Round-Trip*. UK: n.p. DVD.

Poletti, Anna, and Julie Rak. 2014. "Introduction: Digital Dialogues." In *Identity Technologies: Constructing the Self Online*, edited by Anna Poletti and Julie Rak, 3–22. Madison: University of Wisconsin Press.

Potter, Tiffany. 2003. "Writing Indigenous Femininity: Mary Rowlandson's Narrative of Captivity." *Eighteenth-Century Studies* 36, no. 2 (Winter): 153–67.

Pratt, Mary Louise. 1992. *Imperial Eyes: Travel Writing and Transculturation*. London: Routledge.

Probyn, Elspeth. 2005. *Blush: Faces of Shame*. Minneapolis: University of Minnesota Press.

Rachlin, Nahid. 2006. *Persian Girls: A Memoir*. New York: Penguin.

Radhakrishnan, R. 2003. "Ethnicity in an Age of Diaspora." In *Theorizing Diaspora: A Reader*, edited by Jana Evans Braziel and Anita Mannur, 119–31. Malden, Mass.: Blackwell.

Rahimi, Babak. 2011. "Affinities of Dissent: Cyberspace, Performative Networks and the Iranian Green Movement." *CyberOrient* 5, no. 2. http://www.cyberorient.net/article.do?articleId=7357.

Rahimieh, Nasrin. 2007. "Border Crossing." *Comparative Studies of South Asia, Africa and the Middle East* 27, no. 2: 225–32.

Rak, Julie. 2004. *Negotiated Memory: Doukhobor Autobiographical Discourse*. Vancouver: University of British Columbia Press.

———. 2013. *Boom! Manufacturing Memoir for the Popular Market.* Waterloo: Wilfrid Laurier University Press.

Ramazani, Nesta. 2002. *The Dance of the Rose and the Nightingale.* Syracuse: Syracuse University Press.

Reimer, Mavis, ed. 2008. *Home Words: Discourses of Children's Literature in Canada.* Waterloo: Wilfrid Laurier University Press.

Ritivoi, Andreea Deciu. 2002. *Yesterday's Self: Nostalgia and the Immigrant Identity.* Lanham, Md.: Rowman and Littlefield.

Robertson, Geoffrey, QC. 2010. *The Massacre of Political Prisoners in Iran, 1988.* Washington, D.C.: Abdorrahman Boroumand Foundation. http://www.unarts.org/H-II/ref/IMReport1988.pdf.

Saberi, Roxana. 2010. *Between Two Worlds: My Life and Captivity in Iran.* New York: HarperCollins.

Sabety, Setareh. 2010. "Graphic Content: The Semiotics of a YouTube Uprising." In *Media, Power, and Politics in the Digital Age: The 2009 Presidential Election Uprising in Iran,* edited by Yahya R. Kamalipour, 119–24. Lanham, Md.: Rowman and Littlefield.

Said, Edward. 1975. *Beginnings: Intention and Method.* New York: Columbia University Press.

Sarvestani, Nahid Persson, dir. 2004. *Prostitution behind the Veil.* Sweden: Cosmo Film. DVD.

———, dir. 2007. *Four Wives—One Man [Fyra fruar och en man].* Sweden: RealReel Doc. DVD.

———, dir. 2008. *The Queen and I.* Sweden: RealReel Doc. DVD.

———, dir. 2013. *My Stolen Revolution.* Sweden: RealReel Doc. DVD.

Satrapi, Marjane. 2003. *Persepolis I: The Story of a Childhood.* New York: Pantheon Books.

———. 2004. *Persepolis II: The Story of a Return.* New York: Pantheon Books.

———. 2005. *Embroideries.* New York: Pantheon Books.

———. 2006. *Chicken with Plums.* New York: Pantheon Books.

Satrapi, Marjane, and Vincent Paronnaud, dirs. 2007. *Pérsepolis.* France: Sony Pictures. DVD.

———, dirs. 2011. *Chicken with Plums.* France: Celluloid Dreams. DVD.

Scarry, Elaine. 1985. *The Body in Pain: The Making and Unmaking of the World.* New York: Oxford University Press.

———. 1996. "The Difficulty of Imagining Other People." In *For Love of Country: Debating the Limits of Patriotism,* edited by Joshua Cohen, 98–110. Boston: Beacon Press.

Schaffer, Kay, and Sidonie Smith. 2004. "Introduction." In *Human Rights and Narrated Lives: The Ethics of Recognition,* 1–12. New York: Palgrave Macmillan.

———. 2014. "E-witnessing in the Digital Age." In *We Shall Bear Witness: Life Narratives and Human Rights,* edited by Meg Jensen and Margaretta Jolly, 223–37. Madison: University of Wisconsin Press.

Sedgwick, Eve Kosofsky, and Adam Frank. 1995. *Shame and Its Sisters: A Silvan Tomkins Reader.* Durham, N.C.: Duke University Press.

Segall, Kimberly Wedeven. 2008. "Melancholy Ties: Intergenerational Loss and Exile in *Persepolis.*" *Comparative Studies of South Asia, Africa and the Middle East* 28, no. 1: 38–49.

Simon, Roger I. 2005. *The Touch of the Past: Remembrance, Learning, Ethics.* New York: Palgrave Macmillan.

Slaughter, Joseph L. 1997. "A Question of Narration: The Voice in International Human Rights Law." *Human Rights Quarterly* 19, no. 2: 406–30.

———. 2007. "Narration in International Human Rights Law." *CLCWeb: Comparative Literature and Culture* 9, no. 1. http://docs.lib.purdue.edu/cgi/viewcontent.cgi?article=1031&context=clcweb.

Sliwinski, Sharon. 2011. *Human Rights in Camera.* Chicago: University of Chicago Press.

Smith, Sidonie. 1998. "Memory, Narrative and the Discourses of Identity in *Abeng* and *No Telephone to Heaven.*" In *Postcolonialism and Autobiography,* edited by Alfred Hornung and Ernstpeter Ruhe, 37–59. Amsterdam: Rodopi.

Smith, Sidonie, and Julia Watson. (2001) 2010. *Reading Autobiography: A Guide for Interpreting Life Narratives.* Minneapolis: University of Minnesota Press.

Soltani, Neda. 2011. *My Stolen Face.* Amazon Kindle Book.

———. 2012. "The Media Mix-Up that Ruined My Life." *BBC News,* November 14. http://www.bbc.co.uk/news/magazine-20267989.

Spelman, Elizabeth. 1997. *Fruits of Sorrow: Framing Our Attention to Suffering.* Boston: Beacon Press.

Spiegelman, Art. 1986. *Maus I: A Survivor's Tale; My Father Bleeds History.* New York: Pantheon Books.

———. 1991. *Maus II: A Survivor's Tale; And Here My Troubles Began.* New York: Pantheon Books.

Spivak, Gayatri. 1999. *A Critique of Postcolonial Reason: Toward a History of the Vanishing Present.* Cambridge, Mass.: Harvard University Press.

Sullivan, Andrew. 2009a. "The Revolution Will Be Twittered." *The Daily Dish* (blog), *Atlantic,* June 13. http://www.theatlantic.com/daily-dish/archive/2009/06/the-revolution-will-be-twittered/200478.

———. 2009b. "Twitter Ripped the Veil off 'the Other'—and We Saw Ourselves." *Times Online,* June 21. http://technology.timesonline.co.uk/tol/news/tech_and_web/the_web/article6544276.ece.

Sullivan, Zohreh T. 2001. *Exiled Memories: Stories of Iranian Diaspora.* Philadelphia: Temple University Press.

Talebi, Shahla. 2011. *Ghosts of Revolution: Rekindled Memories of Imprisonment in Iran.* Stanford: Stanford University Press.

Thompson, Clive. 2008. "Brave New World of Digital Intimacy." *New York Times Magazine,* September 5.

Tulloch, John, and R. Warwick Blood. 2012. *Icons of War and Terror: Media Images in an Age of International Risk.* London: Routledge.

Van Dijck, José. 2008. "Future Memories: The Construction of Cinematic Hindsight." *Theory, Culture and Society* 25, no. 3: 71–87.

Vaughan, Alden T., and Edward W. Clark. 1981. "Cups of Common Calamity: Puritan Captivity Narratives as Literature and History." In *Puritans among the Indians: Accounts of Captivity and Redemption, 1676–1724,* 1–28. Cambridge, Mass.: Harvard University Press.

"Was Taraneh Raped and Murdered, or Did She Never Exist?" 2009. *The Observers,* August 14. http://observers.france24.com/content/20090814-was-taraneh-mousavi-raped-murdered-did-she-never-exist.

Whitlock, Gillian. 2006. "The Seeing 'I' of the Comics." *MFS Modern Fiction Studies* 52, no. 4 (Winter): 965–79.

———. 2007. *Soft Weapons: Autobiography in Transit.* Chicago: University of Chicago Press.

———. 2008. "From Tehran to Tehrangeles: The Generic Fix of Iranian Exilic Memoirs." *Ariel: A Review of International English Literature* 39, no. 1/2 (January–April): 2–27.

Wilson, Richard Ashby, and Richard D. Brown, eds. 2009. *Humanitarianism and Suffering: The Mobilization of Empathy.* Cambridge: Cambridge University Press.

Yaghoobi, Jafar. 2011. *Let Us Water the Flowers: The Memoir of a Political Prisoner in Iran.* Amherst, N.Y.: Prometheus Books.

Yagoda, Ben. 2009. *Memoir: A History.* New York: Riverhead Books.

"'Zahra's Paradise': An Interview with Amir and Khalil." 2011. *Jadaliyya,* September 13. http://www.jadaliyya.com/pages/index/2607/zahras-paradise_an-interview-with-amir-and-khalil.

Index

Page numbers in italics refer to illustrations.

NIMA NAGHIBI is associate professor of English at Ryerson University in Toronto. She is the author of *Rethinking Global Sisterhood: Western Feminism and Iran* (Minnesota, 2007).